The Paradoxes of High Stakes Testing

How They Affect Students, Their Parents, Teachers, Principals, Schools, and Society

The Paradoxes of High Stakes Testing

How They Affect Students, Their Parents, Teachers, Principals, Schools, and Society

George Madaus
Boston College

Michael Russell
Boston College

Jennifer Higgins
Boston College

INFORMATION AGE PUBLISHING, INC.
Charlotte, NC • www.infoagepub.com

Library of Congress Cataloging-in-Publication Data

Madaus, George F.
The paradoxes of high stakes testing : how they affect students, their parents, teachers, principals, schools, and society / George Madaus, Michael Russell, Jennifer Higgins.
p. cm.
Includes bibliographical references.
ISBN 978-1-60752-027-6 (pbk.) – ISBN 978-1-60752-028-3 (hardcover)
1. Educational tests and measurements. I. Russell, Michael K., 1967- II. Higgins, Jennifer. III. Title.
LB3051.M368 2009
371.26–dc22

2008048550

Printed in the United States of America

CONTENTS

ACKNOWLEDGEMENTS

This book is the culmination of several decades of work in the field of educational testing. Our thinking has been influenced by many people and generously supported by several foundations, granting institutions, and individuals. While there is not room here to name all of those who have influenced our thinking and assisted us with research, we acknowledge the assistance and support of the following. First, we want to thank our spouses, Anne, Liana, and Roger, for their patience and unending support. We are indebted to the Ford Foundation for its financial support and encouragement that made this book possible. We thank Geoffrey and Noreen Boisi, whose gift of an Endowed Chair to the Boston College School of Education has supported research on testing over the years. The Center for Advanced Study of Behavioral Sciences also provided support for work that forms the foundation for much of this book. We thank Janice Petrovich for encouraging us to write this book and Irene Korenfieldl for her assistance throughout the writing of this book. We thank our colleagues, Al Beaton, Thomas Kellaghan, and Walt Haney, for all of their help over the years in reacting to and helping advance our ideas, as well as monitoring us for errors. Robert Linn, John Staudenmaier, Vincent Greaney, Reverend Simon Clyne, Reverend Martin Rafferty, and John Merrow were very generous with their help on various aspects of the book. There are several colleagues at Boston College who have helped us with aspects of the book, including Joseph Pedulla, Brendan Rapple, Yonder Moynihan Gillihan, Stephen Brown, and Kathy Rhoades. We thank Tom Hoffmann and Kevin Keane for creating the visual representations and other artwork in the book. We are grateful to Martha Gowetski for the many hours she spent reading, re-reading, and

The Paradoxes of High Stakes Testing, pages vii–viii

editing drafts. We also acknowledge Mary Howard for the administrative assistance she provided over the years. Finally, we want to thank the many, many graduate students who have worked with us over the years on issues explored in this book.

CHAPTER 1

THE HIGH-STAKES TESTING MANIA

For most of us, testing was an important part of going to school. Beginning in elementary school we took daily quizzes, weekly spelling tests, and unit tests in mathematics, geography, history, and even gym. In middle and high school, there were mid-terms and final exams. Every once in a while, we also took standardized tests, like the California Achievement Test or the Iowa Test of Basic Skills. Sometimes these standardized test results were used for classroom tracking, but for most of us they didn't mean all that much to us.[1]

Yes, there were stakes associated with test performance. But to determine our report card grades our teachers combined scores on the tests they gave us with our grades on homework, projects, papers, laboratory reports, presentations, and other assignments. The standardized tests administered every few years had little or no bearing on our grades.

Today, things are different. Our children and grandchildren still take classroom tests. But in addition, state and federal laws require our children to take state-tests in language arts and mathematics. Soon, testing in science and history will also be mandatory. Today, students entering kindergarten will take a *minimum* of sixteen state tests before graduating.[2] Students who are English Language Learners (ELL) must also take tests in listening, speaking, reading, and writing beginning in kindergarten. Together, these requirements affect nearly 30 million students and have made testing a very

The Paradoxes of High Stakes Testing, pages 1–11

big business that costs states an estimated one billion dollars each year.[3] In addition, states and their schools spend another billion dollars or more each year on tutoring and test preparation materials.[4]

Unlike the thirty to forty-five minute tests our teachers typically made us take, today's state tests often take several hours and are spread across several days. In Bibb County, Georgia, for example, a state or national exam is given to elementary, middle or high-school students in 70 of 180 school days.[5] In Maryland, state testing occurs across 55 days of the school year; in Texas, 51 days (71 if you count field testing); in Michigan it's 50 days. Except for Bibb County, none of these numbers include other tests students may take such as the National Assessment of Educational Progress (NAEP), SAT or ACT college admission tests, Advance Placement (AP) exams or other commercially available standardized tests the local school districts may choose to administer.[6]

In addition to the amount of time students spend taking tests, today's students live in a very different testing environment than most of us experienced; they must deal with more testing, and with the high-stake consequences attached to the results. At last count, 29 states require students to pass state mandated tests to graduate from high school. In some cases, poor performing high school students are directed to seek a GED instead of a standard diploma.[7] At least nine states, and a number of large districts, also use test results to retain students in grade or place them in a remedial class. It is the gravity of decisions like these that cause a state-mandated test to become a "high-stakes" test.

Without a doubt, high-stakes testing policies are well intentioned. State and federal testing policies are intended to focus instruction and learning on the important content and skills that form state curriculum—and they do. In each state, the tests define standards and expectations for student achievement. Test scores provide teachers and schools with information about student performance. They give communities information about the quality of their schools and help parents make informed decisions when choosing a school for their children. High-stakes tests also open doors of opportunity to those previously shut out by holding teachers and schools accountable for student achievement and helping them to focus attention on students previously poorly served. These are all positive outcomes.

It is important that the public acknowledge the positive aspects of high-stakes testing. But, focusing only on the positives masks, the equally important, negative repercussions of high-stakes testing. A sole emphasis on the positive brings to mind the first lines of Johnny Mercer's 1944 hit song:

> You've got to accentuate the positive
> Eliminate the negative
> Latch on to the affirmative
> Don't mess with Mister In-Between.

The many positive outcomes of high-stakes testing are the "affirmative." Other outcomes of high-stakes testing, however, are "negative." For instance, subjects that are not tested, such as art, physical education, foreign languages, and social studies, receive less time and attention. Time for recess and lunch periods are reduced, and in some cases eliminated all together. Students are prohibited from using word processors for classroom papers so that they are used to handwriting the essays required on state tests. Teachers and schools find ways to increase test scores without improving student learning. And over time, these negatives corrupt the accuracy of information about student achievement and school quality.

Mister In-Between is the grey area where the news is good for some students and schools but not for others. For example, high-stakes tests motivate many students and teachers—but not all. Some students and teachers simply ignore the tests and continue doing what they have always done. Others give up and, in the extreme, drop out of school or leave the profession.

The positive, negative, and grey areas are contradictory outcomes produced when high-stakes tests are used to improve student learning and the quality of our schools. These contradictory outcomes make high-stakes testing paradoxical. The paradox results from using test scores for two purposes: First, to identify and help students, teachers, and schools that are not performing well, and second to make high-stakes decisions about those same students, teachers, and schools. These high-stakes decisions set in motion a series of actions by students, parents, teachers, and schools designed to improve test scores. But these decisions also produce unintended negative outcomes. For example, many schools increase attention on students who are at risk of performing poorly on high-stakes tests and increase time on test preparation and drill-and-practice. In response, parents of high-ability students—aka "gifted" students—opt out of public schools for private schools. They believe that private schools, not constrained by accountability requirements and high-stakes sanctions, are able to offer a more challenging, richer curriculum. They perceive that repetitive drills designed to help low-performing students meet high-stakes mandates dilute or preclude the type of instruction their children should receive.[8]

This book is about the paradoxical nature of high-stakes testing. As members of the testing community we value testing, but recognize its limitations. It is crucial that the public also understand that high-stakes testing is a paradoxical policy strategy that affects—for both good and ill—individuals students, teachers, schools, and communities. As we will see, the negative paradoxes of high-stakes testing are predictable and have occurred across the centuries and over continents. The grey areas and negative outcomes associated with high-stakes testing can never be eliminated, but their effects can be moderated if they are understood and acknowledged.

HIGH-STAKES TESTING AND THE NATION

Today, testing is woven into the fabric of our nation's culture and psyche. Chatter about test results can be heard on the playground, at book groups, offices, dinner parties, and the supper table. Testing is a focus of business executives, politicians, policymakers, and think tanks from the right, left, and center. It is an issue of concern for diverse organizations from the Business Roundtable to the National Council of Churches, from the National Governors Association to the Children's Defense Fund. It is a topic for talk show hosts, the media and entertainment industries. Even Disney has tackled the issue of testing by creating a web-site called "What Every Parent Should Know About Standardized Testing."[9]

Children talk about state-mandated tests at the dinner table, while waiting at the bus stop, and during play dates. Children even start thinking about state tests years before they actually take them. As a personal example, during a long Thanksgiving drive home the five-year old son of one of the authors turned from his DVD and asked, "Dad, what is MCAS?" He was told that MCAS was a test that students take starting in third grade. Two years later, when a friend told the son that he was nervous about starting second grade, the son reassured the boy by saying, "Oh, you have nothing to be afraid of this year. You don't need to take MCAS until third grade."

In some schools, ten-year olds now take up to four tests per week focusing on the skills and knowledge their teachers expect will appear on the state test. While some students look forward to taking these tests, other children have trouble sleeping, become sick to their stomachs, and ask to stay home from school. As just one example, a parent of a fifth grade girl attending school in Georgia emailed one of the authors concerned that, "The sheer amount of class time taken up with testing weekly is substantial . . . As her teachers stress how important it is to study for these tests, we find ourselves on most weeknights (and many weekends) helping our daughter to prepare or—more accurately—to cram." Across the nation, the kind of test preparation lamented by the Georgia parent usurps time for autonomous learning—teaching becomes more controlling and learning more narrow.

Like many others across the country, the Georgia parent is troubled that his fifth grader's attitude toward learning and school has changed, and not for the better. "We have watched with distress how over the course of this year our daughter's joy in learning has been dampened, and how she has come to find studying oppressive. I should add that this experience is not ours alone . . . A teacher at the school told us how her 10-year-old son, one of our daughter's classmates, was recently so distraught at the breakfast table one morning that, when she asked him what was wrong, he burst into tears and wailed, 'I've got three tests this week!!!' This from a ten-year old." This parent's concern should not be dismissed as merely anecdotal—it reflects a legitimate concern raised by parents across the nation.

To prepare children for high-stakes tests, some parents turn to gadgets to give their kids a competitive edge. Cell phones present children with practice questions while they wait for the bus. Web sites give students instant feedback on sample tests.[10] Students can download test preparation programs from iTunes onto iPods with video screens.[11] Some popular Japanese style comic books called "manga" are designed to help students prepare for high-stakes tests.[12] There are even toys purporting to improve test performance several years down the road. For example, in 2004, The New York Times ran a story with the headline *For Some Parents It's Never too Early for S.A.T. Prep.* The story focused on the *Time Tracker,* a $34.95 toy on the market that holiday season which purported to help children as young as four better manage their time when taking a high-stakes standardized test years later.[13]

To increase the chances that their children will pass the high-stakes state test, starting in the third grade, some parents enroll their children in tutoring and test preparation courses. For children of the less affluent, No Child Left Behind (NCLB) provides funding for tutoring for two million children.[14] The tutoring and test preparation industry is very lucrative. Revenues are expected to grow to $1.3 billion by 2009.[15] Other parents, concerned that their children may perform poorly on state mandated high-stakes tests, consider sending them to parochial or private schools not subject to state and federal testing mandates.[16]

Hardly a day passes without a newspaper or television news report concerning testing. Average test scores for schools and districts are the focus of headline news stories. There are stories about school scores going up; and headlines about scores going down. There are stories about novel attempts by school administrators to improve student performance on state tests. We read about plans to pay students cash for scoring well on standardized tests.[17] In a story entitled, *The Power of Peppermint Put to the Test,* the Washington Post describes how a school principal ordered 3,600 peppermint candies for students to eat on the day of the test to help improve performance on the Maryland School Assessments.[18] A New York Daily News headline tells us, *Bronx 8th-Graders Boycott Practice Exam But Teacher May Get Ax.*[19] Another story in the Boston Globe tells the moving story of an exemplary 4th grade teacher who must leave in the middle of the semester to serve in Iraq. As a reminder that he was 100 percent behind them, even though he was miles away, the teacher gave each student a pencil inscribed with his name on it to use when taking the state test.[20]

Schools are publicly rated and ranked based on test scores. In turn, the valuation of homes in a community can increase or decrease based on these rankings. When Coppell, Texas, received an "unacceptable" rating on the state test, the superintendent of schools called it the biggest crisis of his career. Some frantic Coppell homeowners called real estate companies to talk about selling their homes "because they [were] afraid that housing values will plunge."[21] Seventeen hundred miles away, the Boston Globe ran an advertisement for a real estate search engine that displayed several houses. One home was crossed out because the taxes were too high. Another was crossed out because the neighborhood was too rural. A third was dinged because the scores on the states math test were below average.[22]

Similarly, there are news stories that compare test scores across districts. In 2006, the Hartford Courant reported that only one third grade boy in the Milner School in Hartford reached the state goal on the reading mastery test, while four miles away in West Hartford, five out of six third graders at the Bugbee School reached the goal.[23] In Massachusetts, the Boston Globe reported that one affluent suburban town wants to "catch up" with its neighbors by getting more students to the advanced level on that state's test.[24]

Stories about testing errors and cheating also make headlines. The media reports on increasing demands for a single national testing program. Reporters write about the need for more testing, in more grades, in more subjects. Editorial arguments in major newspapers tout the value of test based accountability. For example, a September 2007, *New York Times* editorial on the reauthorization of NCLB argued that the country still has a long way to go to reach the ambitious goals set in 2002 when NCLB became law. The editorial opined that, "they will never be met if Congress . . . backs away from provisions that hold schools accountable for how well and how much children learn."[25]

Testing is also the subject of cartoonists. A search of Google Images reveals more than 4,000 cartoons related to high-stakes testing. As just one example, the cartoon by Jimmy Margulies in Figure 1.1 captures an important paradoxical negative outcome of high-stakes testing programs—the intensive emphasis on test preparation.[26]

High-stakes testing also appears on prime time TV. Portraying a lawyer on *Boston Legal*, Michael J. Fox argues before a court that testing is placing undue pressure on teachers. Fox's character expounds, "Instead of teaching children to be innovative our educators are forced to teach to the test . . . it's been documented that nation wide that some teachers have themselves cheated on the tests because their salaries, their bonuses, their job security are linked to the test scores."[27] In a 20/20 broadcast titled *Stupid in America* John Stossel cites test scores as evidence that our schools are failing. In 2006, Oprah Winfrey ran a two-part special called *American Schools in Crisis*. She discussed test scores and used test results as evidence of a crisis, and also praised schools with high-test scores.[28]

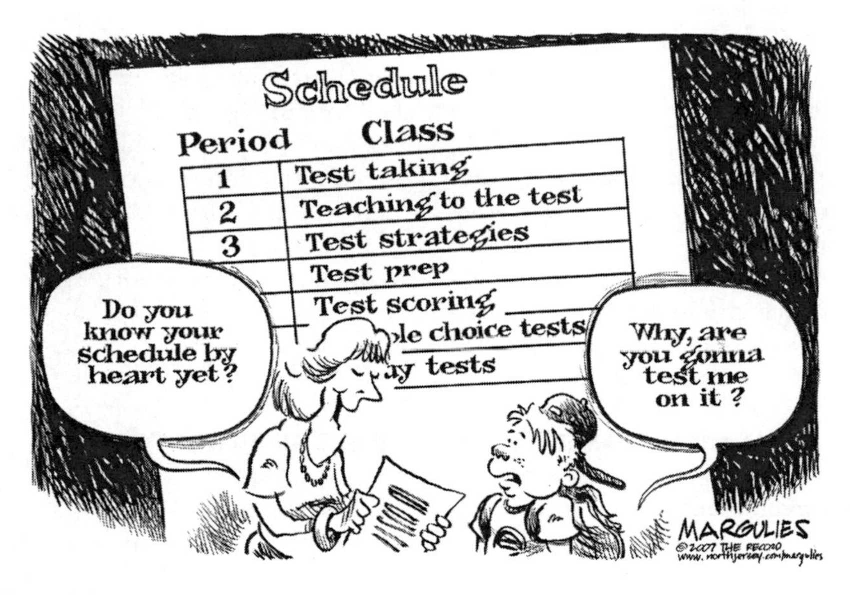

Figure 1.1

Testing also crops up in unexpected places. There is a CD containing songs with titles like "Test the Kids" and "No Child Left Untested."[29] A program for a school string concert reminds parents: "Students with course work/experience in music performance scored 55 points higher on the verbal and 38 points higher on the math portions of the SAT than students with no coursework/experience in the arts."[30]

An award winning Broadway play, titled "The History Boys," contrasts the approach taken by two teachers preparing students for the Oxbridge entrance exam. Mr. Hector emphasizes the pursuit of knowledge as its own reward. Driven by the high-stakes test, Mr. Irwin focuses his instruction on test-taking techniques that will garner higher scores.[31] In a play by August Wilson, titled *Radio Golf,* a handyman describes his reaction to seemingly simple test questions and the consequences that follow:

> They kept me behind in the fourth grade 'cause I wouldn't add twelve and twelve. I thought it was stupid. Everybody knows there's twelve to a dozen and twenty-four to two dozens. I don't care if it's donuts or oranges. They handed me the test and I turned it in blank. If you had seventeen dollars and you bought a parrot for twelve dollars how many dollars would you have left? Who the hell gonna spend twelve dollars on a parrot? What you gonna do with it? Do you know how many chickens you can buy for twelve dollars? They thought I didn't know the answer.[32]

Testing is also a hot political topic. Since the end of World War II testing has been presented as a political solution to educational problems. In 2002, high stakes testing was the principal tool in George W. Bush's plan to improve our nation's schools. In a rare show of bipartisanship, both Republicans and Democrats endorsed the testing requirements of NCLB. In 2007, testing became an even more hot button topic during debates about reauthorizing NCLB.

Indeed, from supper tables to the halls of Congress, from morning newspapers to prime time TV, from kindergartners to the President of the United States, high-stakes testing captivates our nation.

IS HIGH-STAKES TESTING THE BREAD OF REFORM?

For many readers it seems reasonable to use test scores to hold teachers and schools accountable for student achievement. It may also seem reasonable to hold students back if they do not perform to a certain level on a test. And it certainly seems sensible to provide parents with test scores to use in choosing a school for their children or a community when relocating. In each of these cases it seems reasonable to use test scores because they are assumed to be an objective valid measure of effective teaching, student knowledge and skills, and, more broadly, the quality of education. But how reasonable are these assumptions?

For many politicians, and many in the business and testing communities, testing has morphed from a means of obtaining information about the education system to a key strategy for improving educational quality. Testing is viewed as both a system of *monitoring* student performance and a *vehicle of change* driving what is taught, how it is taught, what is learned, and how it is learned. Testing is seen as essential in developing a world class education system, motivating the unmotivated, lifting all students to world class standards, increasing our nation's productivity, and restoring global competitiveness.

A reform tool with these practical uses and desirable societal outcomes would truly be manna from above. Manna to improve our schools, and feed our teachers and students who are often depicted as wandering in a desert of mediocrity.

Manna is generally defined as something valuable—bread from heaven. But manna has another meaning. Exodus recounts that when the Israelites awoke to find "a fine, flake-like thing," they naturally asked, "*manna*"? "What is it?"

Given the paradoxes inherent in high-stakes tests—the positive, negative, and mister-in-between—it is time to ask, "Manna?" What are these tests our children must take? Is high-stakes testing really the bread of reform or are there weevils in the flour? This book addresses the question, "Manna ?"

We begin in Chapter 2 by answering the question, "How did testing become so important?" We examine the progression of testing from a relatively benign educational tool recording the effects of educational reform to a primary tool driving reform. Chapter 2 also explores the unexamined assumptions, values, and ideologies that have given rise to the current emphasis on test results.

Chapter 3 answers the seemingly simple question, "What is a test?" It explains the essential elements of any test. Building on these key elements, Chapters 4 and 5 examine the questions, "What human and cultural factors affect test performance?" and "What technical issues affect test validity?" Chapter 4 describes the relationship between culture and test performance, challenges in defining what is supposed to be measured by a test, the interplay between ideology and the test questions used to measure student performance, and ways in which students interact with test items differently than was intended by the item writer. Chapter 5 examines issues related to test validity, cut-scores, and reliability.

Chapter 6 answers the question, "Why Is It Important to Regard Testing as a Technology?" Many modern technologies are so opaque that we do not think of them as technologies at all. Many of today's technologies are dependent on hidden algorithms that are understood by only a small group of technical experts. In Chapter 6, we learn that hidden algorithms and complex modeling techniques also underpin high-stakes testing. This chapter analyzes current testing programs through the lenses of the history and philosophy of technology.

Chapter 7 addresses the question, "Why is the History of Testing Important?" Since Before the Common Era, tests have been used as a tool to address a variety of political, social, educational, and economic concerns of the power elite. But today's policy makers seem oblivious to this history and its lessons. This history is a story about addressing aspects of testing that acted as a drag, particularly as the number of examinees increased. Testing has continually evolved to meet new demands and integrate other technologies. As we will see, none of today's uses of high-stakes tests, or their paradoxical consequences, are new or unique.

In Chapter 8, we answer the central question, "What Are The Paradoxical Consequences Of High-Stakes Testing?" We recount the many ways in which high-stakes testing affects students, families, teaching, learning, and the curriculum. Across the centuries and continents, there is a wealth of evidence that well intended high-stakes testing produces chronic unintended negative consequences. It is these unintended negative consequences that make high-stakes testing paradoxical.

Chapter 9 explores the question, "What is the Future of Testing?" Not long from now, the marriage of computer-based technologies and the technology of testing will produce tests that are dramatically different than what students take today. In this chapter we foretell the next stages in testing's continuing evolution and describe how today's focus on high-stakes testing inhibits this union.

Chapter 10 raises the question, "Who Is Watching Over High-Stakes Testing?" The benefits and hazards that result from current testing policies are significant for students, educators, and society. What other institution would contemplate subjecting millions of children to a treatment that carries with it serious consequences without first evaluating claims about the treatment? This chapter makes the case for establishing an independent agency that evaluates testing programs before adoption and monitors test use and impact after implementation. The need for an institutionalized means to perform such functions is urgent given the importance of testing for society, testing's fallible nature, and the accelerated growth of high-stakes testing programs.

Given the amount of time, money, and resources our nation is investing to test millions of our children every year from kindergarten through high school, it is essential that we address these eight questions. It is time to ask of high-stakes testing, "Manna?"

NOTES

1. There are a few exceptions. If you lived in New York and wanted a Regents diploma, you had to pass subject matter tests at the end of each school year. If you lived in some southern states during 1970s, you may have taken a minimum competency test for graduation.
2. There are calls to extend NCLB's accountability provisions to testing the achievement of students enrolled in public colleges and universities. For example see Hickok (2006).
3. Sable & Garofano (2007).
4. Eduventures (2006).
5. Hubbard (2006).
6. The numbers for Maryland, Texas, and Michigan came from the state DOE websites that contained the state assessment calendar. We then simply counted the number of unique dates where a test would be administered during the normal school year.
7. The GED is the General Educational Development Tests that are designed to measure the outcome of a high school education.
8. Goodkin & Gold (2007).
9. Arms (2008).
10. Sandoval (2005).
11. Aspan (2007).

12. Bloomberg News (2007). Also see Aspan (2007).
13. Bick (2006); Hays (2004). Another toy, for children 5 and older, is the Geosafari Quiz phone that has over 400 quiz questions and answers for five school subjects. See http://www.youngexplorers.com/itemdy00.asp?c=&T1=Y518884&GEN1=Electronic+Learning+Aids&SKW=ela&PageNo=1#zoom
14. In 2004, only 226,000 or 12 percent of eligible students received such help (Saulny (2006).
15. Hopkins (2004); Saulny (2006).
16. For example see Winerip (2006).
17. See for example Medina (2007). Private money would be used to pay students for between 250 and 500 dollars for perfect scores on standardized tests administered throughout the year.
18. Aratani (2007).
19. Gonzalez (2008).
20. Milton (2008).
21. Schnurman (2005). Reflecting on this story, the reporter stated:

    > That's because the test results were an anomaly, rather than a reflection of the school district's actual performance. Its rating fell, because of a handful of special ed students, whose test scores were matched against their teachers' expectations, rather than a general standard... Not only were residents frantic — they were frantic over a fluke.

    Also see Helderman (2002); Winerip (2005) for additional examples.
22. *Boston Globe* (2008).
23. Green (2006). The reporter, Rick Green, laments that he cannot any find outrage, "News that we have a school where just one precious boy gets our seal of education approval slips by us like dirty water down the drain."
24. Sacchetti (2006).
25. *New York Times* editorial (2007).
26. Margulies (2007).
27. Kelley (2006).
28. See: http://www.oprah.com/tows/pastshows/200604/tows_past_20060412.jhtml.
29. WholeChild Education Reform (date unknown).
30. Needham MA (2006).
31. Bennett (2004).
32. Wilson (2005).

CHAPTER 2

WHY HAS TESTING BECOME SO IMPORTANT?

Why has high-stakes testing so captivated our nation? Without answering this question, one can't fully appreciate the prominence of testing in current state and federal policy or the paradoxical outcomes associated with high-stakes testing programs. We begin this chapter by describing the attraction policy makers and political leaders have had with high-stakes testing for centuries. Building on this historical context, we then recount events since the 1950s that have fueled the growth of high-stakes testing in the United States.

A BRIEF HISTORY OF THE ROLE OF TESTING IN EDUCATIONAL REFORM AND ACCOUNTABILITY

Over the centuries and across nations tests have been employed as bureaucratic tools for a variety purposes. As far back as 200 BC, the Chinese used high-stakes tests to help eliminate patronage and open access to the civil service. England, France, Italy, among other nations, have used high-stakes tests to ensure that students acquire certain skills and establish standards of performance. In 15th century Italy, high-stakes tests were used to hold teachers accountable for student learning. Since then, policy-makers have

The Paradoxes of High Stakes Testing, pages 13–35

used high-stakes tests to hold students and schools accountable and allocate scarce resources.

These various high-stakes testing policies were not meant to be punitive. Instead, these policies were and continue to be sincere attempts to open doors of opportunity and address perceived problems in education. Two facts help explain why policy-makers are attracted to high-stakes testing as a solution to problems in society and education. First, policy-makers realize they cannot directly regulate instruction in classrooms. But, they can indirectly influence instruction by attaching rewards or sanctions to mandated tests. Policy makers have always been aware that a high-stakes test forces teachers to adjust instruction to prepare students for the test.

This faith in the power of testing to shape education is not new or uniquely American. For example, in 1444 the town fathers of Treviso, Italy believed that students would learn if teachers taught "correctly." To motivate the schoolmaster to teach "correctly," his salary was dependent on students' level of attainment on an oral examination.[1] When students did well, the schoolmaster's salary increased. When students did poorly, the schoolmaster was penalized financially.

The Irish Intermediate Education Act of 1878 further demonstrates how policy-makers relied on tests to attain their educational goals. The Act set up a seven-member board charged with developing a system of education for the country and stipulated that secular education in Ireland be promoted by "instituting and carrying on a system of public examinations of students. "Like today's policy-makers, the 19th century Irish realized that a system of high-stakes tests would define educational quality, determine the curriculum, shape teacher's focus, and become the criteria of success for students, teachers, and parents.[2]

In the 19th century, political theorists recognized the need for universal literacy and realized high-stakes tests would promote literacy. In *Wealth of Nations*, Adam Smith reasoned that a literate working class would emerge "by *obliging every man to undergo an examination* [on the central parts of education] . . . before he can obtain the freedom in any corporation, or be allowed to set up any trade either in a village or town corporate."[3] Similarly, John Stuart Mill advocated for a law that would require every citizen to be able to read, write, and possess a minimum amount of general knowledge.

To enforce this law, Mill believed children should be tested yearly. Each year, the range of subjects examined would expand "so as to make the universal acquisition, and what is more, retention, of a certain minimum of general knowledge, virtually compulsory." To ensure that families made an effort to educate their children, Mill attached high-stakes: "If a child proves unable [to pass the test], the father, unless he has some sufficient ground of excuse, might be subjected to a moderate fine, to be worked out, if necessary, by his labor, and the child might be put to school at his expense."[4]

Many aspects of Mill's proposal are clearly present in today's high-stakes testing policies.

Beyond controlling teaching and learning, high-stakes tests have served as an accountability tool that insures value for expenditures of taxpayer's money. The Treviso "payment by results" effort serves as a clear example. The logic behind using high-stakes tests to hold teachers, students, and schools accountable was expressed by Eamon DeValera, the Prime Minister of Ireland. Proposing a system of certification examinations at the end of primary school, he argued successfully before Parliament in 1941:

> ...if we want to see that a certain standard is reached and we are paying the money, we have the right to see that something is secured for that money. The ordinary way to test it and try to help the whole educational system is by *arranging our tests in such a way that they will work in a direction we want.*[5]

Like many of today's policymakers, DeValera believed that high-stakes tests provide the evidence that determines whether taxpayers' money is well spent. This reasoning is reflected clearly in President Bush's reliance on high-stakes tests to evaluate the success of educational programs. When asked whether he thought No Child Left Behind was working, Bush replied:

> Listen, the whole theory behind No Child Left Behind is this: If we're going to spend federal money, we expect the states to show us whether or not we're achieving, you know, simply objectives, like literacy, literacy in math, the ability to read and write.
>
> And, yes, we're making progress. And I can say that with certainty, because we're *measuring*....Instead of just spending money and hoping for the best, we're now spending money and saying, *Measure.*[6]

Bush's use of high-stakes tests to measure the outcomes of education reflects a larger belief in the use of metrics to determine the success of any policy. As Ken Mehlman, the former chairman of the Republican National Committee describes, "If you can't measure it, it's not worth doing, because then you [don't] [sic] know whether you're being successful. That's how you avoid hope being your strategy."[7]

For contempory policy makers, and many in the business community, testing has moved from a means of obtaining information about students and the education system to a key strategy for improving student learning and educational quality. Testing is viewed as both a system of monitoring and a vehicle of change that is consciously used to dictate the ends of the instructional system, and change teacher behavior and classroom instruction.[8]

The belief in the efficacy of high-stakes tests to monitor and shape education, as well as foster accountability has great resilience. The rise of high-stakes testing in the United States is rooted in the idea that the correct system of rewards and punishments will motivate obstinate, dispirited, lazy, or recalcitrant students, as well as their teachers, to try harder.[9]

There are three assumptions underlying policies that use high-stakes tests as a motivating device. First, the greater the reward offered for success or the punishment for failure, the harder students and teachers will try. Second, all teachers and all students will respond to the rewards and punishments in essentially the same way. Third, student and teacher effort is maximized when rewards are distributed on a competitive basis.[10] Although these assumptions are very seductive, they beg two questions. Are these assumptions accurate? And what do high-stakes tests actually motivate people to do? As we shall see throughout this book, responses to high-stakes testing policies produce serious paradoxical consequences for students, parents, teachers, schools, and society.

What factors have contributed to the growth and importance of testing?[11] Standardized tests were used extensively during World War I to identify recruits for officer candidate training. Shortly after the war ended, commercial standardized tests were introduced to our schools. However, until the 1960s, standardized tests had little or nothing to do with state or federal policy. Educational testing policies were, by and large, a local decision. New York was the sole exception. Throughout the 20th century, New York used its Regents examinations as a policy tool to award a Regents diploma to students who pass.

In the 1950s, policies regarding testing began to change. Over the next fifty years, a number of events and federal legislative acts solidified the importance of high-stakes testing in American society. Today high-stakes testing is the primary strategy employed by federal and state governments to monitor and reform the educational system.

The 1950s: Sputnik and the National Defense Education Act

In 1957, the Soviets launched a space satellite called Sputnik. This event sparked nation-wide concern about the United States' competitiveness with the Russians in mathematics and science education. H-bomb creator Edward Teller voiced this fear, "We have suffered a very serious defeat in a field where at least some of the most important engagements are carried out: in the classroom."[12] Similarly, the noted scholar Arthur Bestor phrased his concern this way: "We have wasted an appalling part of the time of our young people on trivialities. The Russians have had sense enough not to do so. That's why the first satellite bears the label 'Made in Russia'."[13] Sputnik-inspired concern produced the National Defense Education Act (NDEA) of 1958—the first major effort by the federal government to reform American education.[14]

To secure Congressional support for federal intervention in elementary and secondary education, the Act was justified as essential for our national defense: "The Congress hereby finds and declares that the security of the nation requires the fullest development of the mental resources and technical skills of its young men and women."[15] The act was a landmark in the expansion of educational testing. The NDEA authorized funds for local testing programs in both public and private systems. For the first time, the federal treasury funded testing at both the state and local levels.[16]

The 1960s: The Civil Rights Movement and Federal Legislation

In the 1960s, federal legislation increased the importance of testing in two distinct ways. First, test results were used to document the need to increase educational opportunities for disadvantaged and minority children. Second, tests were then used to judge the success of various reform programs.

Authorized by the Civil Rights Act, the Equal Educational Opportunity Survey (EEOS) contributed greatly to the exponential growth of educational testing. Commonly known as the Coleman Report after its lead author, the report prompted a dramatic shift in the way people judged school quality.[17] Prior to the report, school quality was judged by *inputs* such as school funding, the state of the physical plant, the number of books in the library, the quality of science and foreign language laboratories, and teacher qualifications. The EEO report shifted the focus of school quality from *inputs* to *outputs*. To measure outputs, the report focused on student test scores. This focus on test scores contributed to the prominence of testing as an accountability tool.[18]

The Elementary and Secondary Education Act of 1965 (ESEA) also increased the importance of educational testing. For the first time, financial assistance was provided to school districts serving high concentrations of low-income families and to state departments of education to develop their capacity to administer state-wide testing programs designed to measure student achievement. [19]

Finally, the National Assessment of Educational Progress (NAEP) raised the use of tests to monitor public education to the national level. Administered periodically to samples of students across the nation, NAEP tested students in various grade levels on mathematics, reading, and science, and occasionally other subjects.[20] Although NAEP results are not used to make high-stakes decisions about individual students or schools, data are used to monitor national and more recently state attainment levels.

NAEP opened the door for the federal government to directly fund, on a continuing basis, the gathering of nationally representative achievement test data. NAEP also reinforced the shift from inputs to outcomes to appraise educational quality. In turn, NAEP data has been used to support calls for educational reform in the 1970s, 1980s, and 1990s, with each call resulting in new testing programs.[21]

The 1970s: The SAT Score Decline and Education for All Handicapped Children Act

During the 1970s, two major events increased the nation's focus on educational testing. First, a decline in SAT test scores was highly publicized. Between 1963 and 1977, the national average SAT verbal score declined by nearly 50 points, and the average math score dropped by about 30 points. This unprecedented decline in test scores sparked intense scrutiny and debate over the quality of high school education.

A special panel concluded that the decline in SAT scores had two causes. It was determined that prior to 1970, the drop in scores was most likely due to "compositional changes" in the population of students taking the SAT. Over a decade, the number of women and minorities taking the SAT increased. Many of these "new" test-takers tended to earn lower SAT scores in comparison to previous test-takers who were predominantly middle- and upper-class white males. After 1970, the continuing decline in SAT scores was believed to result from the waning quality of schools and schooling.[22] As occurred in the 1960s, concern about decreasing quality of schools led to new efforts to reform schools. In turn, tests were used to evaluate the success of these reforms.

The second major event was the enactment of the Education for All Handicapped Children Act of 1975, known as P.L. 94-142.[23] The act mandated that handicapped children have their specific needs identified, receive individual educational plans (IEP), and receive proper placements. The criteria for determining specific learning disabilities included a severe discrepancy between a student's achievement and intellectual ability in one or more of the following areas: oral expression, listening comprehension, written expression, basic reading skills, reading comprehension, mathematical calculation, and mathematical reasoning. Educators turned en masse to standardized tests to measure and document these gaps.

The 1980s: The Courts, Wall Chart, and A Nation at Risk

With good reason, the *New York Times* education writer, Fred Hechinger, described the 1980s as the "Testing Decade."[24] In this decade several major events bolstered the nation's reliance on educational tests. First was the 1981 landmark decision by the United States Fifth Circuit Court of Appeals in *Debra P v Turlington.* Advocates for Debra P. filed a lawsuit when she was denied a high school diploma because she failed the Florida minimum competency graduation test. The court ruled the state's use of the test as a high school graduation requirement was permissible, as long as it measured what was taught in the state's classrooms.[25] The federal court's decision established a precedent for using scores from a state-mandated high-stakes test as a high-school graduation requirement.

A second event occurred in 1984 when Terrence Bell, President Reagan's Secretary of Education, introduced the "wall chart." The federal government used the wall chart to make state-by-state comparisons of not only educational resources and processes, but also "outcomes" including college admissions test scores like the SAT and ACT. According to proponents, the wall chart "signaled a revolution of sorts in the reporting of facts and trends in American education."[26] Unfortunately, this "revolution" improperly used college admissions test scores for a purpose for which they were never intended.[27] Indeed, independent research on the wall chart data quickly showed that the states with the highest college admissions test scores tend to be those in which smaller proportions of students take the tests. Despite these serious problems, the inclusion of SAT and ACT scores on the "wall chart" solidified the perception that test scores were a valid measure of school quality.

As important as *Debra P* and the "wall chart" are in the story of testing's expansion, they pale in comparison to the tectonic shift caused by the 1983 release of *A Nation at Risk,* a report produced by the National Commission on Excellence in Education. Anyone interested in national issues during the 1980s will remember the splash of media coverage caused by *A Nation at Risk.* Like the response to Sputnik, *A Nation at Risk* blamed our educational system for world events that were perceived to threaten our nation.[28] The report dramatically warned, "Our once unchallenged preeminence in commerce, industry, science, and technological innovation is being overtaken by competitors throughout the world... a rising tide of [educational] mediocrity threatens our very future as a Nation and a people."[29] The Commission, in effect, argued that the professed decline in America's economic competitiveness was in no small measure due to the performance of the educational system and, by implication; reform of the system would help to cure the country's economic ills.[30]

Like the Sputnik scare, the Commission also employed a powerful war metaphor placing blame on the educational system for its inaccurate assertion that our economic competitiveness had declined: "[i]f an unfriendly foreign power had attempted to impose on America the mediocre educational performance that exists today, we might well have viewed it as an act of war... We have, in effect, [for the last two decades] been committing an act of unthinking, unilateral educational disarmament."

How did they reach this conclusion? The Commission relied on test scores from multiple sources to assert that the nation's schools were failing.[31] Like policy makers in the preceding decades, the report then embraced testing as a policy tool to improve the quality of education. The report recommended that:

> standardized tests of achievement (not to be confused with aptitude tests) should be administered at major transition points from one level of schooling to another and particularly from high school to college or work. The purposes of these tests would be to: (a) certify the student's credentials, (b) identify the need for remedial intervention, and (c) identify the opportunity for advanced or accelerated work. The tests should be administered as part of a nationwide (but not Federal) system of State and local standardized tests. This system should include other diagnostic procedures that assist teachers and students to evaluate student progress.[32]

In a follow-up study later that year, the Commission found that 35 states had enacted testing requirements and 44 had strengthened graduation requirements since the publication of *A Nation at Risk*.[33]

As seen in previous decades, policy makers in the 1980s relied on test scores to argue that there was a problem in our educational system. Policy makers then called for increased testing in order to determine whether reforms were effective. As the 1980s drew to a close, testing was widely accepted as an essential tool for improving education.

The 1990s to the Present: Goals 2000, Individuals with Disabilities Education Improvement Act, and No Child Left Behind

The 1990s saw yet another round of educational reform proposals which increased the prominence of high-stakes testing in America. The first major reform proposal, enacted into law in 1994, was the Goals 2000: Educate America Act. This Act established eight goals for American education.[34]

In tracing the growth of testing, Goals 2000 is important for two reasons. First, it called for the establishment of "world class" standards that would identify what all students should know and be able to do to live and work in the 21st century. To help authorities determine whether the standards were being met, high-stakes tests are administered. Once high-stakes tests are put into place, they become the de facto standards. For teachers, the content of the tests define what they teach. This is an important paradoxical outcome that is discussed further in Chapter 8.

Second, Goals 2000 called for a national—but not federal—testing program to monitor progress toward the eight goals and the attainment of the "world class" standards.[35] While the idea of a national test had broad appeal, it was never developed. Instead, many states developed their own standards and testing programs.[36] Although none of the goals established by Goals 2000 were ever reached, testing was once again promoted as the policy tool of choice to hold schools and individuals accountable and reenergize our nation's schools.

In 1997, the Individuals with Disabilities Education Act, or IDEA, was enacted. IDEA had important implications for testing because it required that students with disabilities participate in both the general curriculum and assessments of achievement administered by districts and states.[37] The 2004 reauthorization of IDEA continued the expectation that students with disabilities take standardized tests and achieve at levels commensurate to peers without disabilities.[38] This testing requirement was prompted by a belief that if they did not participate in state and local assessment programs, students with disabilities would receive an unequal and inferior education. Here again, tests were used as a tool to alter instruction.

Testing's extraordinary growth that began in the 1950s reached a pinnacle in 2002 when the No Child Left Behind Act was passed.[39] Like policymakers in the past, President Bush used test results to justify the need for the No Child Left Behind Act. He singled out a lack of growth in the NAEP results and argued that the Third International Mathematics and Science Study showed that the U.S. was performing below many of its industrialized competitors.[40] Like past policymakers, Bush turned to testing to improve the quality of educational. Echoing the Ireland's former Prime Minister DeValera, Bush argued:

> We've got to hold people accountable... I do believe that in return for taxpayers' money that the local folks ought to develop accountability measures that tells us all whether or not children are learning to read and write and add and subtract. It is so important to have an accountability system become the cornerstone of reform in America.

The President then declared:

> And you'll hear people say, well, you can't test because it's racist to test. Folks, let me tell you this as plainly as I can: It's racist not to test. It is racist not to measure. Because guess who gets shuffled through the system—children whose parents don't speak English as a first language. It's so much easier to quit on some newly-arrived to our country. It's too hard to educate this person; we'll just move him through. We'll ask him how old they are and put them here, regardless of whether they can read and write. Inner-city kids—it's

> so much easier to walk into a classroom of inner-city kids and say, these kids are too hard to educate, we'll move them through.[41]

President Bush's remarks justifying NCLB clearly illustrate a trend that began in the '50s to use tests to highlight shortcomings in education and to then use tests to eliminate these shortcomings.

WHY ARE CALLS FOR INCREASED TESTING SO CONVINCING?

Like a cyclone, reliance on tests to first identify and then solve educational problems has spiraled and gained strength over the last six decades. During each decade, the funnel cloud of testing has expanded and its impact on our educational system has become more pronounced. The testing cyclone reached full strength with the passage of No Child Left Behind, requiring 30 million students to take high-stakes tests each year.

There are three major reasons why calls for increased testing have been so convincing. First, tests are attractive because they provide quantitative information about students and schools that confers the appearance of fairness, impartiality, authority, and precision.[42] Second, education has long been an easy target for criticism and a convenient scapegoat for perceived societal, economic, and security concerns.[43] Third, to persuade the public that testing is a viable solution to educational problems, proponents of test-based educational reform have employed three effective tactics—a slippery-slope argument, a powerful story line, and the use of pseudo-facts and pseudo-events.

Test Scores are Quantitative

Our society trusts numbers. We like tests because they provide numeric scores.[44] Our society believes test scores are fair, impartial, and precise. Using tests to make important judgments about students, teachers, schools, or the educational system as a whole, creates the impression that these judgments are objective and therefore fair.

This faith in test scores, however, requires a "willed ignorance" about the limitations of high-stakes tests.[45] This willed ignorance is driven by what the eminent sociologist, Robert Merton, call an "imperious immediacy of interest." As he describes, this interest creates "a paramount concern with the foreseen immediate consequences [that] excludes the consideration of further or other consequences of the same act."[46] For proponents of high-stakes testing, there is both a willed ignorance and an imperious immediacy of interest that leads proponents to turn a blind eye to the fallibility of test scores, and the paradoxical, chronic negative consequences of using test scores to make high-stakes decisions.

While tests open doors of opportunity for some, proponents choose to ignore that tests also close doors for others. Proponents overlook the fact that decisions based on state testing programs in elementary school influence the education a student receives. These test-based decisions affect the focus of instruction, the curriculum offered, a student's placement in elementary, middle, and high school, and, for some, whether they graduate or pursue higher education.

Instead of seeing test takers as unique individuals and schools as complex institutions, willed ignorance also allows proponents of high-stakes testing to use the same one-size-fits-all test to quantify and objectify students and their schools. Given the diversity of students and the complexity of teaching and learning, proponents choose to ignore that relying on the same single quantitative measure for all students and schools as the key reform tool is analogous to using only a sledge hammer to renovate a house.

Education is an Easy Target for Attack

Political theorist William Connolly identifies four criteria that make an institution in society an easy target for attack by policy makers.[47] First, the institution can be easily portrayed as a threat to a common identity. Second, the institution can be used to deflect what would otherwise be seen as defects or failings in the political or the business communities. Third, the institution is strategically weak enough to be subjected to punitive measures. Finally, the institution is resilient enough to emerge again as a scapegoat if the proposed reform remedies fail.

The educational system meets all four of Connolly's criteria. Fear of military weakness sparked by Spuntik in the 1950s, and concern about economic competitiveness since the 1980s led policymakers to blame schools for threats to the nation's security and economic competitiveness. Focusing blame on education obscures the failings of business, military, and political institutions. Given its costs and dependence on tax dollars, the educational system is in a strategically weak position to fend off attacks. Yet, education's critical importance for society assures its resilience, that in turn makes it available for blame when reforms fail or new societal problems arise.

It's not that each of 110,000 public schools can't be made better. But as the late John Kenneth Galbraith argued, we make a serious error "in undue generalizations as to the quality of American education."[48] There are some very real, serious educational problems. But to generalize these problems to all students or all schools is a mistake. By and large, problems are specific to certain types of schools—poor, rural, and urban—and groups of students—poor, inner-city children, cultural and linguistic minorities, immigrants, and increasingly the non-college bound. Nonetheless, over the past six decades, critics have used test score data to make generalization across all students and schools, making it appear that the educational system is failing.

This focus on the educational system, as a whole rather than specific groups of students or schools, makes a one-size fits all testing program an attractive solution. But, paradoxically, mandating a universal testing program makes it difficult to accurately delineate, diagnose, and treat underlying specific causes of educational problems. Moreover, as we will see in Chapter 8, mandated testing programs that link rewards or sanctions to test scores chronically triggers a number of unintended and often negative consequences.

The Slippery Slope Argument

To press the message of failing schools and the accompanying need for high-stakes tests, proponents use "slippery slope" arguments to portray individuals or the nation sliding down a perilous slope to cataclysm. While slippery-slope arguments are applied to a host of issues—TV violence, gay marriage, healthcare reform, the war on terror—they are widely used to justify educational reform. As an example, William Bennett, the former U.S. Secretary of Education, once alleged that:

> [o]ver the past three decades we have experienced substantial social regression. Today the forces of social decomposition are challenging—and in some cases, overtaking—the forces of social composition .... *Unless these exploding social pathologies are reversed, they will lead to the decline and perhaps even to the fall of the American republic.*[49]

As we see in Bennett's allegation, conclusions designed to both frighten and capture the moral high ground are smuggled into the premises of slippery slope arguments.

Slippery slope arguments also portray the future as unavoidably unpleasant if certain things are allowed either to happen, or, in the case of education, certain reforms aren't put in place. This was clearly the case, for example, when *A Nation at Risk* alleged that our nation had committed "an act of unthinking, unilateral educational disarmament."

In addition to employing scare tactics, reform supporters often become blindly nostalgic, viewing their own education through the hazy lens of memory. Implicit in many of their arguments and conclusions is the idea that schools were "really better then," or that today's schools have slipped badly, relative to schools of yore. But how can this be when some fifty years ago critics were also arguing that schools were slipping badly?[50]

A Powerful Story Line

To generate mass mobilization and widespread support for a reform agenda, it is essential to have a good story line that justifies the need for reform. A good story line presents an argument that is believable, dramatic, and appears to be based on certain knowledge about the crisis.[51]

Rallying support for a policy initiative requires understandable, consensual, and legitimating social knowledge which is often presented with a facade of apparently unambiguous, doubt free facts.[52] As an example, the authors of *A Nation at Risk* built such a façade using correlations between the test scores of recent graduates and indices of productivity to connect education to an alleged loss of competitiveness.

The need for a powerful story line by those pushing for test-based reform partially explains the disdain for and disregard of data that contradicts the "education in crisis" story line.[53] When building the story line, embarrassing or inconvenient data are willfully ignored. For example, *A Nation at Risk* omitted stronger factors that could explain a slower growth rate in productivity, such as decreased national investment in research, poor management decisions, transition to a service economy and downsizing, possible decreases in the quality of production, and an increase in the use of drugs and alcohol.

The need for understandable and unambiguous facts explains why the technical complexities of testing are never mentioned in the rush to promote high-stakes testing programs. As Gusfield explains, "Summarizing research in ways which eliminate qualifications and uncertainties maintains the smoothness of the story line."[54] Smoothness is important because the appearance of certainty is an essential rhetorical device used to persuade skeptical, recalcitrant, and indifferent people to embrace policy recommendations.

Creating a smooth storyline was clearly evident in the Twentieth Century Fund's 1983 report entitled, *Making the Grade.* It opens by asserting "The nation's public schools are in trouble. By almost every measure . . . the performance of our schools falls far short of expectations."[55] Yet, buried in the appendix of this same report is a commissioned background paper that examined all available information, including test scores, and concluded "[n]othing in these data permits the conclusion that educational institutions have deteriorated badly."[56] Ignoring this finding in the main body of the report safeguarded the smooth storyline.

Like *Making the Grade*, other reports and legislative actions, including *A Nation at Risk*, AMERICA 2000, and No Child Left Behind were not about research. They were a call to, and a justification for, action. Data, technical issues, or alternative interpretations that raise questions or cast doubts about such action plans are unwelcome, and ignored.[57] As Richard J. Samuelson of the *Washington Post* explains:

> By casting their agendas as reforms, political advocates don't aim to stimulate debate and discussion. They aim to suppress it. They aim to stigmatize adversaries as nasty, wrongheaded, selfish or misinformed. If you're in a debate, you want to be the "reformer" and you want the other guy to be the "obstructionist." Once you've achieved that, you're halfway to victory. You've shifted the contest away from substance—an argument over principles and practicality—and toward symbolism, where your symbol is superior.[58]

There is a basic pragmatic motive for presenting a strongly negative and, unqualified, narrative about public education. Media attention is absolutely necessary to get the reform message to the public.[59] The Bush administration was well aware of this fact when it paid the conservative commentator Armstrong Williams to portray NCLB in a favorable manner.[60]

Implicitly or explicitly, various groups and commissions considering education realize that the media looks for simple descriptions of and solutions to complex problems. The press values factoids, definitive sound bites, and a clear case of cause and effect. As the media critic Robert McChesney argues, today's press coverage of policy debates lacks a critical analysis of the arguments on both sides. This, however, was not the intent of our founding fathers:

> They wanted to set up a press system that would challenge people in power. You couldn't have self-government unless you had a press that stood outside those in power. *And [the Founders] assumed everything [those is power] tell you had to be subject to examination. Took nothing for granted. That's the problem we have. And we [the press] say, Well, we'll let people in power debate it, and we'll report it and you decide. That's not journalism. That's stenography.*[61]

An example of McChesney's displeasure with the press was its uncritical reporting of assertions about the quality of education that used NAEP scores to characterize the achievement of students nationwide. The press willfully ignored concerns raised by many test experts regarding the technical merit of the NAEP scores.[62] Clearly, nuanced descriptions, exceptions, complexity, and technical details are not as sensational and compelling as the "education is in crisis" argument.[63]

The Creation of Pseudo-Facts and Pseudo-Events

In addition to creating slippery-slope arguments with a powerful storyline, policy elites also use pseudo-facts and create pseudo-events in order to market their policies.[64]

Pseudo-facts present statistics in a misleading fashion in order to support a story line. Misleading statistics are often used to bolster claims that the economy and America's schools are degrading. As an example, a 2005 article in *Fortune* magazine, entitled "America Isn't Ready [Here's What to Do About It]," offered the seemingly alarming statistic that China produces 600,000 engineers and India 350,000 to the United States' 70,000. Based in part on these data, the article opines, "We're not building human capital the way we used to. Our primary and secondary schools are falling behind the rest of the world's."[65]

Gerald Bracey, who specializing in correcting disinformation, writes in a *Washington Post* Op Ed article, "These numbers [from the *Fortune* story] attained seemingly impeccable credibility when they were featured in a press release last October in a report from the Committee on Science, Engineering, and Public Policy, a joint group from the National Academy of Sciences, National Academy of Engineering, and Institute of Medicine."[66] Bracey points out that The *Fortune* statistics in the Academies' report were then picked up by major newspapers. And he points out that business groups also used the statistics to link the sensitive subject of outsourcing and off-shoring to the supposed short fall of US engineers.[67] Evoking the specter of Sputnik, our schools were alleged to have let us down yet again.

A study by researchers at Duke University, however, found that in fact "the United States annually produces 137,437 engineers with at least a bachelor's degree while India produces 112,000 and China 351,537. That's more U.S. degrees per million residents than in either other nation."[68] Nonetheless, Bracey reports:

> even after the Duke report and other demurrals, these spurious throngs of Chinese and Indian engineers remain alive and well, appearing, for example, in a Newsweek opinion piece last winter by Education Secretary Margaret Spellings. Commerce Secretary Carlos M. Gutierrez repeated the numbers in March to a meeting of the National Association of Manufacturers, and Sen. John W. Warner (R-Va.) cited them in April during an appearance at a Fredericksburg science expo for middle-school students.[69]

Such pseudo-facts, actually urban myths, take on a life of their own and continue to be used to denigrate public education.

In contrast to pseudo-facts, which are the outgrowth of data that is either misinterpreted or embraced despite its inaccuracy, pseudo-events are purposefully engineered by policy makers to sell a story line. Pseudo-events include National Press Club news conferences with on-the-spot TV coverage; interviews on morning and Sunday TV shows; press briefings; "news releases;" news leaks; photo ops; ceremonial appearances by politicians at gatherings such as the "education summits;" and presidential visits to schools.

It is important to realize that pseudo-events are not spontaneous. They are planned for the convenience of the media, in order to create news, heighten and disseminate the elite's message, and help to provide a "common discourse" about an issue.[70] Unlike propaganda, which is an appealing falsehood, the pseudo-events peddle ambiguous truths that are made "more vivid, more attractive, more impressive, and more persuasive than reality itself."[71]

For those who challenge testing policies promoted through pseudo-facts and pseudo-events, it is nearly impossible to receive the same level of media attention as the policymakers. Critics of testing programs generally do not hold positions of power that provide easy access to the press. As a result, it is nearly impossible to create pseudo-events that attract widespread media attention. In addition, the complexities and paradoxes of testing do not lend themselves to short sound bites. Yet, correcting pseudo-facts often requires discussing technical issues that are difficult for the press to convey to the general public.

WHY ARE HIGH-STAKES TESTING POLICIES BIPARTISAN?

Why do test-based accountability proposals resonate across the political and ideological spectrum, left, right, and center? How does one explain the similarity of the role of testing in the education bills of the George H. W. Bush and Bill Clinton administrations? Why did Senator Edward Kennedy (D, MA) strongly support the enactment of George W. Bush's NCLB?

What at first seems like bipartisan unity around a common national problem and its remedies is a more complicated story. Using testing scores, both sides implicate the public schools as a cause of the growing sense of loss in the American economic and social dream, and want the schools reformed, but for different reasons.

On one hand, Democrats strongly believe in the efficacy of governmental programs and of public education, in particular, to reduce social and economic inequality. From this perspective they see the need to reform the schools in order to restore education's image as one of the principal institutions of governmental efficacy. On the other hand, Republicans—who believe in smaller government, getting the government off the backs of the people, individual responsibility, and the efficacy of free-market forces—see failing schools as a testimony to an inefficient large governmental bureaucracy. Viewed from this perspective, opening education to energetic market forces will reform the public schools by reducing governmental bureaucracy and interference.

But why do both sides advocate educational accountability through a system of high-stakes achievement tests? First, as the retired Yale professor of psychology, Seymour Sarason describes, such a system has "surface plausibility" in an age of "quality control in education."[72] Second, test scores formed the basis for describing the crisis in education in the first place; therefore, what better criterion of the success of reform programs than improved test scores. Third, a testing system has appealing symbolic value to both parties; symbols of failure, low test scores, will be replaced by a symbol of success, world-class standards embodied in tough tests.

Advocates on both sides view a high-stakes testing system as a cheap, efficient, self-justifying technological fix. As we develop in Chapter 6 testing is a technology, and, therefore, plays well to the mentality that technical solutions are less painful than solutions that require social or political change.[73] Like all tools, tests are incorrectly regarded as value neutral. Using tests as a reform tool conceals the political aims of a reform. Unable to legislate classroom behavior, policy makers realize that testing is a tool that motivates educators to alter instructional process.

For Democrats specifically, test scores provide evidence that government programs can be made to work. For Republicans, the very same test scores provide evidence that existing bureaucracies are inefficient, incentives for teachers and students to work harder, and criteria that form the basis of school choice and voucher plans.

The purpose of a technological fix, such as high-stakes testing, is control or power over a social problem. Unfortunately, neither Democrats nor Republicans seem to realize that such fixes rarely work as intended and produce the paradoxical consequences which we detail in Chapter 8.[74] Seymour Sarason, in his *Letters To a Serious Education President,* captures the paradoxes of a high-stakes testing program:

> Isn't it surprising that proponents of the program never (but never) say anything about possible negative side effects, or can imagine unintended consequences, or indicate that they are aware of the minuscule improvements (if any) of state-mandated programs?[75]

For Democrats, the irony is that a high-stakes testing system—certainly an energetic government intervention—has the potential to diminish pluralism across the curriculum, teaching, and learning. In addition, such a system might lessen the control that individuals have over decisions that affect their lives. For Republicans, the paradox is that a testing system like NCLB requires *more* federal regulation, not less. Furthermore, such a system has the distinct potential to tightly regulate cherished school-choice proposals. If the primary criterion for making a choice is to judge the quality of a school by its performance on mandated tests, then the potential impact of free-market forces on education is constricted to a narrow concept of quality, that is, whatever the test measures. Consequently true control of schools by the people through informed choice criteria is constrained.

CONCLUSION

The steady rise of testing as a policy tool in education since the 1950s stems from the following perceptions: tests provide objective measures of student learning and document deficiencies in the educational system; schools and teachers will respond positively to a testing regime; and without test-based reform, our international competitiveness and subsequent economic well-being is in jeopardy. As we traced above, over the past sixty years calls for increased testing have employed strong storylines publicized through pseudo-events and aided by the media that relies heavily on pseudo-facts provided by advocates of test-based reform. But calls for test-based educational reform consistently ignore the technical nature of testing, the fallibility of tests, and the unintended negative consequences that inevitably emerge. In the chapters that follow, we explore these issues in greater detail. But before doing so, it is essential to understand what a test is.

NOTES

1. Aries (1962).
2. Madaus & Greaney (1985).
3. Smith (1846, p. 352, emphasis added).
4. Mill (1961, p. 352).
5. Ireland. Dail Eireann (1941, col. 119, emphasis added).
6. Bush (2005).
7. Frontline/WGBH (2005).
8. Kellaghan & Greaney (2001).
9. Webb, Covington, & Guthrie (1993).
10. Kellaghan, Madaus, & Raczek (1996).
11. For brevity's sake, we confine our analysis to national rather than state initiatives, although state-level decisions have contributed to testing's growth as well.
12. Teller (1957, p. 65).
13. Bestor (1958, p. 69); Rickover (1957, p. 91); Trace (1961, p. 3).
14. Another Cold War controversy that affected schools came to be known as the muscle gap. When John F. Kennedy ran against Richard Nixon for president, he argued there was a "missile gap" between the U.S. and Russia. A large part of his platform was that the U.S. had to regain its role as "Number 1" in many

areas. After his election, Kennedy asserted that American children needed to be more physically fit, because there was also a so-called "muscle gap." He worked with the President's Council on Youth Fitness to implement his idea that every student should exercise for 15 minutes every day, and there was a large-scale advertising campaign associated with the effort.

15. National Defense Education Act of 1958, Section 101.
16. Ironically, we managed to defeat Soviet communism despite our abandonment in the 1970s of Sputnik-inspired math and science curricular reforms in favor of a basic skills/minimum competency reform agenda.
17. Coleman et al. (1966, p. 53). The report's startling conclusion was that "[s]chools bring little influence to bear on a child's achievement that is independent of his background and general social context." The media erroneously simplified this conclusion as "schools don't make a difference." Although inaccurate and counterintuitive, the "schools don't make a difference" mantra contributed to the stereotype of failing schools and to the widespread adoption of high-stakes testing programs.
18. Haney, Madaus, & Lyons (1993); Madaus, Airasian, & Kellaghan (1980).
19. Not surprisingly, test results then became the yardstick used to measure the success of Title I as well as other federal interventions such as Head Start and Follow Through.
20. Over the years, details of NAEP's administration, such as the frequency of assessment and in the grade level targeted, have changed. Currently, assessments are conducted every second year on samples of students in grades 4, 8, and 12. Eleven instructional areas have been assessed periodically. Most recent reports have focused on reading and writing, mathematics and science, history, geography and civics. Data have been reported by state, gender, ethnicity, type of community and region.
21. NAEP led to the development of new scaling, reporting, and sampling techniques.
22. Wirtz (1977, p. 46–48).
23. Since 1975 the Education for All Handicapped Children Act has been changed in several major ways. In 1986, amendments extended the right to free and appropriate public education for children with disabilities to include preschoolers aged 3 to 5. In 1990, the Education of the Handicapped Act amendments were renamed as the Individuals with Disabilities Education Act. Two new categories of disability were added (autism and traumatic brain injury) and various kinds of service coordination were mandated (Hardman, Drew, Egan, & Wolf, 1993).
24. Hechinger (1990).
25. For a detailed description of minimum competency testing see Airasian, et al. (1979). For a treatment of the Debra P case and its impact, see Madaus (1983).
26. Ginsburg, Noell, & Plisko (1988, p. 1).
27. Haney et al. (1993).
28. See Madaus (1995) for an analysis of error in the economic and educational assertions in *A Nation at Risk*.
29. National Commission on Excellence in Education (1983a).

30. Similar dire warnings were echoed in the Twentieth Century Fund's *Making the Grade* that opened with, "The nation's public schools are in trouble. By almost every measure... the performance of our schools falls far short of expectations" (Twentieth Century Fund Task Force on Federal Elementary and Secondary Education Policy (1983). In 1987, Bill Clinton, then governor of Arkansas, affirmed this catastrophic diagnosis in declaring, "Educational reform in the eighties was born of a national consensus that America could not maintain its economic, political, or military leadership in the world, or continue to offer its own children the promise of a brighter tomorrow without much better schools" (Clinton, 1987, p. 5).
31. The indicators of this "mediocrity" were results from the National Assessment of Educational Progress, the SAT score decline, studies of functional literacy, data from the International Assessment of Educational Achievement and test scores from the Department of Defense.
32. Op. cit., p. 28.
33. National Commission on Excellence in Education (1983b).
34. The Goals 2000 Act grew out of an "education summit" where President George H. W. Bush and the National Governors Association, headed at that time by Governor Clinton, announced six National Education Goals, later augmented to eight. These goals included:
    1. All children will start school ready to learn.
    2. The high school graduation rate will increase to at least 90%.
    3. By the year 2000, all students will leave grades 4, 8, and 12 having demonstrated competency over challenging subject matter including English, mathematics, science, foreign languages, civics and government, economics, arts, history, and geography, and every school in America will ensure that all student learn to use their minds well, so they may be prepared for responsible citizenship, further learning, and productive employment in our Nation's modern economy.
    4. By the year 2000, the Nation's teaching force will have access to programs for the continued improvement of their professional skills and the opportunity to acquire the knowledge and skills needed to instruct and prepare all American students for the next century.
    5. U.S. students will be first in the world in science and mathematics achievement.
    6. Every adult American will be literate and will possess the knowledge and skills necessary to compete in a global economy and exercise the rights and responsibilities of citizenship.
    7. Every school in America will be free of drugs and violence and will offer a disciplined environment conducive to learning.
    8. By the year 2000, every school will promote partnerships that will increase parental involvement and participation in promoting the social, emotional, and academic growth of children.
35. It is important to note that Goals 2000 called for a national test rather than a federal test. A federal test is one developed and administered by the federal government. A national test, like the SAT, is one used across the nation, but

developed by an independent, non-governmental organization. The idea of a federal test was not accepted politically at the time.

36. Goals 2000 established the National Education Standards and Improvement Council. The Council was charged with examining and certifying national and state content, performance, and opportunity-to-learn standards as well as the assessment systems voluntarily submitted by states.
37. McLoughlin & Lewis (2005).
38. Hallahan & Kaufmann (2006).
39. Contributing to this extraordinary growth in testing was the bureaucratization of education. Following World War II, control of American schooling became increasingly centralized. With increased centralization came increased bureaucratization and tests became a necessity. Test scores expedite formal and impersonal administrative procedures, such as accountability and the definition of merit.
40. Bush (2001).
41. Ibid.
42. Porter (1995).
43. See Berliner (1993); Berliner & Biddle (1995); Tanner (1993).
44. See Porter (1995) for more details.
45. The author Gary Wills (2000) argues that "willed ignorance" is "so useful that one protects it, keeps it from the light, in order to continue using it."
46. Merton (1936).
47. Connolly (1991).
48. Galbraith (1992).
49. Bennett (1994, emphasis in the original).
50. See Bestor (1958, p. 72).
51. Boles (1982); Gusfield (1981).
52. Gusfield (1981, p. 63). See also Keenan (1993); McCormick (1993).
53. There are a number of excellent sources of contrary, positive evidence about our public schools. Here are just a few:
    - Haney's (2001a) examination of the so-called "Texas Miracle".
    - Bracey (1992); Bracey (1993); Bracey (1997); Bracey (2004a); Bracey (2004b). Bracey's annual lament, substantiated by a careful compilation of evidence, that there is good news about the public schools but that it is ignored or receives short.
    - Berliner's (1993) compilation of data, which undercuts 13 malignant myths about the public schools, such as: today's youth do not seem as smart as they used to be; they cannot think as well as they used to; our top students are not as good as they were; the performance on standardized achievement tests reveals gross inadequacies; we don't produce enough mathematicians and scientists to maintain our competitiveness in world markets; and the U.S. is an enormous failure in international comparisons of test performance. They also examine the consequences of high-stakes testing. See also Berliner (1993); Nichols & Berliner (2005).
    - The Sandia National Laboratories study, which found steady or slightly improving trends in public education on nearly every measure examined,

despite dramatic demographic changes in our schools. See Carson, Huelskamp, & Woodall (1992); Huelskamp (1993).

- The Organization for Economic Cooperation's "statistical portrait of American education that is far more favorable than several studies undertaken in recent years by American educators." See Cellis (1993, p. 1).
- Rotberg's (1990) and Westbury's (1992, 1993) de-mystifying of international comparisons. Westbury, for example, showed that American students who took algebra scored above the Japanese average on the Second International Mathematics Assessment.

54. Gusfield (1981).
55. Twentieth Century Fund Task Force on Federal Elementary and Secondary Education Policy (1983, p. 3).
56. Peterson (1983, p. 59).
57. The United States, at the time of *A Nation at Risk,* and well into the 1990s was the most productive and competitive nation in the world (Kotkin & Kishimoto, 1988; Nasar, 1993; The Economist, 1994b). In fact, the Japanese Ministry of Labor issued a detailed report showing Americans had higher productivity and more buying power per hour of labor than workers in Japan, Germany, France, and England. In terms of the key indicator—purchasing power per hour of manufacturing work—Americans out-produced the Japanese by 62 percent. Americans also enjoyed higher productivity figures in agriculture, service and retail sectors (Reid, 1992) . In 1992 the United States led six other Organization of Economic Co-Operation and Development (OECD) countries—including Germany and Japan—in real growth in Gross Domestic Production with a percentage change of 2.8 (Economic Focus,1993). It was true that the American economy was not the overwhelmingly dominant power it was for a quarter century after World War II—a period when the economies of the rest of the world were recovering from the shambles of the war (Dionne, 1992). It was also true that productivity had slowed in rate of growth relative to other countries, but then the rates of growth of other countries were not nearly as steep as they approached the rate of the U.S. (Berliner, 1993).
58. Samuelson (2004, A25).
59. Boles (1982).
60. Writing in the *New York Times,* Robert Pear reported, "Federal auditors [found] that the Bush administration had violated the law by purchasing favorable news coverage of President Bush's education policies, by making payments to the conservative commentator Armstrong Williams... In a blistering report, the investigators, from the Government Accountability Office, said the administration had disseminated 'covert propaganda' inside the United States, in violation of a longstanding, explicit statutory ban" (Pear, 2005).
61. Now with David Brancaccio (2005, emphasis added).
62. Koretz & Deibert (1994); Stufflebeam, Jaeger, & Scriven (1991); Stufflebeam, Jaeger, & Scriven (1992).
63. Soukup (1993).
64. Boorstin (1961); Boorstin (1989).
65. Colvin (2005).
66. Bracey (2006, p. B03).

67. Bracey quotes Professor Ron Hira of the Rochester Institute of Technology to this effect.
68. Bracey (2006, B03).
69. Ibid.
70. Boorstin (1989).
71. Op cite, p. 277.
72. Sarason (1993, p. 109).
73. Volti (1992).
74. Ellul (1964); Ellul (1990); Eulau (1977); Fielder (1992); Hall (1977); Winner (1977); Winner (1986).
75. Sarason (1993, p. 112).

CHAPTER 3

WHAT IS A TEST?

Tests are a common and important part of schooling. Yet, most people are not familiar with how they are made or how they function. An important reason for this lack of knowledge is that testing is a technology. Like most technologies, be it a light bulb, telephone, or automobile, most consumers are not concerned with how they are made or how they function. Such concerns are the province of those who develop and sell them.[1] Instead, most people are interested in how the technology can be used.

After a test is constructed, it may be used for a variety of purposes. Some of these uses, such as measuring student attainment in Algebra 1, are an appropriate use of the technology. Other uses, like using an IQ test to determine readiness for kindergarten, are inappropriate. But there is much more to tests than the many ways they are used. This chapter provides a more complete answer to the question "What is a Test?"

In education, the word "test" describes a tool used to systematically obtain a sample of what a student knows or can do. Sometimes the word "assessment" or "examination" is used synonymously with the word "test." Whatever name you choose, at its core, the technology of testing contains three fundamental ideas that are essential to understanding what a test is.

First, a test measures a specific body of knowledge or set of skills which testing experts refer to as a *domain*. Second, a test is a *sample* of knowledge, skills, or ability from the larger *domain* of interest. Third, this *sample* is used to make an *inference* about the student's probable performance on the larger *domain* of interest and allows users to *describe* or make *decisions* about

The Paradoxes of High Stakes Testing, pages 37–60

an individual or group of test takers. Let us examine each of these ideas in more detail.

A TEST FOCUSES ON A SPECIFIC DOMAIN OF INTEREST

Tests are designed to measure a specific body of knowledge, skills, abilities, or an attribute. For example, a test might measure such things as knowledge of biological terms, ability to write a coherent essay on a current events topic, understanding of the checks and balances in the U.S. Constitution, or ability to rebuild an engine. The area of interest is called the *domain* of a test.

There are three reasons why it is important to understand what a domain is. First, the concept of a domain is central to understanding the two remaining features of a test—sampling and inferences. Second, an understanding of a domain empowers people to ask whether the domain is the correct one given the uses to which the test is put. Third, understanding what a domain is exposes serious problems and misperceptions that result when an improper name is tagged to the domain.

An essential step in creating a test is to clearly define the domain. Some domains can be simple, such as a list of 1,000 vocabulary words. Others are more complex, like the domain of 4th-grade arithmetic problems.

Imagine a department store, called The Arithmetic Depot, which contains all the possible 4th-grade arithmetic problems. As depicted in Figure 3.1, these problems can be organized into infinitely long aisles. One aisle might contain all addition problems; another, multiplication problems; and still another, word problems. Each aisle is what test experts call a sub-domain.

Each sub-domain could be further organized into smaller sections. For example, one section of the addition aisle could contain problems involving single digits while another section contains problems involving three

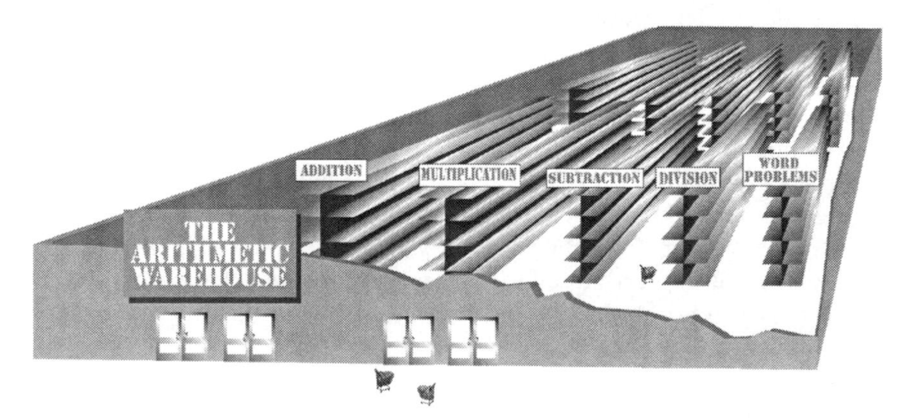

Figure 3.1 Domain of 4th-grade arithmetic.[2] To view a color version of this figure, please visit www.infoagepub.com/madaus_paradoxes.

or more digits that require carrying.[3] Test experts sometimes refer to these sections as facets and refer to the problems as items. Once the domain, sub-domains, and facets are clearly specified, a test can be constructed to measure either the entire domain or a particular facet of it.

A domain like 4th-grade arithmetic is fairly straightforward and determining the skills and knowledge that form the domain sparks little controversy. However, specifying the domain for history, social studies, multiculturalism, areas of science, arts, and literature can be very controversial. People do not always agree on what is important, what is permitted, and what is taboo for these subjects.[4]

In reality, the domains for today's high-stakes tests are defined by the standards or curriculum frameworks established by state departments of education (see Figure 3.2). The role that state standards and curriculum frameworks play in defining the test domain explains, in part, why the process of developing these standards and frameworks can be contentious. Perhaps the most publicized example is the debate about whether "Intelligent Design" should be included in the science standards and curriculum frameworks. Once standards and frameworks are established, they become the de facto domain for test construction.

While Figures 3.1 and 3.2 represent rather typical content, or achievement domains, test domains in education are not limited to academic or curricular areas. A test domain might focus on topics such as skills for a particular occupation or on more abstract traits called *constructs.* Examples of constructs are "intelligence," "motivation," "honesty," "competence,"

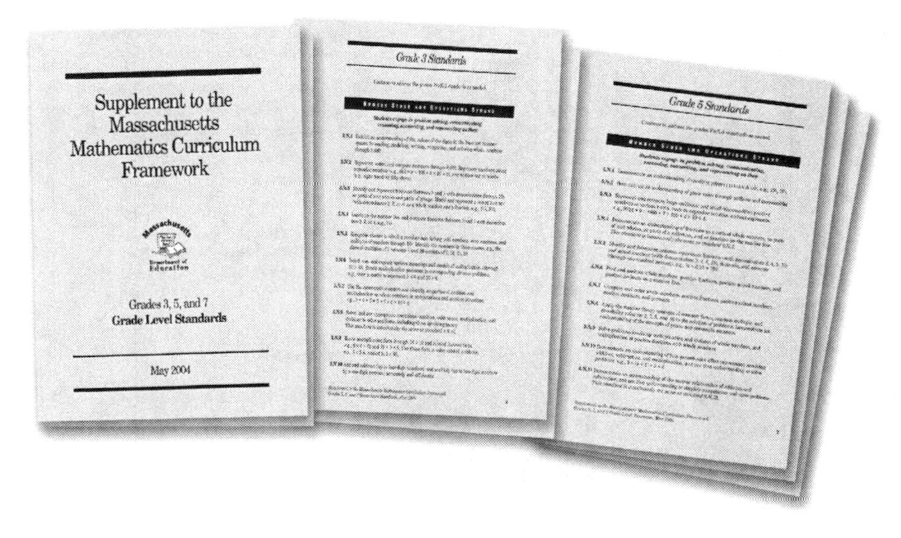

Figure 3.2 The domain of a curriculum framework. To view a color version of this figure, please visit www.infoagepub.com/madaus_paradoxes.

"functional literacy," "aptitude," "problem-solving ability," "memory," "self esteem," and "spatial ability."

The American Educational Research Association defines a construct as a "theoretical idea developed to explain and to organize some aspect of existing knowledge."[5] Quotes are used to set off the label for a construct (e.g., "intelligence") because the label is an artificial application of a term to a set of closely related behaviors. Constructs are not directly observable. Instead, a term is employed to label a set of observable behaviors that are believed to be the product of the construct.

Take "intelligence" as an example. "Intelligence" cannot be observed directly. We cannot simply look at a person and see "intelligence." Instead,

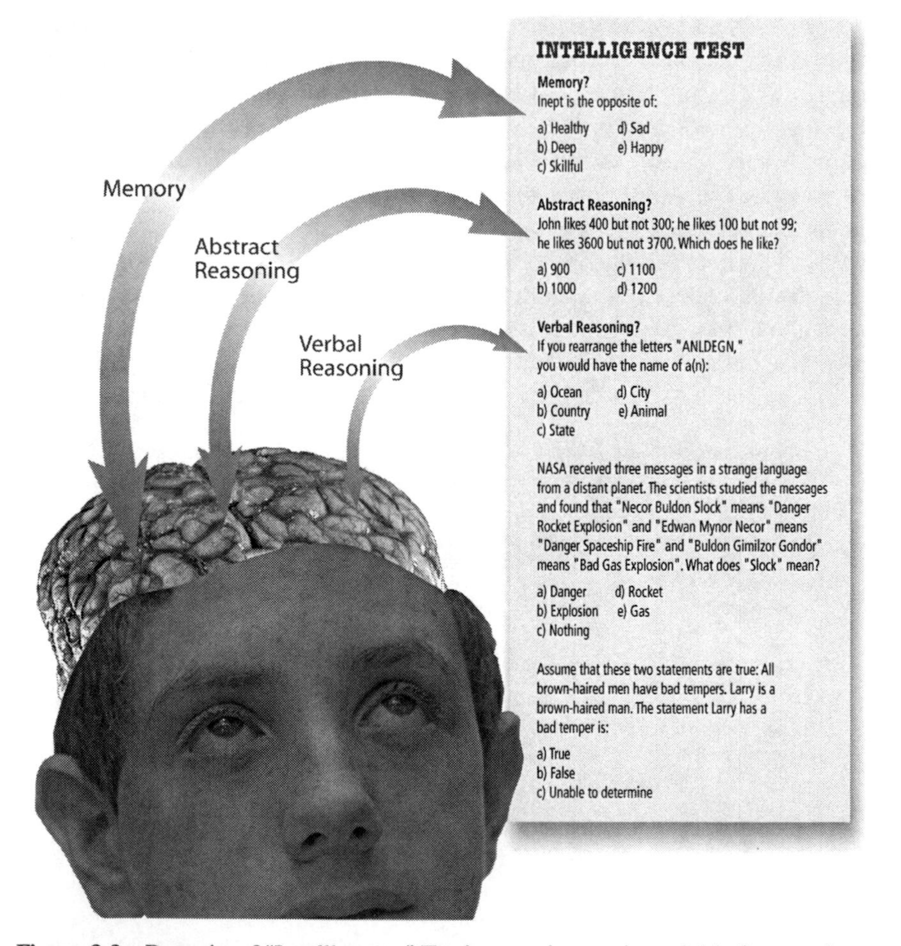

Figure 3.3 Domain of "Intelligence." To view a color version of this figure, please visit www.infoagepub.com/madaus_paradoxes.

it is through a person's behaviors that we infer "intelligence." As depicted in Figure 3.3, correctly defining words, solving abstract problems, and re-arranging letters to create a different word are all behaviors that are believed to be the product of "intelligence." Moreover, the degree to which individuals are able to consistently demonstrate these behaviors, becomes a measure of the amount of "intelligence" the person is believed to possess.

Like 4th-grade arithmetic, a given construct can be divided into sub-domains. Figure 3.3 shows that the construct of "intelligence" can be divided into sub-domains such as memory, abstract reasoning, and verbal reasoning.

A TEST IS A SAMPLE FROM THE DOMAIN

The second basic concept is that a test is a *sample* of behaviors from the domain of interest. In most cases, the behavior takes the form of answers to questions that make up the test. Thinking back to The Arithmetic Depot depicted in Figure 3.1, a domain is comprised of all possible items that could be used to measure the domain. These items can be grouped into sub-domains and a facet within a sub-domain. An enormous number of items are associated with many domains of interest—so many that we could never have students answer all of them. A test developer, therefore, selects a sample of items to *represent* the domain. This sample becomes a measure of performance on the entire domain.

Assembling a sample of items to create a test for a domain is analogous to testing the purity of water in a lake. It would be impossible to test all of the water in a lake. Instead, samples are taken at different locations. The results from these samples represent the purity of water in the entire lake. The same logic applies to a test—performance on the sample of items is used to represent performance across the entire domain that the test is intended to measure.

Figure 3.4 illustrates the concept of *sampling* from the domain of 4th-grade arithmetic. In this example, a limited number of items from each of the four sub-domains are combined into a single test that represents the larger domain we call 4th-Grade Arithmetic.

The sample of items that make up the test, and represent the domain, are generally developed according to a test specification plan. Test specifications provide a detailed blueprint for constructing the test. This blueprint describes in detail such matters as the number of items on the test; the proportion of test items representing each part of the domain; the type of items to be used; the time allocated to take the test; and the statistical characteristics of the item such as the difficulty and readability levels.

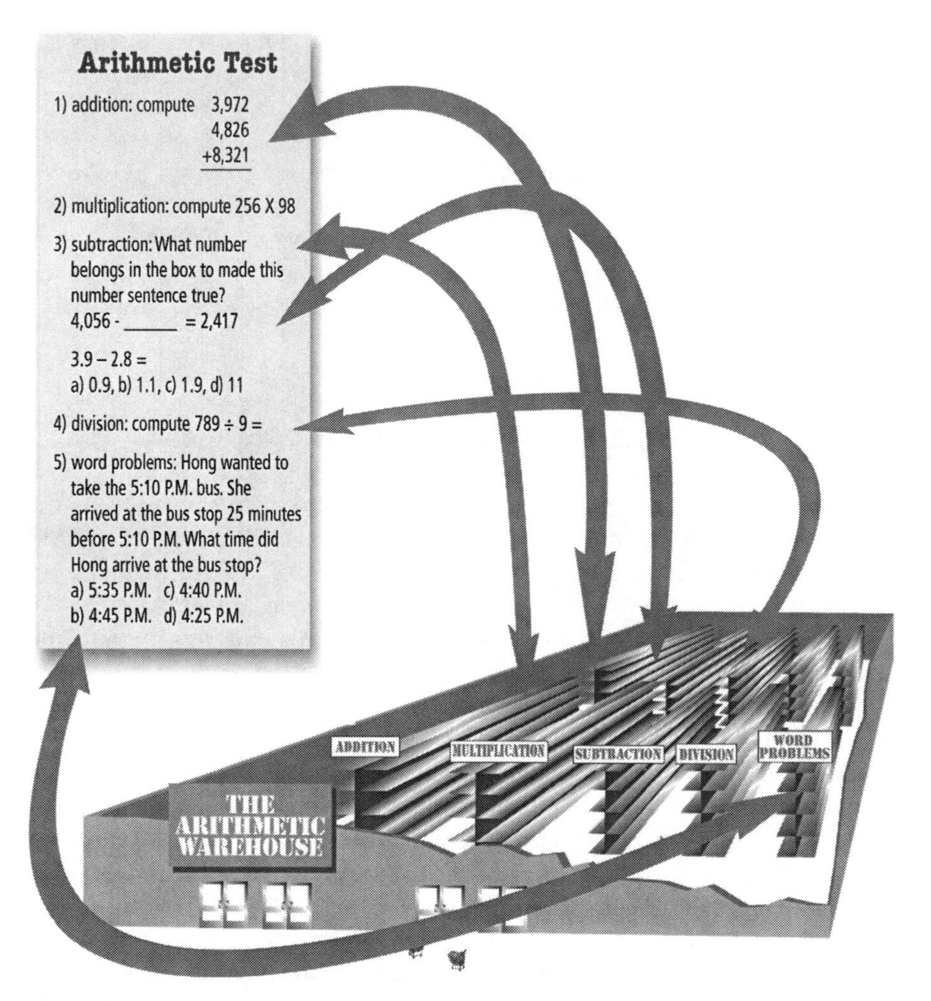

Figure 3.4 Sampling from the Domain of 4th-Grade Arithmetic. To view a color version of this figure, please visit www.infoagepub.com/madaus_paradoxes.

A CLOSER LOOK AT TEST ITEMS

The items sampled from the domain are the basic building blocks of a test. Each test item contributes one or more points to a student's total test score. There are only two types of test items, selection and supply. The item type chosen—selection or supply—should be governed by what one wants to measure within the domain. Selection items, which involve recognition of information, pose a direct question and ask a student to *select* an answer from a limited list of options. Most often, selection items take the form of multiple-choice questions, but can also be presented as true-false or matching items.

Supply items ask a student either to *supply* an answer, which involves recall, analysis or synthesis of information, or to *perform* a task. Supply items most commonly take the form of essays or short written responses. But supply items can present tasks such as conducting a chemistry experiment, assembling a portfolio of artwork, diagnosing and repairing a car, or building a piece of furniture.

Let us examine selection and supply items in more detail.

Selection items are the most common item type used by commercially available standardized tests. They are attractive for several reasons. Because a selection item has only one correct answer, it is fast, easy, and relatively inexpensive for a machine to score students' answers. This efficiency makes it possible to administer a test to a large number of students across a state or the nation. Since it takes a small amount of time for students to respond to a selection item, many more items can be sampled from the domain. For example, 40–50 multiple-choice items can be administered in the same time it would take to answer a limited number of essay items or performance tasks. This larger sample of items increases the reliability of a test's score.

Multiple-choice items have two parts. The first is called the "stem," which presents the problem or the question. The second part is the options from which students select an answer. Incorrect options are called distracters. Figure 3.5 displays the two parts for a multiple-choice item. In this example, the stem establishes the problem students are to solve, i.e., how many airplanes are on the ground. The options allow the student to make a selection from among one correct answer and three distracters.

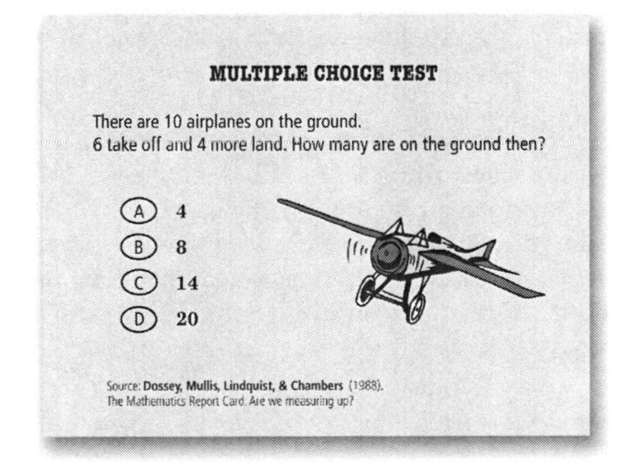

Figure 3.5 Typical multiple-choice item.[6] To view a color version of this figure, please visit www.infoagepub.com/madaus_paradoxes.

MATCHING TEST

On the line to the left of each invention in column A,
write the letter of the person in column B who invented it.
Each name in column B may be used only once or not at all.

Column A	Column B
____ (1) telephone	A. Eli Whitney
____ (2) cotton gin	B. Henry Ford
____ (3) assembly line	C. Jonas Salk
____ (4) polio vaccine	D. Henry McCormick
	E. Alexander Graham Bell

Figure 3.6 Typical matching item. To view a color version of this figure, please visit www.infoagepub.com/madaus_paradoxes.

A true–false question is a multiple-choice item with one correct response and one distracter. As shown in Figure 3.6, a matching item is a set of multiple-choice item stems with common response options. A single option can be the correct answer for more than one stem.

At times, the efficiency and simplicity of selection items is so attractive that test developers ignore a domain's complexity and rely solely on selection items even though these items may be inappropriate for measuring the domain. For example, rather than asking a person to produce a writing sample, some "writing" tests used during the middle of the 20th century consisted solely of multiple-choice questions. Scoring such tests was a speedy endeavor, but did not provide an authentic measure of a student's writing ability.

Supply items are being used increasingly by many state testing programs to measure domains like writing and math competency. Supply items ask the test taker to produce a tangible product that can then be evaluated according to some preset criteria. Examples include essays, oral presentations, experiments, journals, demonstrations, portfolios, paintings, drawings, plays, dances, poems, and investigations. Figures 3.7–3.10 illustrate various types of supply items.

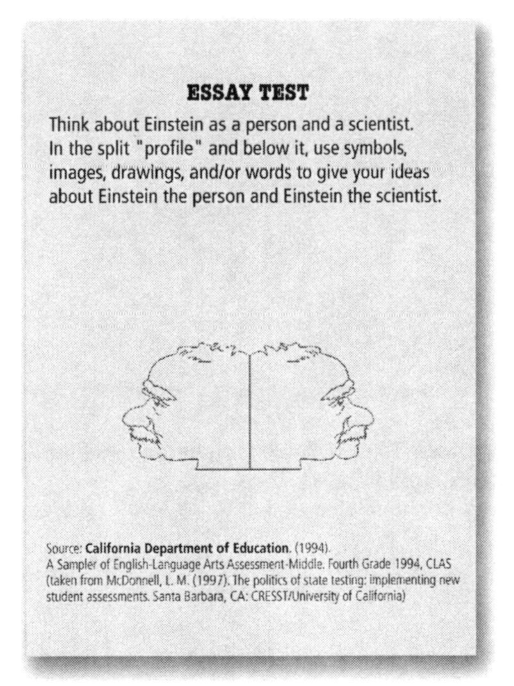

Figure 3.7 An essay question. To view a color version of this figure, please visit www.infoagepub.com/madaus_paradoxes.

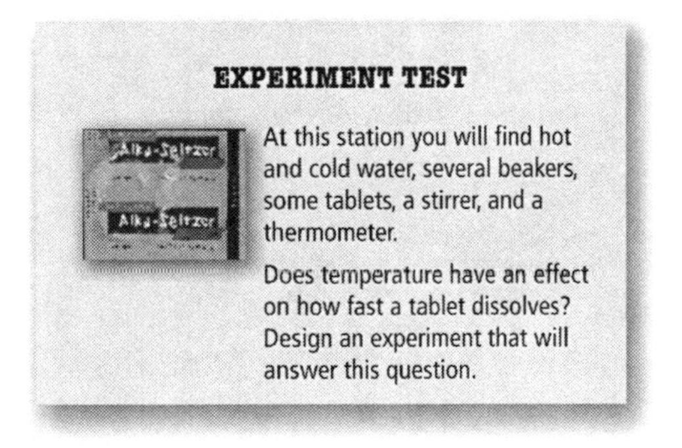

Figure 3.8 Conduct an experiment. To view a color version of this figure, please visit www.infoagepub.com/madaus_paradoxes.

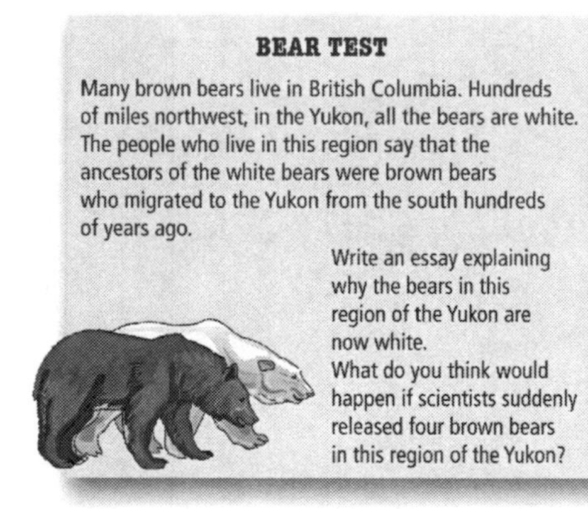

Figure 3.9 Genetics item. To view a color version of this figure, please visit www.infoagepub.com/madaus_paradoxes.

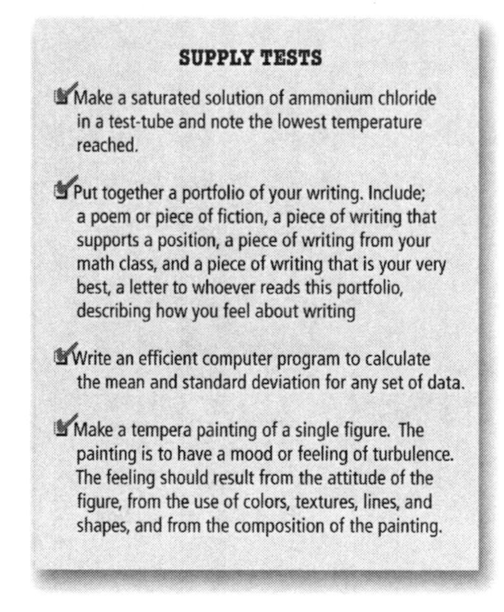

Figure 3.10 Other examples of supply items. To view a color version of this figure, please visit www.infoagepub.com/madaus_paradoxes.

Supply items are attractive because they require students to produce responses in their own words and to demonstrate their skills. The time required to complete supply tasks, however, often limits their use to just a few samples on most tests. This limitation can affect the reliability of the information provided by the test.

USING A TEST TO MAKE INFERENCES AND DECISIONS

A student's performance on the sample of items that form a test is useful *only* if that performance enables accurate *inferences* about a student's probable performance on the *entire* domain. *Domain performance, not test performance, is really the interest in any testing situation.* A student's score on a test is only of value if it represents how the student is likely to perform on all possible items in the domain.

Figure 3.11 illustrates this fundamental concept for the 4th-grade arithmetic domain. Based on the person's performance on the test represented in Figure 3.11, an *inference* is made about the student's 4th-grade arithmetic attainment. While a sample of items from the domain is used to form the test, the focus of attention should not be on how the student performed on the actual test. Rather, the focus should be on how the student is performing within the domain of interest. The situation is the same as testing the purity of lake water. The samples of water and test items are trustworthy only if they are representative of all the water in the lake or all items in the domain.

In addition, the water purity test is used to decide whether or not to treat all of the water in the lake, not just those locations where samples were drawn. Similarly, a decision to provide further instruction based on a student's test performance should focus on the domain itself, rather than on the content of the specific items used to represent the domain.

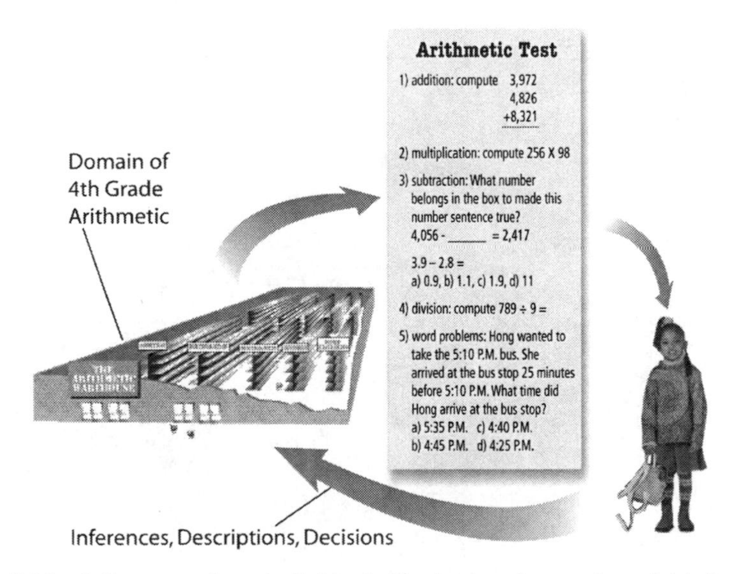

Figure 3.11 Inferences about individuals. To view a color version of this figure, please visit www.infoagepub.com/madaus_paradoxes.

Finally, just as the results of a water purity test do not tell us why water is polluted, a test score does not tell us *why* an individual performed poorly. In other words, achievement tests, especially those used for high-stakes testing, are not diagnostic.

In addition to using a test to make an inference about an individual student, test scores are often combined to make inferences about a group or groups of students, such as all children in a particular school or the subset of Hispanic students in the district. In most cases, group inferences rely on the average test performance of all students in that group (or at least of all the students for whom a test score exists). As illustrated in Figure 3.12, the average score for a group of students on a test is used to make inferences about the group's performance in the domain of 4th grade arithmetic.

Test scores can be further aggregated to make inferences about the performance of much larger groupings. As an example, test scores can be aggregated across students in a state to make inferences about the achievement level for the state.

Norm-Referenced and Criterion-Referenced Tests. Two types of tests are used to measure student achievement. Norm-referenced tests compare the performance of an individual student to the performance of a group of students, referred to as a norm-group. A norm-group is a sample of students that represent a specific population. A representative sample of students

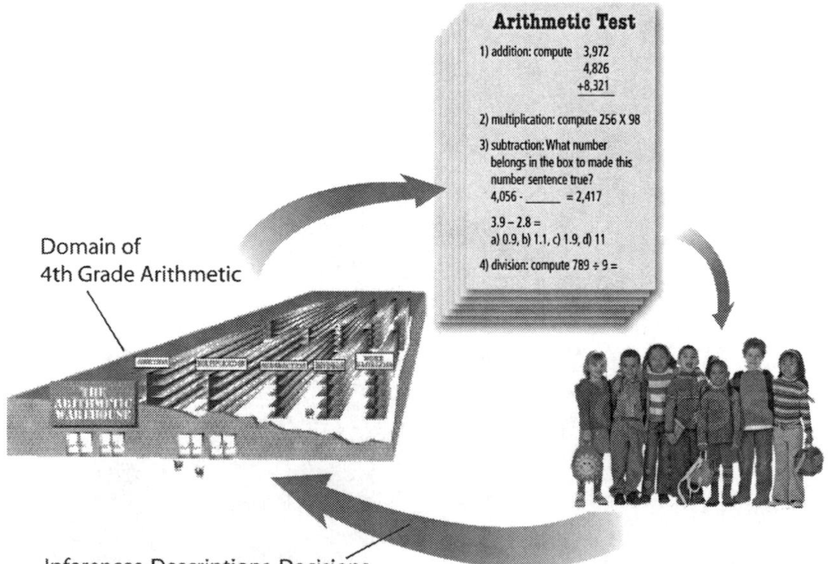

Figure 3.12 Inferences about group performance. To view a color version of this figure, please visit www.infoagepub.com/madaus_paradoxes.

from across the nation forms a National norm-group. A sample of students from urban schools across the nation would form a National Urban Schools norm-group. And a sample of students from a specific state, say California, would form a California norm-group. What is important to remember about a norm-referenced test is that the score reported for a student is dependent on both his performance and the performance of the norm-group to which he is compared.

A criterion-referenced test compares the performance of an individual student to an established standard or criterion. For a high-stakes test, the criterion is a test score that separates people into one performance level or another. Unlike a norm-referenced test, criterion-referenced tests do not consider how other examinees performed when reporting a student's test performance. The only comparison is between the student's performance on the test and the score needed to be classified into a specific performance level.

The type of decision to be made about a student should determine whether to use norm-referenced or criterion-referenced test. When one is interested in how a student's performance compares to other students in the nation, state, or a specific type of schools, a norm-referenced test is appropriate. When one wants to determine whether a student is performing at a specific level or has mastered specific skills or knowledge, a criterion-referenced test should be used. Today, most high-stakes tests are criterion-referenced.

Inferences to Different Domains

Occasionally, test results are used to make inferences about probable performance on a domain different from the one tested. As an example, Figure 3.13 shows how an SAT score, which reflects a combination of verbal and mathematical skills, is used to make inferences about a variety of issues such as a student's future college freshman grade point average, how state K–12 educational systems compare, or a student's eligibility for athletics or a scholarship.

Tests are also used to make inferences about an individual or a group, based on the performance of a separate group of test takers. As an example, inferences about teacher quality or effectiveness are based on the performance of his or her students' test performance. Similarly, inferences about the quality of a school are based on the test performance of all of the students within that school.

To summarize, test performance on a sample of items drawn from the domain is used to make an inference about a student's or a group's performance relative to either the domain or to an entirely different domain

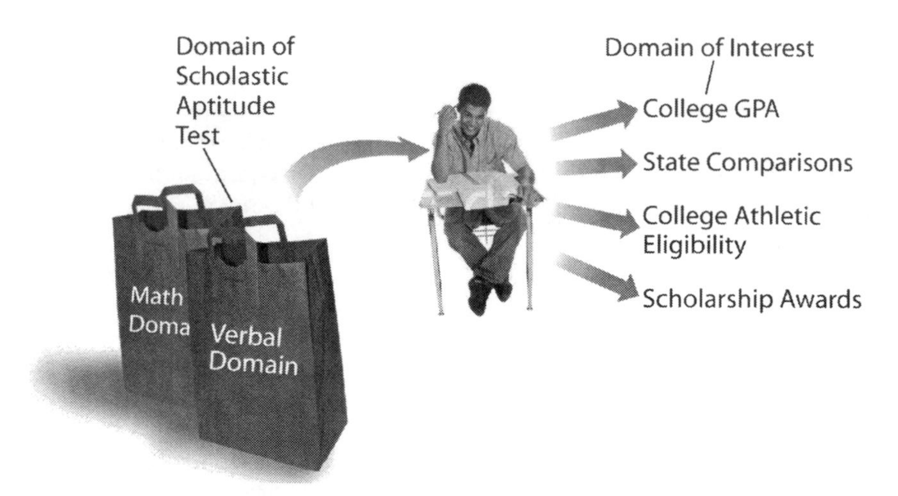

Figure 3.13 Inferences about a different domain. To view a color version of this figure, please visit www.infoagepub.com/madaus_paradoxes.

of interest. Based on the inference, the test results are used to describe and/or make decisions about an individual student or group of students. Describing students and making decisions about them is the reason the test was constructed and administered in the first place.

The descriptions and decisions based on test performance can be influential—good or bad—in the lives of individual students, groups of students, teachers, and schools. The paramount *raison d'etre* for testing is to make consistent, appropriate, and accurate inferences about student or group performance in a domain so that the subsequent descriptions and decisions are also consistent, appropriate, and accurate. Two concepts essential for making good descriptions and decisions based on test performance are *test reliability* and *test validity*.

Test Reliability

Test Reliability is a measure of the consistency and dependability of test scores. Reliability answers the question: "How likely is it that a student would obtain comparable scores if the test was taken multiple times?"[7] Just as one would expect a scale to show the same weight—within a pound or so—if you stepped on the scale several times, a reliable test provides a consistent estimate of the student's performance on the domain. If you stepped on a scale 10 times and it showed about the same weight, you would have more confidence in its accuracy than if you had only stepped on it twice. Similarly, as the number of items from the domain included on a test increases, test reliability increases because there is more information to estimate how well the student is likely to perform across the domain. As discussed above, more selection than supply items can be administered in a given amount of time, allowing test developers to increase test reliability.

Despite the efficiency and low cost of scoring selection items, critics argue that selection items do not provide a full measure of the skills and knowledge students should develop. Instead, these critics advocate for the use of performance tasks such as conducting an experiment, writing a persuasive essay, or producing a portfolio. To build a reliable test using only performance tasks, research shows that the test should contain approximately nine items to represent the domain when making decisions about *individual* students.[8]

Regardless of how well a measurement tool is made, it is never perfect. Whether it is a blood-pressure gauge, Pap smear test, PSA tests for prostate cancer, breathalyzer, radar gun, or fingerprint matching, the resulting measures are fallible.[9] As just one example, *error* is associated with cholesterol tests. This error results from physical changes that occur regularly within the person being tested and in the laboratory analysis. This error means that when a person tested for cholesterol receives a reading of 220 mg/dl, the person's actual cholesterol level falls somewhere between 187 and 267.[10] No matter how well constructed, educational tests also produce fallible scores. A test's fallibility results from two types of error: *measurement error* and *human error.*

Measurement Error. Measurement error occurs when factors other than a student's actual level of achievement randomly affect his or her score. There are three categories of measurement error.

First, there are factors specific to an individual on the day of the test such as illness, motivation or concentration levels, an emotional upset just before the test, family problems, not having eaten breakfast, and so on. Second, there are situational factors such as a hot or cold testing room, the time of day, the length of testing, outside noise, disorder, or other distractions. Third, differences in how scorers interpret a student's response or have varying concepts of the correctness of an answer or the quality of a performance affect measurement error. [11]

Measurement error affects individual students randomly. Depending upon the day a test is taken, a student may or may not experience and be affected by such things as an illness, cold weather, or a noisy classroom. Similarly, the luck of the draw dictates who scores a student's responses to supply items.

Human Error. Human error can be divided into two parts. The first involves specific people-related mistakes like creating faulty test items or making mistakes when programming scoring software, calculating results, calibrating scoring machines, and handling answer sheets. The second is latent errors. These are general managerial or policy missteps, such as unrealistic timelines for reporting results that increase the likelihood of people-related mistakes.[12] For example, in 2008, major errors occurred on the British Key Stage Two high-stakes test when Educational Testing Service Global attempted to score and return results for more than 10 million essays within a tight timeframe.[13]

Human errors can adversely affect classifications and subsequent decisions. For example, due to a calibration error, the passing score for the 1976 version of the Armed Services Vocational Aptitude Battery (ASVAB) was incorrectly set. As a result, more than 300,000 recruits who normally would have been rejected because of low scores were admitted into the military.[14] More recently, storing answer sheets in a damp environment led to the mis-scoring of the 2005 fall administration of the SAT. As a result, 4,400 students received lower SAT scores than they should have while 600 students received higher scores.[15]

For a high-stakes test, measurement and human error can seriously affect individual students. A student may be misclassified, mislabeled, misplaced, inappropriately retained in grade, or denied a high school diploma due to measurement or human error. It is essential, therefore, for parents, teachers, and policymakers to take measurement error and the possibility of human error into account when a test score is used to make a high-stakes decision.

Test Validity

Test validity is a complex concept that has evolved over the past fifty years. Here, we provide a synopsis of the importance and fundamentals of test validity, particularly as it relates to high-stakes tests.[16]

The 1999 *Standards for Educational and Psychological Testing* describe validity as "the most fundamental consideration in developing and evaluating tests."[17] Test validity evaluates the accuracy of the inferences and appropriateness of decisions made based on a test score. It is incorrect simply to assert, "This is a valid test." Instead, claims about validity vary depending on how a test is used. As an example, using a score from a state achievement test to make inferences about how well a student is meeting the state's learning standards will be more valid than using that same test score to make decisions about whether the student is ready for a driver's license. An evaluation of test validity must focus on the accuracy of a *specific* inference and the subsequent decisions or descriptions made about an individual or group based on that inference.

Test validity is a matter of degree, not a simple dichotomy of valid or not valid. Evaluating test validity is an ongoing process of accumulating different types of evidence about the correctness of an inference made from a test score. Inferences, however, are always problematic. Test validity offers a reasoned *defense* for an inference, decision or description, but not *proof.* A truthful validation study seeks evidence that not only confirms, but also might cast doubt on, the accuracy of inferences and appropriateness of decisions based on a test's results.

Evaluating test validity requires multiple studies that focus on four aspects of a test. The first aspect, *test content*, addresses the question: "Does the content of the test provide a representative sample of the domain, and is this sample appropriate for the intended test use?" Determining the appropriateness of the test content for a given use requires consideration of the characteristics of the students who will take the test (e.g., age, grade level, language, etc.), and the intended inferences and decisions based on the test score.

Evidence that the test represents the content of the domain usually involves knowledgeable people making *judgments* about the appropriateness of each item and how well the sample of items represents the domain.[18] Examining test content is necessary when evaluating test validity, but it is far from sufficient.

The second aspect of test validity focuses on the *cognitive skills and abilities* the test is meant to measure and addresses the questions: "Do the items require students to apply the thought process and skills that the test purports to measure? Are unrelated skills and thought processes required for students to do well on the test? Can students do well on the test without applying the skills and thought processes of interest?" In other words, does the test measure the skills and knowledge of interest without requiring students to apply skills and knowledge that are not of direct interest? As an example, an arithmetic test intended to measure students' ability to add and subtract that is composed entirely of word problems would require students to apply reading skills in addition to the arithmetic skills of interest. Students who may know how to add and subtract may perform poorly on this test simply because they are poor readers. Nonetheless, the inference made based on the test score is about the students' arithmetic abilities, not their reading skills. A validity study must examine the extent to which unrelated skills and knowledge may affect students' ability to demonstrate the skills that the test purports to measure.

The third aspect of test validity accumulates evidence about the *relationship between other variables* and the test score. Depending on how the test scores are used, this aspect of test validity may address questions such as: "Do the test results correlate with performance on other tests that measure similar skills and abilities? Are the test results consistent with what a student is able to do in the classroom? Do the test results accurately predict what they claim?"

As an example, for a state test that is used to determine whether students can read proficiently, one might compare performance on the state reading test with performance on a different reading test. Results for the 2004 Mississippi state test, for example, categorized 87% of 4th graders as proficient in reading, yet on the National Assessment of Educational Progress only 18% of Mississippi 4th graders were proficient in reading.[19] Such data shed light on whether results from these tests support accurate inferences and decisions about students' reading ability.

For a test that is used to predict future performance, one might examine the correlation between students' test scores and how well they actually perform in the future. As an example, SAT scores are used to predict students' grade point average in the freshman year of college. The extent to which students' SAT scores and actual freshman GPA are correlated is an index of the predictive validity of the SAT.

The final aspect of test validity focuses on the *consequences of test use* and addresses the question, "What are the positive and negative consequences that result from a test's use?" When examining this question, a validity study must consider the impact of the test's use on individual students, groups of students, teachers, schools, and communities. Chapter 8 is devoted to consequences associated with high-stakes tests.

As we detail in the next chapter, test developers and testing programs typically collect evidence about test content and use it to make claims about test validity. Robust validity evidence, however, requires that all four aspects of test validity be examined and reported.

Traditionally, the four aspects described above formed the cornerstones of test validity. Today, however, the use of a single test score to categorize students into a distinct performance level and to make high-stakes decisions based on that categorization introduces a fifth aspect of test validity—the use of cut-scores. The next section examines cut-scores in detail.

Cut-Scores

A cut-score is a predefined test score that separates one performance level from another. For years, cut-scores have been used to help inform decisions about admission, placement, and retention in grade. In each case, admission officers, teachers, and school administrators took the initiative to establish cut-scores for a standardized test that was *not* designed to categorize students into distinct performance levels. This use of cut-scores improved the efficiency of decision-making and created a perception of numerical "precision." Establishing these cut-scores was an informal, arbitrary, seat-of-the-pants operation performed by admission officers, teachers, and school administrators with little to no attention paid to the validity of the resulting classifications and decisions.

For today's high-stakes testing programs, however, the situation is very different. As mandated by No Child Left Behind, today's high-stakes tests are designed for the specific purpose of classifying students into distinct

Leap 21 Performance Level Cut Scores

For Grade 8 English Language Arts

402-500	Advanced
356-401	Mastery
315-355	Basic
269-314	Approaching Basic
100-268	Unsatisfactory

Figure 3.14 LEAP Cut Scores.[20] To view a color version of this figure, please visit www.infoagepub.com/madaus_paradoxes.

performance categories. In essence, state testing programs collapse a broad range of scores (e.g., 0%–100% of items correct) into just a few points.

As an example, the actual score a student obtains on the Louisiana state test (LEAP) can range from 100 to 500. As shown in Figure 3.14, a student's actual score is used to categorize him/her into one of five levels of performance—Advanced, Mastery, Basic, Approaching Basic, and Unsatisfactory. For the LEAP, a cut-score of 269 established the dividing line between Unsatisfactory and Approaching Basic. As a result, students whose scores range from 100 to 268 are placed in the Unsatisfactory category while students between 269 and 314 are categorized as Approaching Basic.

Setting Cut-Scores

Cut-scores for most high-stakes tests are determined by having a group of knowledgeable people make judgments about the performance level needed to answer each question on the test.[21] Those individual judgments are then aggregated across all judgments.[22]

In one widely used method called bookmarking, the test questions are ordered along a scale based on the percentage of students who answered each item correctly during a pre-test. Judges receive a description of what a student at each performance level is expected to be able to do. The judges are then asked to place—or bookmark—each test item at a point on the score distribution they believe separate one attainment level from another. Each judge then determines where the cut-score for each performance level should be set. Next, the judges discuss discrepancies in their scores. Judges then individually repeat the bookmark procedure two more times. Finally, the average cut-score across all judges is calculated for each performance level. These averages define the final cut-scores for the test.

Given the use of a test score to categorize and label each student, it is essential to examine the accuracy of classifications. Like the cholesterol test mentioned earlier, categorizations based on cut-scores for a high-stakes test contain error.

Error and Cut-Scores

A test produces a single numeric score. This score represents an *estimate* of how well a student is performing within the domain of interest. With any estimate, there is error. As an example, Figure 3.15 displays the estimated path of Hurricane Rita on the morning of September 21, 2005 approximately *three days before* its landfall. The black line represents the estimated path that Rita will follow based on information available at that time. The white cone represents the *error* associated with the estimated path. On September 21, there was a reasonable chance that the actual path would fall anywhere within this cone.

Like estimating the path of a hurricane, a test score estimates an examinee's "true" performance within a domain. Test scores, like all estimates, contain error. Using the error associated with a test score, one can create a band within which a student's "true" performance falls. This error band is analogous to the cone that predicts the range Rita's predicated track. The

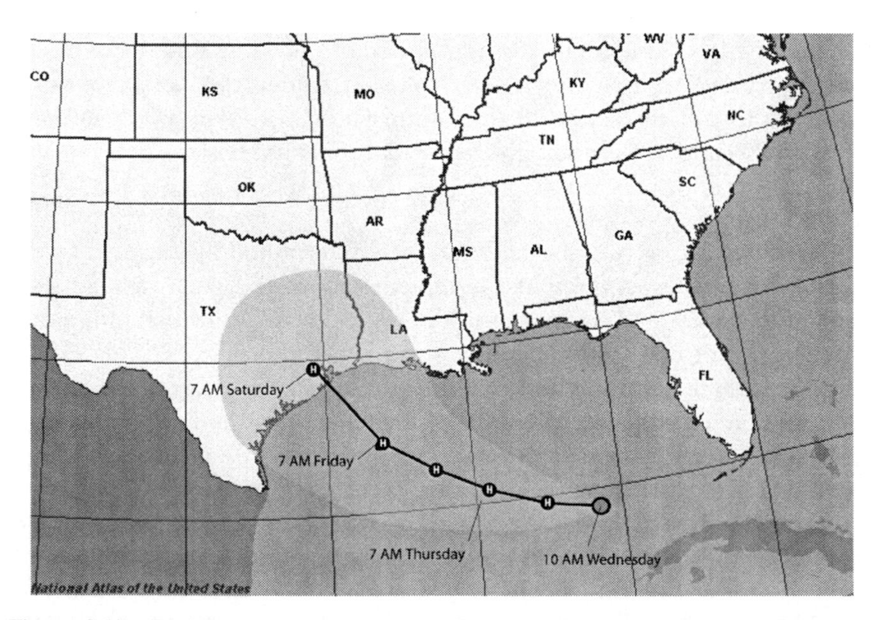

Figure 3.15 Projected path of Hurricane Rita one day and two days out. To view a color version of this figure, please visit www.infoagepub.com/madaus_paradoxes.

error associated with a test score is particularly important when examining students whose test scores are close to a cut-score.

As seen in Figure 3.16, Sue's test score (represented by a dot) is above the cut-score for Failing so she is classified as Basic. Her error band, however, extends below the cut-score. Based on her obtained score, she may be falsely classified as Basic when she may in fact be failing and in need of additional instruction. On the other hand Steve's test score is below the cut-score for Basic, so he is categorized as failing. Steve's error band, however, shows that his "true" performance level could be in the Basic level. If this is the case, he would be falsely classified as Failing and the resulting decisions—remedial instruction or being denied a diploma—would not be warranted. As we explore in the next chapter, high-stakes testing programs pay far more attention to students like Steve than to students like Sue.

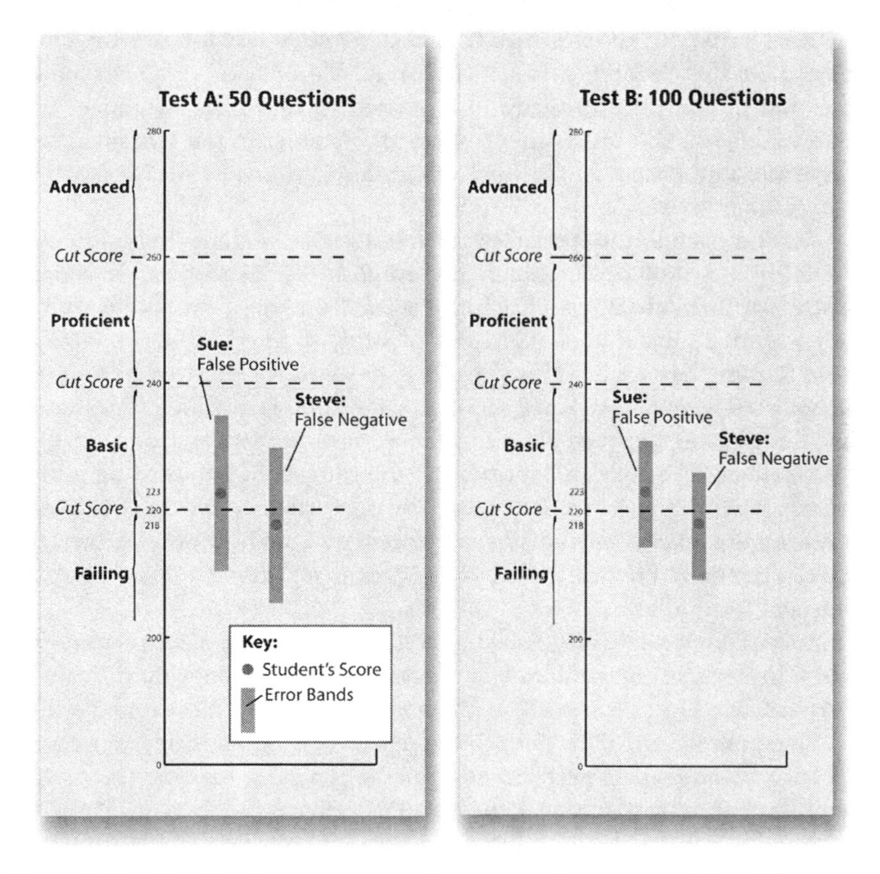

Figure 3.16 Classification error around cut scores for two tests with a different number of items. To view a color version of this figure, please visit www.infoagepub.com/madaus_paradoxes.

As in projecting Hurricane Rita's path, the more information that is currently available, the more accurate the estimate is. Looking at Figure 3.15 for Rita, the band is narrower one day out from its position on September 21, than two or three days out. This occurs because there is more reliable information available to estimate the path one day out than three days out. Similarly, as we see in Figure 3.16, the width of the error band for a test becomes smaller as the number of items or score points on the test increases. This occurs because there is more information available to estimate the "true" score when a test contains a larger number of items.

SUMMARY

In this chapter, we answered the question "What is a test?" by describing the three crucial characteristics of a test. First, a test focuses on a particular domain. Second, a test is a sample of behavior or performance from that domain. And, third a test is used to make an inference from performance on the test to probable performance on the larger domain of interest, and based on that inference; descriptions or decisions about the test taker are made.

Thinking back to the myriad of tests we took as students, it is clear how this definition works. Whether math, English, social studies, or science class, the tests made by our teachers focused on the most recent unit of study within a subject area. This unit of study defined the domain of interest. Rather than asking every possible question related to that unit, the teacher's test contained a small set of questions, most of which represented what the teacher believed were the most important ideas from the unit. This small set of questions represented the sample of behavior or performance within the domain. Based on our performance on that sample of questions, the teacher then made an inference about how well we knew the material contained in that unit and, in most cases, made a decision about our grade for that unit.

Similarly, high-stakes tests used by each state follow the same procedures. State standards or curriculum frameworks define the specific domain of interest. A test blueprint specifying how the domain will be sampled is then developed. Based on that blueprint, a set of test items is developed and piloted. The items that perform best during the pilot become the sample used to measure what students know and can do on the domain. Based on the resulting test scores, an inference is made about how well a student is performing in comparison to the standards. This inference is then used to make a variety of decisions about individual students, groups of students, teachers, and schools.

While this chapter has provided an answer to the question "What is A Test?," there are a number of issues that complicate the interpretation of test scores and test use. These issues stem from both the technical complexities of creating a high-stakes test and how people interact with a test. It is these technical and human issues that make testing a fallible technology. In Chapter 4 we explore the human factors that affect test performance and the subsequent use of test scores. In Chapter 5 we examine the technical issues that affect the accuracy of inferences made based on test scores. As we will see, these technical issues raise important issues that are often overlooked or ignored by those who use tests to make decisions about students, teachers, and schools.[23]

NOTES

1. Winner (1986).
2. Graphics: Figures 3.1–3.4, 3.11–3.14, and 3.16 by Kevin Keane, © 2006. Figures 3.5 and 3.7–3.10 by Thomas M. Hoffmann ©1997. Figure 3.15 from the *Washington Post* September 21, 2005.
3. Not all test domains can be so easily divided into sub-domains or facets in this way.
4. These ideological/political fights over the curriculum are by no means limited to the United States. Consider the debate in Great Britain over the English National Curriculum. Committee members of the School Examination and Assessment Council argued that empathy (putting oneself in the place of historical figures) was more important than knowing about the history of Britain (Graham & Tyler, 1993).
5. American Educational Research Association, American Psychological Association, & the National Council on Measurement in Education (1985, revised 1999, p. 29).
6. Dossey, Mullis, Lindquist, & Chambers (1988).
7. There a number of ways to estimate test reliability. For more information on test reliability, see American Educational Research Association, American Psychological Association, & National Council on Measurement in Education (1999).
8. See Gao, Shavelson, & Baxter (1994); Shavelson, Baxter, & Pine (1992); Shavelson, Gao, & Baxter (1993).
9. For information on challenges to fingerprinting, see Spector (2002). For information on bullet matching, see Lichtblau (2005).
10. See Brigden & Heathcote (2000); Moore (1989); The Michigan Diabetes Research and Training Center).
11. Feldt & Brennan (1989).
12. An on going study of human errors between 1976 and 2007 has documented 169 reported human errors in educational tests. The majority of these are on national tests (e.g. SAT) or state level tests and occurred since 1997 when test-based school reform efforts began in earnest in many states. There are

undoubtedly other errors that have gone unreported or unrecognized, A detailed treatment of human error in testing through 2003 can be found in Rhoades & Madaus (2003). http://www.bc.edu/research/nbetpp/reports.html. The update to 2008 is in the process of being posted.

13. Woolcok (2008).
14. National Commission on Testing and Public Policy (1990). Also see Sticht (1988). It is interesting to note that several subsequent studies showed that, as a group, these enlistees performed only somewhat less well than those who actually passed the ASVAB, while numerous individual enlistees who benefited from the error fared as well or better.
15. Sanchez (2006).
16. For more on test validity, see Messick (1989).
17. American Educational Research Association et al. (1999, p. 9, emphasis added).
18. The extent to which the content of the test is aligned with the domain is the aspect of validity most commonly evaluated by test developers and testing programs.
19. For example the *New York Times* reported that on the Mississippi state test 87% of fourth graders were proficient but on NAEP only 18% were categorized as proficient. The director of assessment said the state has its own definition of proficient (Saulny, 2005). In addition, in 2004, Florida had almost as many schools receiving grades of A as B through F combined. Under NCLB, however, more than 80% of schools failed to meet standards (Waite, 2004).
20. Louisiana Department of Education website, 2002–2003 Annual Report http://www.doe.state.la.us/lde/uploads/1703.pdf
21. Another method is called contrasting groups. It is used in medicine to determine cut-points for diagnostic or treatment decisions. For example, to set a cut-score for decisions about the blood's acceptability, pathologists plotted the distributions of the serum glutamic pyruvic transaminase of healthy individuals and those with hepatocellular damage. The overlap area allowed pathologists to estimate for various cut-scores, the number of false positive and false negative classifications (Colton, 1974).
22. See Horn, Ramos, Blumer, & Madaus (2000) for a more complete description of different standard-setting techniques used to determine cut-scores.
23. For an excellent treatment of issues surrounding testing see, National Research Council (2007).

CHAPTER 4

WHAT HUMAN AND CULTURAL FACTORS AFFECT TEST PERFORMANCE?

Testing is an integral part of American education. For most readers, a school where you and your children never, ever took a test is unimaginable. But it is important to recognize that the way testing is viewed and approached in our society is class and culturally determined.[1] Family and cultural background influence the way students view and interact with tests.

HOW DOES FAMILY BACKGROUND AFFECT TEST PERFORMANCE?

Richard Rothstein of the Economic Policy Institute offers a number of examples of how family backgrounds and experiences in the home can influence students' behavior in the classroom and on high-stakes tests. Among others, he describes how parents whose job requires them to collaborate are more likely to have their children figure out answers themselves. He tells how children whose parents are professionals are generally more inquisitive and take a more active approach to learning than children whose parents are from the working-class. He also finds that parents with professional jobs speak more 2,000 words an hour to their children compared

The Paradoxes of High Stakes Testing, pages 61–76

with 1,300 words for working-class parents and only 600 for mothers on welfare. Finally, Rothestein notes that for every one reprimand toddlers of professionals receive six encouragements. In contrast, working-class children receive only two encouragements per reprimand, and welfare children receive one encouragement for every two reprimands.[2] Rothestein argues that these and other home experiences influence how students respond to the demands of schooling.

A recent analysis of National Assessment of Educational Performance (NAEP) reading test scores also examined the influence of home factors on test performance. This analysis revealed that collectively, single-parent families, parents reading to a child every day, hours a child spends watching television, and the frequency of school absences explained two-thirds of the differences in reading scores.[3] The relationship between test performance and home factors calls into the question the use of test scores to judge school quality without considering class related factors that also influence learning and test performance.

HOW DOES CULTURE AFFECT TEST PERFORMANCE?

In addition to class, cultural values affect how an individual student experiences school in general and testing in particular. High-stakes testing incorporates two culturally held values. The first is that achievement is an individual accomplishment. The second value is that individuals must display their accomplishment publicly.

Most middle-class children are socialized to accept these two values. They come to school with an understanding of what testing is about, and that tests are meant to evaluate and judge them on their achievement. Early on, middle class children assume the role of information givers.[4] Prior to entering school, they are "tested" by their parents. Babies are repeatedly asked to point to their nose, bottle, shoes, and so on. Toddlers are asked "where is the truck" or point to the horse in a picture. Preschoolers are asked about stories in books, and people and events in their lives.

Prior to attending school, children with different backgrounds are not asked by adults to be "information givers."[5] As a result, many of these children do not have a clear idea of what testing is about when they initially encounter it in school. For example, this is true for many American Indian children. Rather than emphasizing the development of verbal skills, Indian cultures socialize children through nonverbal communication and emphasize spatial skills, sequential visual memory, and motor skills. Tribal cultures also emphasize sharing and working together. In contrast, the tests they encounter in school focus primarily on verbal skills and force the child to work alone.[6]

As an example, research focusing on Navajo children found that they learn through repeated observation and self-initiated self-testing. Mistakes are not publicly acknowledged and public questioning does not occur. When a Navajo encounters traditional educational testing for the first time, they see it as an evaluative tool. They must learn what their middle-class Anglo peers already know—testing is an evaluative task that forces them to publicly display their knowledge, skills, and competencies whether or not they feel ready to do so, and that they are judged and labeled by their test performance.[7]

Another study that focused on a young Ojibwa student documents how different cultural values influence behavior and the evaluation of that behavior.[8] When tested, several professionals recorded that the student stared into space, completed tasks very slowly, and gave "non-reality-based" responses to questions. Based on these reactions, they concluded the student had learning and behavioral problems. However, it was later determined that the boy's response stemmed from a special relationship he had with his traditional Ojibwa grandfather. His grandfather encouraged the boy's dreaming—whether it occurred by day or by night—and often discussed the nature of dreams with him. The boy's dreaming was consistent with the Ojibwa's value of *mu-zhi-tum-ing*, which means feeling what you do not see, or subjectivity. The Ojibwa place less value on *ga-na-wa-bun-daw-ming*, which means seeing without feeling, or objectivity.[9] Tests tend to promote the values of objectivity, the importance of factual knowledge and "right" answers, and rapid visible performance. In so doing, tests devalue subjectivity, feelings, reflection, introspection, and discernment.[10]

American Indians are not the only people who have a culture clash with tests. The test performance of minorities, recent immigrants, bilingual students, and females all are affected by cultural aspects of testing.[11] This is not to argue that school children from non-majority cultures may not need to adapt to the ways of the majority culture, including high-stakes testing, if they are to succeed. Nonetheless, cultural influences on test performance begin at a very young age and affect how an individual student and groups of students are perceived and treated throughout their time in school.

CONFLICTING ASSUMPTIONS ABOUT STUDENT LEARNING

As we saw in Chapter 3, an essential step in developing a test is to clearly define the domain of the test. Defining a domain for a high-stakes test is contentious. Over the last century, conflicting assumptions about how students develop and learn have influenced the definition of many important domains.

As the influential psychologist Jerome Bruner points out, "Different approaches to learning and different forms of instruction—from imitation, to instruction, to discovery, to collaboration—reflect differing beliefs and assumptions about the learner—from actor, to knower, to private experiencer, to collaborative thinker."[12] Disagreement about how students learn and how they should be taught create conflict over the value of different approaches to teaching reading and mathematics—phonics versus whole-language instruction, and the drill-and-practice techniques many of us experienced in school versus the open-ended discovery practices that many of today's students encounter.

As we will see in Chapter 8, high-stakes tests define what is taught. Given this, it is impossible to underestimate the national, state, and local controversies that arise over the content that forms the domain of some tests. Witness the national battle that ensued over teaching Evolution, Creationism, and Intelligent Design in a 9th grade biology class in a Pennsylvania school district. Controversy over the inclusion of intelligent design as part of the biology domain prompted the President of the United States to weigh in on the side of teaching intelligent design. A federal judge, however, ruled that intelligent design was not science because it included a supernatural explanation of creation and therefore could not be included in the biology curriculum.[13]

The Name of a Test Conveys Powerful Cultural Meanings

Words like "intelligence," "ability," "competence," "honesty," "aptitude," "readiness," and even "achievement" are used to name the construct a test purports to measure. While these words are familiar to everyone, a universally shared understanding of what they mean when used to name a test is by no means guaranteed. People's interpretation of test performance is based on the affective, connotative, emotional, and metaphorical baggage associated in their minds with the word used to name the test.[14]

Intelligence, for example, means different things to different people. For many, the name "intelligence or IQ test" conjures up the image of an innate, stable ability to reason. Many believe that intelligence is largely genetic.[15] For others, the word "intelligence" refers to street smarts. To still others, there are multiple intelligences that include such things as verbal intelligence, musical intelligence, and visual/spatial intelligence.[16] And in the testing community, some people use a circular definition that intelligence is whatever an "intelligence" test measures.

Not surprisingly, the meaning people give to the word intelligence influences the way in which they interpret a student's score on an "Intelligence"

Test and, in turn, how that student is treated. In *Stories in an Almost Classical Mode*, Harold Brodkey offers an example:

> I did well in school and seemed to be peculiarly able to learn what the teacher said—I never mastered a subject, though—and there was the idiotic testimony of those peculiar witnesses, IQ tests: those scores invented me.
>
> Those scores were a decisive piece of destiny in that they affected the way people treated you and regarded you; they determined your authority; and if you spoke oddly, they argued in favor of your sanity. But it was as easy to say and there was much evidence that I was stupid, in every way or... as my mother said in exasperation, "in the ways that count."[17]

For Brodkey, his teacher's interpretation of his high scores led her to regard him favorably and give his speech the benefit of the doubt.

The experience of many minority children in school is a powerful example of the other side of the IQ coin. As early as 1918, Charles Judd, then director of the School of Education at the University of Chicago argued that "unsatisfactory school results [can] be traced to the *native limitations in the ability* of [the] child or to the home atmosphere in which the child grows up."[18] When these children scored low on an English-language IQ test, they were too often treated quite differently than high-scoring children, despite the fact that when they took the test they were at a disadvantage for cultural and linguistic reasons.[19]

Simply changing the name of a test can alter people's perceptions of that test and their *attitudes* about *test use*.[20] For example, in the late 1970s, Florida's high school graduation test name was changed from the Functional Literacy Test—popularly called the Funci Lit—to the Florida State Student Assessment Test—Part II (SSAT-II). The name change was in response to the damaging effects associated with the negative label "functional illiterate" given to those who failed to pass the Funci Lit. The new name was neutral to the point of not conveying any image whatsoever of the domain measured by the test.

In the 1980s and '90s, many people recoiled at schools using "intelligence" test scores for admission to kindergarten or promotion to the first grade. Their attitudes, however, changed, when a test with the same kinds of questions was named a "readiness test." [21] It was acceptable to say a child is not ready, but not acceptable to say the child is not smart or intelligent enough for kindergarten or first grade.

Does the Test Measure the Correct Domain?

It seems obvious to ask whether the domain measured by a test is appropriate for an intended use. But too often the question is never asked. The "readiness test" for young children is one example. As we saw in Chapter 2, the Department of Education's infamous "wall chart," which used SAT scores to rank states on student achievement, is another example. The fundamental problem with the Wall Chart was that the SAT was not designed to sample the domain of skills and knowledge developed by public schools. Rather, the SAT's domain was defined as a subset of skills and knowledge believed to be predictive of success during the first year of college, much of which is developed outside of school.[22]

Another example is the use of a high school reading test to screen job applicants. Many employers might think that "basic reading skills" are essentially the same in school and on the job. The ability of school-based tests of basic reading skills to predict job performance, however, varies enormously from job to job. A comprehensive review of literacy and reading performance found that literacy associated with basic academic skills has little impact on job performance. Many workers are able to perform jobs competently even when the reading material is well above their tested reading levels on academic tests.[23]

Edward Hall's work on the use of English-language tests to screen foreign students wishing to study in America provides a further example. Although many foreign students passed academic language tests, Hall found that they were often unable to understand their instructors in American classrooms.[24]

Whether it be determining readiness, ranking schools or states by student achievement, or making any decision based on test scores, it seldom occurs to the general public to ask the question, "Is this the correct domain?" The answer to this question, however, is central to appropriate test use.

IDEOLOGY AND TEST ITEMS

Just as domain specification can be controversial and subject to ideological fights, the items used to measure a domain are not immune to ideological criticism. For example, on the 1994 10th-grade California Learning Assessment System English test, questions were removed as a result of protests by concerned organizations. In one case, a test question about Alice Walker's story *Roselily*—about a black unwed mother—was removed from the test because a conservative Christian group believed the story and associated test question were anti-religious. In a second case, instructions asking students to express their feelings about stories they read on the test were removed. Although the test was measuring students' writing skills and used a prompt that asked students to write a letter that conveyed their feelings about a school policy, a representative of the Traditional Values Coalition successfully argued that it was not the role of the school to test children on their feelings.[25]

The Christian right was not the only offended group. Another story, *Am I Blue* by Alice Walker, was removed because it was seen as "anti-meat-eating" and because 10th graders should not be asked to comment on the fact that animals have to be killed to put meat on the table.[26] Still another question that focused on a passage from Annie Dillard's memoir *An American Childhood* in which she described a snowball fight as a "charming and delightful reminiscence" was purged from the 8th-grade test because the passage was deemed too violent for children to contemplate.[27]

Differences in ideology also lead to conflicts over mathematics items. On mathematics tests, complex supply items have led to a clash over the nature of mathematics, how it is learned, and how it should be taught. Consider this item from a test given to 8th graders in California:

> A forest fire has destroyed 3,000 trees. To prevent erosion, new trees must be planted. Students from your school want to help replant the trees. Each student is given two trees to plant. On the first day of replanting, one student plants both his trees in the forest. On the second day, two students plant their trees. On the third day, four students plant their trees, and so on. How many days will it take to replant the forest on this schedule?
>
> Explain your answer to the principal so that you can help convince her to help get students involved in replanting the forest.

The item was attacked in the *San Francisco Chronicle* because the scoring rubric awarded a lower score to students who got the right answer but did not provide an adequate explanation for their answer, while a higher score was awarded to students who provided a wrong answer but accurately described how they determined their answer.[28]

In the case of the math test, the test developer was placing more value on students' meta-cognitive skills, their ability to recognize the thought processes they used when solving a problem, and their subsequent ability to express those processes in written form. The *Chronicle*, however, placed more value on obtaining the correct response despite the student's inability to record how this response was reached.

HOW STUDENTS INTERACT WITH TEST ITEMS

A crucial factor in test development is the quality of a test's items or questions. Item preparation is not an easy task. It is an art, not a science. Adults write the items that children and adolescents must answer. Test items must stand alone without benefit of detailed context to further define the situation or problem. Test takers scrutinize each item very carefully; therefore, each word, diagram, graph, or equation in an item must unambiguously establish the task. The presentation of an item or its directions can cause some examinees to get the item wrong even though they have the necessary knowledge, skill, or ability, while other students without the knowledge, skill, or ability get it right.

In a review of the *The Oxford Murders*, Thomas Jones captures the difficulty faced by item writers:

> It used to be Kalman's job to set questions for school IQ tests. "[H]e spent his whole life preparing logical series, of the most basic kind... given three symbols in sequence, please fill in the fourth symbol." He also had to mark students' papers, and in the process discovered a curious thing: there were always a very few exam scripts in which all but one of the answers were right, and the one mistake was never an error he'd have expected. *Asking the candidates to justify their answers, Kalman found that each 'incorrect' solution was rather 'another' possible and perfectly valid way of continuing the series, only with a much more complicated justification.*[29]

Kalman's approach of asking students to explain why they answered test questions the way they did is crucial in trying to determine how different students experience the same item(s). Asking them to explain their answer is the only way to shed light on why some get an item wrong for sound reasons, and why some get it right for mistaken ones.

The cognitive psychologist Jerome Bruner insists that knowing what children *do* is not enough; we need to know what they *think* they are doing and their reasons for doing it.[30] To illustrate, Bruner presents a quote from Howard Gardner: "We must place ourselves inside the heads of our students and try to understand as far as possible the sources and strengths of their conceptions." Neither Bruner nor Gardner was referring specifically to why students answer test questions the way they do, but their observations are spot on.[31]

Two studies looked specifically at why students answered questions the way they did and shed light on the limitations and fallibility of test items for some students. First, Clifford Hill and Eric Larsen, in their study of how children answer questions on 3rd-grade reading tests, describe the dilemmas facing item writers, and the test company that assembles those items to form the test.[32] Test developers must maximize test reliability and validity by covering different kinds of content and skills that form the domain. But they must also build a test that takes into account the limited attention span of children and can be administered in a single class period.

These conflicting technical and administrative demands limit the total number of words that can be used on a multiple-choice test. Item writers, therefore, must omit contextual material from the story on which a reading test question is based. The resulting de-contextualized passage can lead children astray. When faced with an abridged reading passage, children must construct their own context. Hill and Larsen argue that when this happens children are primed to select the multiple-choice option that is closest to the context they have constructed.

Second, a study by Walter Haney and Laurie Scott asked young children to explain why they chose a particular answer to items on commonly used standardized achievement tests.[33] Figure 4.1 illustrates their findings.

When asked why they chose the incorrect cabbage option, a number of students explained that the cabbage, which was not in a pot, had been picked and therefore no longer needed water. Perfectly good reasoning on the child's part, but unanticipated by the item writers who designated the cactus as the correct answer. For this test, children who chose the cabbage distracter were marked wrong. While it may seem trivial to focus on a single problematic item on a test, such an item can have an adverse impact on the classification and subsequent treatment of students who are within a point or two of a cut-score.

Another important design limitation of both selection and supply items is that little is known about how a standardized procedure performs in slightly different contexts, and how different contextual presentations affect answers. Very slight alterations in test design can lead to very different descriptions of student performance. An illustration of this problem is the seemingly dramatic drop in the National Assessment of Educational Progress (NAEP) reading scores from 1984 to 1986. This drop was so large that people thought it improbable, and it became known as the infamous "reading anomaly."

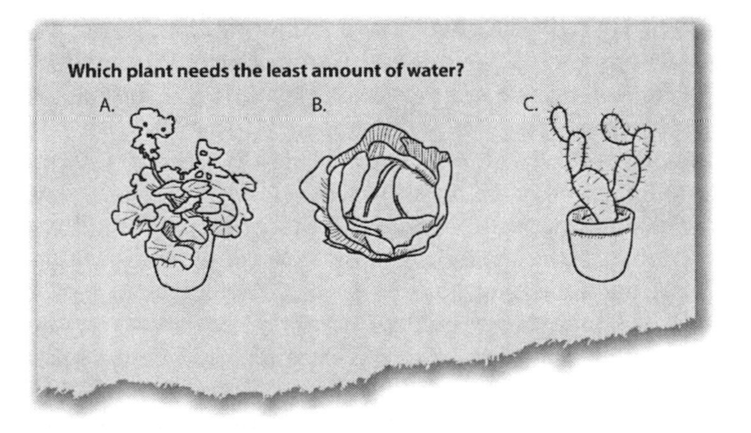

Figure 4.1 Problematic multiple choice test item. To view a color version of this figure, please visit www.infoagepub.com/madaus_paradoxes.

Researchers Albert Beaton and Rebecca Zwick showed that posing the same questions but making slight, innocuous changes to the test's appearance explained the drop in test scores.[34] Little changes like switching the order of the questions—e.g. item 3 becomes item 7; using stapled instead of saddle-stitched test booklets; having students fill in an oval rather than circle a letter to mark their answer; and using brown or black instead of blue print conspired to produce a very misleading description of progress in reading performance in our nation's schools. In other words, the changes in test scores, used to make inferences about changes in student achievement, was affected by subtle changes in the test format rather than changes in students' actual skills and knowledge.[35] These findings are powerful given the tendency of many to accept a quantitative test score as an infallible pronouncement about students' attainment or No Child Left Behind's use of test scores as an index of average yearly progress.

HOW STATES RESPOND TO INCORRECT OR AMBIGUOUS TEST ITEMS

Sometimes test items are simply bad or problematic. Although infrequent, items can contain more than one correct answers or no correct answer at all. For example, during the 2001 administration of the Massachusetts Comprehensive Assessment System (MCAS) math test, two 10th-graders found one multiple-choice item for which all of the answers provided were correct.[36] To nullify the offending item, the DOE decided not to score it.

Test officials often claim that removing the item corrects the problem, because the item does not affect the scores. Not scoring the offending item, however, does not remediate the disruption experienced by knowledgeable test-takers who try to find a solution to a faulty question. In the case of the faulty MCAS item, one of the students who discovered it reported that he worked for more than five minutes on the item, which should have taken only one or two minutes.

An event that occurred during the 2000 Summer Olympic Games demonstrates the residual impact of faulty items, even if they are not scored. Svetlana Khorkina, international favorite to win a gold medal in the women's gymnastics competition, failed to win the coveted prize. Khorkina ranked first after scoring a 9.812 on the floor exercises. She then moved to the vault, where she uncharacteristically landed on her hands and knees.[37] After a string of similar mishaps, event officials rechecked the vault's height. It was set at 120 instead of 125 centimeters, a difference of a little less than two inches. The vault was raised and the affected gymnasts were allowed to repeat their vaults. But the damage was already done. Khorkina was unable to regain her momentum or her confidence, and she declined another attempt on the apparatus. She left the event in 10th place, far behind her initial standing, and ended the competition in 11th place after a fall on the uneven parallel bars. Like the incorrect vault height, the inclusion of a faulty item(s) on a test can affect the performance of examinees on subsequent test items.

When faulty items are brought to the attention of state departments of education, officials often dismiss the challenges. For example, in 1988, John Anderson, a high school English teacher from Bell Buckle, Tennessee, brought an ambiguous question on the Tennessee High School Proficiency Test to the attention of Department of Education. At that time, public school students had to pass the state test to obtain a high school diploma. Mr. Anderson noted that a few students at his school had failed the test by one question. He further noted they had chosen another viable, but according to the test developers "wrong," answer for the ambiguous item. State officials turned down Mr. Anderson's request to review the question, stating that 98.6% of the state's students had chosen the keyed response, and therefore it must be correct.

Mr. Anderson then sought the opinions of experts in English and in psychometrics.[38] The experts supported Mr. Anderson's position and relayed their findings to the Department of Proficiency Testing. The director of the department indicated that grammarians within the Division of State Testing were consulted and stood by the single response that the Department originally deemed correct. In addition, the Department maintained that Mr. Anderson's complaint was nullified by the fact that 98.6% of students selected the "correct" response, suggesting that such a high percentage of students could not be wrong. The Department seemed to erroneously assume that the percentage of students selecting an option defines item veracity. The incident concluded with a ruling against Mr. Anderson's claim, preserving the students' "failing" classification.[39]

PROBLEMS WITH SUPPLY ITEMS

Many people believe tests that require students to produce, rather than select, answers provide a better opportunity for students to demonstrate their knowledge and skill. However, like multiple-choice tests, open-response items are not without problems. Focusing only on writing tests, there are at least four issues that affect an individual's test score.

First, instead of testing students' writing skills, writing tests sometimes measure the effectiveness of test preparation. The Irish Primary Certification Exam, used to certify the successful completion of primary school, is an example. The Exam contained an essay question that changed every year. To prepare for the essay question, many students were simply taught to begin their essay using an all-purpose opening paragraph. As seen in Figure 4.2, this strategy led many students to begin their essays with the same stock opening, regardless of the prompt. This example from Ireland shows that writing exams may not necessarily measure writing, but instead students' ability to recall rehearsed responses that earn a passing mark.

A second issue with writing tests is that the length of an essay can influence those scoring the test. When analyzing the scoring of the SAT essay test, Lee Perelman, an MIT professor, found that the longer the essay the higher the score. Perelman demonstrated that when an essay is scored on length alone, the resulting score is identical to the reported score more than 90% of the time.[41]

This relationship between the length of an essay and its score is probably not surprising to most readers. Many of us remember writing as much as we could in hopes of earning a higher score. In his autobiography *Growing Up,* Russell Baker recounts how the length of an essay worked to his benefit. At the end of his freshman year in college, Baker dropped physics and calculus and concentrated on literature, history, and economics where "examinations usually *posed essay questions permitting a glib writer to bluff his way through.*"[42]

Baker's reminiscence calls to mind the story of an Irish grandmother who pins a Holy Ghost medal beneath her grandson's lapel in preparation for his "A" level science exam, which 18-year-olds in Northern Ireland took to qualify for higher education.[43] She asks her grandson what science is about. When he tries to explain at length, she interrupts, "If y'can blether as well with your pen—you'll do all right."[44]

A third issue relates to how the method used to assess writing ability affects test performance. One of the authors has conducted a series of experiments in which students write an essay using either paper-and-pencil or a computer.[45] Across grade levels and subject areas, these studies have consistently found that students who are accustomed to writing with a computer perform significantly worse when they must use paper-and-pencil to write their essay. Similarly, students who usually write with paper-and-pencil perform much worse when they are forced to write on a computer. This difference is about as large as the change over a year in students' scores on commercial standardized tests. A student, nonetheless, possesses the same knowledge and skill whether typing or writing a response. However, the method used to measure the trait of interest affects students' ability to demonstrate the degree to which they possess the trait in question. This paper-versus-computer effect is a classic example of what the testing community calls a trait-method issue.[46]

A fourth issue is that the appearance of an essay influences the person who is scoring a student's response. Several studies have found that readers award lower scores to the same essay presented with "sloppy" penmanship

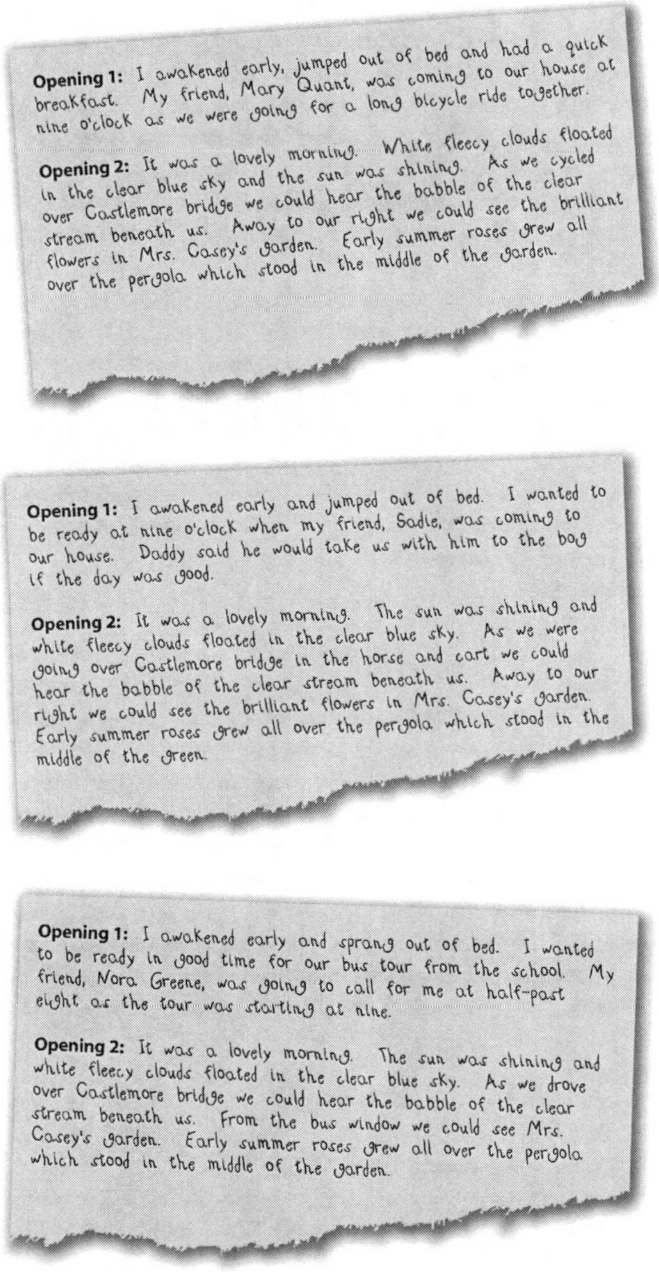

(a)

Opening 1: I awakened early, jumped out of bed and had a quick breakfast. My friend, Mary Quant, was coming to our house at nine o'clock as we were going for a long bicycle ride together.

Opening 2: It was a lovely morning. White fleecy clouds floated in the clear blue sky and the sun was shining. As we cycled over Castlemore bridge we could hear the babble of the clear stream beneath us. Away to our right we could see the brilliant flowers in Mrs. Casey's garden. Early summer roses grew all over the pergola which stood in the middle of the garden.

(b)

Opening 1: I awakened early and jumped out of bed. I wanted to be ready at nine o'clock when my friend, Sadie, was coming to our house. Daddy said he would take us with him to the bog if the day was good.

Opening 2: It was a lovely morning. The sun was shining and white fleecy clouds floated in the clear blue sky. As we were going over Castlemore bridge in the horse and cart we could hear the babble of the clear stream beneath us. Away to our right we could see the brilliant flowers in Mrs. Casey's garden. Early summer roses grew all over the pergola which stood in the middle of the green.

(c)

Opening 1: I awakened early and sprang out of bed. I wanted to be ready in good time for our bus tour from the school. My friend, Nora Greene, was going to call for me at half-past eight as the tour was starting at nine.

Opening 2: It was a lovely morning. The sun was shining and white fleecy clouds floated in the clear blue sky. As we drove over Castlemore bridge we could hear the babble of the clear stream beneath us. From the bus window we could see Mrs. Casey's garden. Early summer roses grew all over the pergola which stood in the middle of the garden.

Figure 4.2 Responses to Irish Primary Certification Exams' Writing Prompts[40]
(a) A bicycle ride (1946); (b) A day in the bog (1947); (c) A bus tour (1948). To view a color version of this figure, please visit www.infoagepub.com/madaus_paradoxes.

than those with "neat" hand-writing.[47] Presenting an essay in handwritten or typed form also influences the grader. One might think that typed responses receive higher scores than handwritten responses. In fact, however, the opposite generally occurs—typed responses receive lower scores.[48] Readers have higher expectations for typed text, consider typed text to be a final product, and can more easily see spelling, punctuation, and capitalization errors.[49] Together, these factors lead readers to be more critical of typed responses. This presentation effect is also an example of a trait-method problem.

Together, the method of assessment—paper-and-pencil versus computer—and the effect that the presentation of the student's response has on the scorer create a catch-22 for test developers and test-takers. On the one hand, allowing a student who is accustomed to writing with a computer to use a computer during testing will enable him to better demonstrate his writing ability. On the other hand, when his essay is scored, the student may receive a lower score because the reader has higher expectations for printed responses. This catch-22 is one of the many paradoxes of high-stakes testing and another example of its fallibility.

SUMMARY

Developing, administering, and using a test to make educational decisions seems like an easy process—simply assemble a set of questions that cover the skills and knowledge that you want to test and give that test to students. But, as we have seen in this chapter, creating a test is just the beginning. A range of human, cultural, ideological, and political factors influence the content of a test, the types of items used, the name given to a test, how the examinee interacts with the test, and how scores are interpreted. Along with the technical issues explored in the next chapter, these human and cultural factors explain in part why it is challenging to make a single test that works across a very diverse body of students and schools.

NOTES

1. See, for example, Henry (1963) and Hall (1977).
2. These examples come from an interview with Richard Rothestein by Lewis Diuguid of the Kansas City Star (Diuguid, 2005). Also see Rothstein (2004).
3. Barton & Coley (2007).
4. Deyhle (1986).
5. Also see Tyler (1979).
6. Locust (1988).
7. Deyhle, op cit.

8. The Ojibwa are sometimes referred to as Chippewa.
9. McShane (1989); National Commission on Testing and Public Policy (1990, p. 13).
10. In 2005, the National Indian Education Association raised concerns about No Child Left Behind and its associated testing requirements that caused major disruptions in schools directly impacting Native culture-based education. Among the report's findings were: a) Schools send the message that if Indian children would just work harder they would succeed, b) The few successes achieved have clearly been at the expense of Native languages and cultures, and c) American Indian children internalize the system's failures as their own personal failures (National Indian Education Association, 2005).
11. National Commission on Testing and Public Policy (1990).
12. Bruner (1996, p.50). For a discussion of how views of the learner have influenced the mathematics curriculum over time, see Madaus, Clarke, & O'Leary (2003).
13. For an analysis of Judge John E. Jones' findings, see *Washington Post* (2005).
14 The power of using the right word to label a test is profound. As feminists have come to realize, whoever names the world owns it. Therefore, the name given a test domain must be chosen with great care, since naming the test reifies it. When people take the name of a test literally they are no longer like the Wizard of Oz who knew green glasses made Oz green, they believe that Oz *is* green (Turbayne, 1962).
15. The Oxford scholar Peter Medwar observes that such a belief "makes Nature herself an accomplice in the crime of political inequality" (Medwar, 1982, p. 177).
16. Gardner (1997).
17. Quoted in Kermode (1988, p. 3).
18. Judd (1918, p. 152, emphasis added). Also see Gould (1981).
19. The 2007 Emanuele Crialese film, *The Golden Door*, about the turn-of-the-century voyage of a poor family from rural Sicily to the United States contains a scene where the immigrants are given a non verbal IQ test at Ellis Island. It is a powerful example of how cultural and family background affects how they perceived the task presented to them and the dire consequences of being returned to home for failure.
20. Madaus (1983).
21. National Commission on Testing and Public Policy (1990). Attributed to Lorrie Shepherd in Cunningham (1989). Also see Shepard & Smith (1986); Shepard & Smith (1988a); Shepard & Smith (1988b).
22. The Educational Testing Service (ETS) President Gregory Anrig summarized his "serious reservations" about using SAT scores to make state comparisons, in a letter to then Secretary of Education Lauro Cavazos:

    The SAT is not designed to reflect the outcome of instruction in high school and therefore is not sensitive to a great many changes in the high school curriculum or to changes in subject matter.... Given the tenuous relationship of SAT scores to changes in high school instruction and the lack of representativeness of the scores, the state rankings are likely to be in serious error and small changes from year to year meaningless (Anrig, 1990).

23. Stedman & Kaestle (1987 Winter). Datta found that "there may be *domains* of basic skills that differentiate skilled from less able employees and that these *domains* differ substantially from what the schools teach" (Datta, 1982, p. 168, emphasis added)).
24. Hall (1977).
25. Asimov (1994a).
26. Asimov (1994c). Also, the CA Board of Education Chair McDowell said that "Am I Blue" was withdrawn "because it might be viewed as advocating a particular nutritional lifestyle" and "seemed to violate rural children's family occupations." It was this quote that made the press start calling the reason for being withdrawn as "anti-meat eating."
27. The book Banned says "Groups on the religious right also lobbied the Board of Education about Annie Dillard's "An American Childhood," stating that a snowball fight depicted in that story was too 'violent.'" A CRESST report about the politics of state testing reports reported that it was two state board of education board members that objected to the story because the snowball fight was too violent. See Holt (1996) for details.
28. Saunders (1995).
29. Jones (2005, p. 29–30, emphasis added).
30. Bruner (1996).
31. Gardner (1991, p. 253).
32. Hill & Larsen (2000).
33. Haney & Scott (1987).
34. Beaton & Zwick (1990).
35. These finds are for groups not for individual students.
36. Lindsay (2001).
37. Harasta (2000).
38. One of the experts in English was Claire Cook, the former Editorial Supervisor of MLA Publications. George Madaus was one of the psychometrics experts.
39. Rhoades & Madaus (2003).
40. Madaus & Greaney (1985). These examples, and many more, were provided by a school inspector who collected them during the 1940s.
41. Winerip (2005).
42. Baker (1984, p. 208, emphasis added).
43. There is a separate exam for each subject.
44. Maclaverty (1979, p. 41).
45. Russell (1999); Russell & Haney (1997); Russell, Higgins, & Hoffmann (2004); Russell & Plati (2001). This effect was also replicated for the NAEP writing test by Horkay, Bennett, Allen, Kaplan, & Yan (2006).
46. Campbell & Fiske (1959).
47. Bull & Stevens (1979); Chase (1986); Markham (1976); Marshall & Powers (1969).
48. Powers, Fowles, Farnum, & Ramsey (1994).
49. Russell & Tao (2004a); Russell & Tao (2004b).

CHAPTER 5

WHAT TECHNICAL ISSUES AFFECT TEST VALIDITY?

Examining the validity of test-based inferences, descriptions, and decisions is the heart and soul of testing. Unless a test is valid for its intended purpose there is no reason to use it. The *Standards for Educational and Psychological Testing* describe at length the importance of examining and reporting on test validity.[1] In this chapter we begin by examining how high-stakes testing programs deal with the central issue of test validity. We then examine several issues that affect the validity of using cut-scores to classify students.

STATE TESTING PROGRAMS AND TEST VALIDITY

Despite the fundamental importance of validity, the breadth of most validation studies of high-stakes state testing programs is limited. A 2006 study examined the information that all 50 states provided about their testing programs. As seen in Figure 5.1, all 50 states published summaries of test results on their website.

Forty-six states provided detailed information about test schedules, and 45 states provided sample test items on their websites. However, only 24 states made technical reports about their tests publicly available on-line. Of these 24 states, three did not mention validity.[2] As seen in Figure 5.2, across

The Paradoxes of High Stakes Testing, pages 77–93

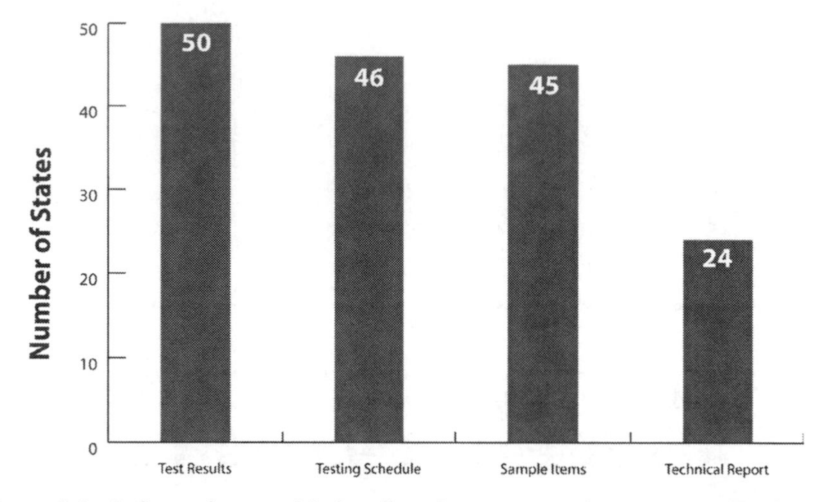

Figure 5.1 Information provided on-line about state testing program. To view a color version of this figure, please visit www.infoagepub.com/madaus_paradoxes.

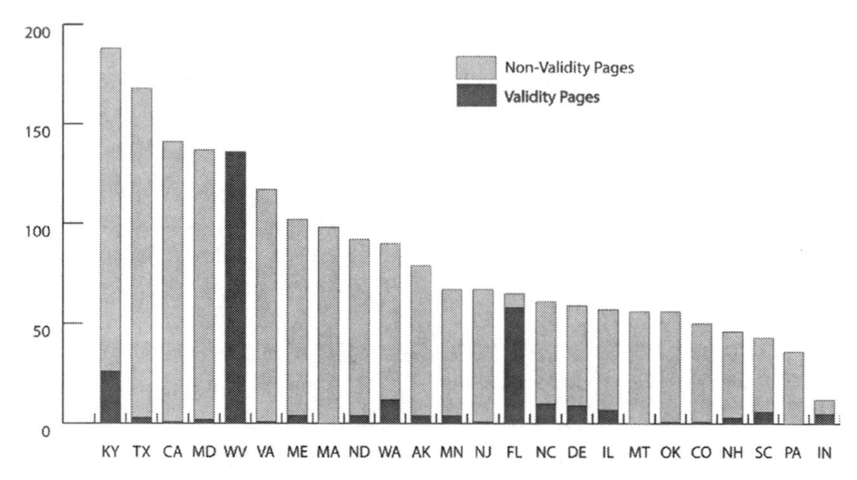

Figure 5.2 Number of technical report pages dedicated to test validity. To view a color version of this figure, please visit www.infoagepub.com/madaus_paradoxes.

all 24 states that provided an on-line technical report, only 298 of 2,023 (14.7%) pages focused on validity.

It is interesting to note, however, that two states—West Virginia and Florida—dedicated nearly all of their technical reports to the issue of test validity. When these two states are removed from the analysis, the remaining states dedicated only 5.7% of pages in their technical reports to test validity.[3]

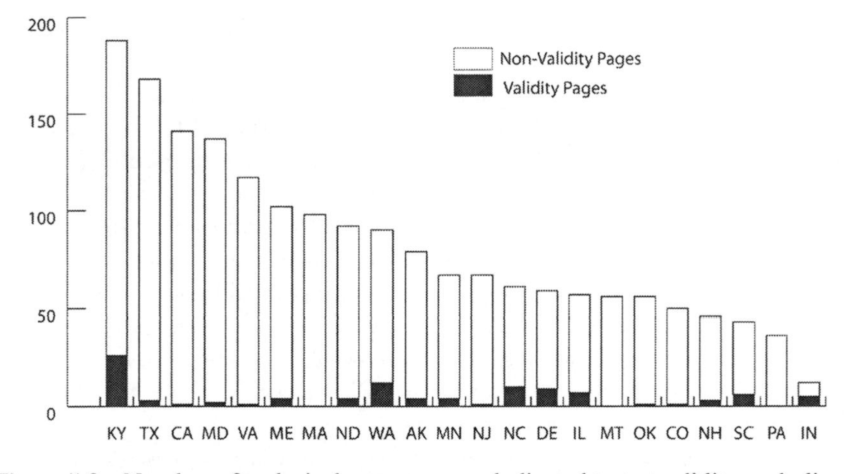

Figure 5.3 Number of technical report pages dedicated to test validity excluding West Virginia and Florida. To view a color version of this figure, please visit www.infoagepub.com/madaus_paradoxes.

CONFLICTS OF INTEREST CAUSE A FOCUS ON CONFIRMATORY EVIDENCE

Two impediments to high quality validation studies are time and expense. A larger issue, however, is the conflict of interest faced by test developers and those invested in a testing program. Test developers have vested financial and professional interests in the test. State departments of education and the federal government have vested political, financial, administrative, and management interests in a testing program.

These apparent and real conflicts of interests often limit validation studies to the collection of evidence that confirms preconceived beliefs about the quality and benefits of a testing program. Absent, however, are efforts to examine evidence that may call into question the testing program. Pursuing disconfirming evidence—asking questions that may challenge a test's validity—poses unknown risks. And, when one is afraid of potential answers, it is difficult to ask challenging questions. For this reason alone, examining evidence that goes beyond the statistical or psychometric quality of a test is a threatening proposition.

Several examples bear witness to the limited scope of most validity studies. In 2005, Connecticut filed a lawsuit challenging a testing provision of No Child Left Behind. Connecticut argued that since there is no significant validity evidence that testing at every grade results in positive consequences for students and their schools, states should not be required to test at every grade.[4]

In Massachusetts, a decade passed before the Department of Education began formally examining disconfirming evidence regarding the validity of its writing test. As described in chapter 4, students accustomed to composing written responses using a computer under-perform on the state writing test that requires all students to produce hand-written essays.[5] In response to this validity problem, the state has raised concerns that allowing some students to use computers during the writing test would complicate administrative procedures, increase the cost of the testing program, and affect the standardization of testing conditions. While these concerns are legitimate, they have nothing to do with the core validity question about the accuracy of inferences made about student writing.

Another example from Massachusetts relates to promises made about its testing program to improve the quality of public schools and hold schools accountable for student learning. Between 2001 and 2005, the Department of Education highlighted improvements in the passing rates for its high school exams. Yet, when students who passed the state test went on to attend pubic colleges in the state 37% needed remedial help.[6] Texas also reported improvements in the results of its high school tests over the last decade. Increased passing rates suggest that students are performing at a higher level and have acquired better academic skills. And yet the performance of college-bound students on the states' college entrance exams remained stagnant, despite rapid improvements in high school test scores.[7] Further, in 2007 the *Commission for a College Ready Texas* reported that almost half of college freshmen in the state take remedial classes. The Commission observed that passing the state's high school graduation test does not guarantee a student is ready for college.[8]

As a final example, one might think that if a state's test scores are improving, then more students will graduate from high school. The opposite pattern, however, has occurred in several states. For example, Texas has seen a noticeable decrease in its graduation rates, particularly for minority students. When Massachusetts introduced a graduation requirement linked to performance on the state test, a similar decrease in its graduation rate occurred during the succeeding years. This pattern occured in several other states and large urban areas as well.[9]

It is important to recognize that validity is not an all-or-none concept, it is a matter of degree. Evidence regarding college readiness and graduation rates does not mean a state's testing program is "invalid." But it does point to the importance of examining the variety of consequences that may or may not flow from the use of a high-stakes test and take steps to remedy negative consequences.

WILLED IGNORANCE OF THE CONSEQUENCES OF HIGH-STAKES TESTS

Despite the importance of examining consequential validity, some advocates of high-stakes testing programs flat out ignore consequences. For example, in 1991, Chester Finn, former Assistant Secretary for Research and Improvement at the U.S. Department of Education took issue with the distinguished test expert[10] Robert Linn's call for validity studies of high-stakes tests that examined the consequences of test use. Finn argued that studying consequences was naïve. He said that Linn "has sorely confused the world of the technical with the world of the political... I must describe [Linn's paper] as a classic example of what can happen when 'experts' are turned loose in the policy pasture."[11]

Finn's argument is revealing and troubling. He argues that policy goals trump recommendations of technical experts regarding test validation. He also implies that it is not important to consider the consequences a high-stakes test can have for an individual student. But, can you imagine a political leader ignoring the advice of medical experts to examine the effects that a new medication or treatment has on individual children?

While it is a generally held opinion that consumers should adhere to the advice of the product developers, as is done when installing an infant car seat or when taking medication, the advice of test developers and contractors often goes unheeded in the realm of high-stakes decision-making.[12] For example, Eugene Paslov, the then president of Harcourt Brace's testing division, said that standardized tests should not be used as the sole determinant of who graduates from high school and who does not.[13] He stated, "When these tests are used exclusively for graduation, I think that's wrong."[14] Massachusetts Board of Education Chairman James Peyser responded, "Obviously [the test contractors'] job is to provide a service, not to make policy. No, we don't need them on board."[15] This willingness of a government leader to openly dismiss advice from test experts is another demonstration of the political limits placed on validation studies. Politics and policy issues aside, the accuracy of an inference from a test score and ensuing consequences are issues at the very heart of testing. The real and present danger comes from those who labor in the "policy pasture" ignoring the advice of technical experts when they call attention to the fallible nature of high-stakes tests and their unintended consequences.

ISSUES AROUND CUT-SCORES

As we saw in Chapter 3, a cut-score is used to sort students into one of two performance levels. The process of setting cut-scores is subjective and many factors influence the outcome. Just as subtle changes to the format and layout of the 1994 NAEP reading test led to changes in student performance, minor changes to the standard-setting procedures can create changes in where cut-scores are set. For example, altering the definition of a given performance level or changing the directions given to the panel will affect the placement of the cut-score. Changes in the composition of the panel that sets the cut-scores may also affect the outcome. And, any change to a cut-score can affect a student's classification. But beyond the method used to set a cut-score there are several other issues that affect the validity of classifications made based on cut-scores.

THE NORMATIVE NATURE OF CUT-SCORES

A cut-score establishes an objective criteria for student classification—your score is either above or below the cut-score. However, the procedures used to set cut scores depend heavily on subjective, norm-referenced decisions. Panel members base their judgments on their experiences working with students—a normative frame of reference. Raters are also supplied with information about the percentage of students that answer each item correctly. This information is also normative. Therefore, the process of determining the cut-score is fully dependent on normative data and judgments.

Walker Percy, a well-known physician and novelist, points out that normative judgments are at the root of all classification procedures in both the physical and social sciences:

> [T]he scientist, in practicing the scientific method, cannot utter a single word about an individual thing or creature insofar as it is an individual but only insofar as it resembles other individuals. This limitation holds true whether the individual is a molecule of NaCl or an amoeba or a human being....We all remember taking science courses where one was confronted with a *sample of* sodium chloride or *a specimen* of a dogfish to dissect. Such studies reveal the properties shared by all sodium chloride and by all dogfish. We have no particular interest in this particular pinch of salt or this particular dogfish.
>
> But perhaps we are a bit startled when we are told that this same limitation applies to psychiatry. In the words of Harry Stack Sullivan, perhaps the greatest American psychiatrist: "To the degree that I am a psychiatrist, to this same degree I am not interested in you as an individual but only in you and your symptoms insofar as they resemble other individuals and other symptoms."[16]

Percy's argument underscores that normative comparisons are inescapable when classifying objects or people. While we may call a test criterion-referenced, at its root it is norm-referenced.

No doubt, the normative reality of "criterion-referenced" testing creates confusion among policy makers and test users. For example, in 1993 Sir Ron Dearing, the Chairman of the National Committee of Inquiry into Higher Education in Great Britain, recommended reforming the "criterion referenced" Standard Assessment Test (SAT). To establish that students had successfully completed a given stage of education, Dearing proposed to give a test to a random sample of students. The median score for that sample of students would be the criterion for successfully completing a given stage.[17] In effect, Dearing's proposal would establish a normative scale and anyone who performed above average would be classified as successful.

Dearing's proposal is similar to practices during the early 20th century in America. At the time, it was thought that test scores could be interpreted in terms of absolute proficiency or achievement. Standards for proficiency, however, were invariably based on the median test performance within a given district.[18] Given the nature of educational measurement, this reliance on normative data is inevitable but is rarely acknowledged.

THE CONTINUOUS NATURE OF KNOWLEDGE AND COMPETENCIES

Skills, knowledge, and competencies are continuous in nature. We cannot simply draw a line in the sand and say that people on one side posses a skill, knowledge or competency while those on the other side do not. Yet, a cut-score attempts to do just that—a single point on a test score continuum is used to classify a student's level of attainment. Quite simply, this problem is unavoidable once the decision is made to establish a cut-score.

What are the implications of dichotomizing the continuous nature of knowledge, skills, and ability? Consider two students. Johnny's score is one point below the cut. Mary is one point above the cut. Although their scores are only one point apart, their classifications make them appear very different. Johnny is labeled as needing improvement while Mary is classified as proficient.

Now, consider a third student. Joe scored ten points higher than Mary, which was the top score within the proficient category. Because Mary and Joe share the same classification they are likely to be treated similarly. Yet, isn't Mary's level of knowledge or skill more like Johnny's than Joe's? If Johnny will receive additional instruction to boost his performance, wouldn't Mary also benefit? The problem is even more serious when the cut-point separates students labeled as failing from those who pass.

As we explore below, problems that result from using a cut-score to classify students are further complicated by measurement error. If tested again,

Johnny might very well score one point higher and Mary one point lower, switching their classifications.

COMPARING CLASSIFICATIONS ACROSS DIFFERENT TESTS

Policy makers and the media often compare classifications across tests. As an example, the percent of students classified as proficient on a state test are often compared to the percent of students proficient on a national or international test. The normative nature of establishing cut-scores, however, makes these comparisons suspect.

Under No Child Left Behind each state sets cut-scores for its own tests that classify students into one of four categories. All but three states employ their own unique test, their own method, and group of expert judges to set cut-scores.[19] Given the differences in tests and cut-score setting procedures used across states, what does it mean when students are classified as failing, needs improvement, proficient, or advanced on a state-by-state basis?

The meanings of the classifications categories are not comparable from state to state for at least three reasons. First, the domains measured by the various state tests differ in subtle and not so subtle ways. As an example, the cannon for eighth grade mathematics differs across states. Second, the tests used by some states are much easier than in others.[20] Finally, to meet No Child Left Behind requirements, some states set a much lower bar when setting cut-scores than do others. Together, these differences create a situation in which proficient in Massachusetts does not mean the same thing as proficient in Texas, or any other state, in terms of what students know and can do.

The incomparability of student classifications became clear in 2005 when the percentage of students performing at each of the four levels specified by No Child Left Behind were compared to the classifications based on the National Assessment of Educational Progress (NAEP). For its Fall 2004 4th grade mathematics assessment, Connecticut reported that 79% of students performed at or above the proficient level. Yet NAEP's spring 2005 results for Connecticut classified only 42% of students as at or above proficient in mathematics. Similarly, Texas reported that 80% of students met its 2005 standard on its Spring 2005 4th grade mathematics assessment, yet Texas' NAEP's spring 2005 mathematics assessment classified only 29% of students as at or above proficient.

Not surprisingly, the disparity between how states and NAEP classified students caused confusion within the media. A *New York Times* headline proclaimed, "Students Ace State Tests but Earn D's From U.S."[21] The *Wash-*

ington Post opined, "Students Show Few Gains since 'No Child': Math Up Slightly, Reading No Improvement."[22]

But there is a problem with interpretations such as these. While there is no doubt that the standards set on various state tests are indeed low, the media coverage assumes that the NAEP cut-scores are valid—the gold standard against which all other students classifications are to be compared. Yet, there are at least two reasons to question the accuracy of NAEP classifications. First, NAEP is a "drop from the sky" event. Unlike high-stakes state tests or college admission tests, where the results are seen as very important, a "drop from the sky" test does not have personal repercussion for students. For this reason, it is unclear how seriously students take the NAEP test.

Second, there is no external evidence for the validity of NAEP classifications. Consider NAEP data from 1992 and 1994. In grade 12, only 2 percent of students were classified at the advanced level. That same year, about 50 percent of all seniors took either the SAT or ACT. Many readers would consider a person who scores above 600 on the SAT as advanced. About 16 percent of those taking the SAT score higher than 600. This constitutes about 8 percent of all seniors, which is four times as high as the 1994 NAEP advanced category percentage.[23] In other words, high achievement on NAEP is defined differently from high achievement on college admission tests.[24] While some readers may believe that a score of 600 on the SAT is not a high enough bar for advanced, this very disagreement illustrates the challenge of setting cut-scores and comparing classifications across tests.

CONTROVERSIAL NATURE OF SETTING CUT-SCORES

With respect to the validity of NAEP classifications, there has been controversy since their creation in 1990. An independent evaluation found that the National Assessment Governing Board "failed to produce dependable achievement levels for use in interpreting NAEP results... [and] *failed to produce evidence that the users of NAEP results can and are likely to make appropriate use of the levels in reaching valid conclusions about the meaning of NAEP results.*"[25] The National Assessment Governing Board rejected this evaluation and attempted to cancel the evaluators' contract. However, a subsequent evaluation conducted by the General Accounting Office also found that the standard-setting work was seriously flawed.[26]

Since then, several other organizations, including the National Academy of Science, the National Academy of Education, and the Center for Research in Evaluation, Student Standards and Testing have questioned the validity of the NAEP performance levels. These conclusions about the NAEP performance levels were based in part on the process used to determine the performance levels. As the National Research Council described, "It is clear that the current processes are too cognitively complex for the raters, and there are notable inconsistencies in the judgment data . . . Furthermore, NAEP achievement-level results do not appear to be reasonable compared with other external information about students' achievement."[27]

Remember, the process of establishing cut-scores is arbitrary and depends upon subjective decisions. For this reason, alone, it is imperative that high-stakes criterion-referenced testing programs collect and examine independent external evidence to support their classifications of students.

THE POLITICS OF CUT-SCORES

Neither the establishment nor validation of cut-scores is immune to politics. When policy makers passionately embrace a program, any exposure of its shortcomings by outsiders is quickly denounced. Despite concerns about the validity of the NAEP cut-scores, political leaders have resisted calls to modify the NAEP achievement levels. In fact, concerns raised by the independent evaluators hired by NAGB, were dismissed. NAGB ignored technical, statistics, and psychometric data regarding the inadequacy of the performance levels. Instead they relied on the opinions of governors, members of Congress, and the executive branch who believed the performance levels were useful in meeting their political goals.[28]

More than a decade later, researcher Gerald Bracey notes that resistance to altering the NAEP performance levels still exists. Bracey argues that this resistance stems from a desire by leaders like Rod Paige, the former Secretary of Education, to use the NAEP achievement levels to shame states into doing better.[29] This strategy of shaming schools was examined by the columnist George Will, who titled his article, "Shame: School Reform's Weak Weapon." In his article, Will described Paige's strategy of shaming as one that exerts "power to embarrass states if their results on the National Assessment of Educational Progress (NAEP) . . . reveal that they are not progressing."[30] Use of NAEP to shame schools into "reforming" depends on the questionable assumption that the NAEP performance levels are themselves valid.

Politics also influences cut-scores and performance levels. For example, in 2005, the Massachusetts' Commissioner of Education, David Driscoll proposed raising the cut-scores that had been established by the state's standard setting committees. He argued that arbitrarily raising the standards would better prepare students for college and better meet the goals of No Child Left Behind.[31] A New York Times article reported that state legislators in South Carolina also proposed ignoring the cut-scores set by their standard setting committees. In South Carolina, however, the politicians wanted to lower that state's cut-scores because the current standards made it too hard for schools to meet No Child Left Behind requirements.[32]

To eliminate arbitrary decisions made about cut-scores in some states and to assure comparability across states, some people have argued that the country needs to create a national test.[33] While such a test would certainly eliminate arbitrary changes to state cut-scores, it would be difficult to reach consensus about the content of, and the cut-scores for, such a test. Recall how politics and ideology can affect curriculum and testing programs. These problems are serious at the state level; it is hard to imagine them being any less serious nationally.

RELIABILITY OF CUT-SCORE CLASSIFICATIONS

The accuracy of student classifications is an essential aspect of cut-scores. When employing any test—medical, chemical, or educational—measurement error, and sometimes human error, occurs. Measurement error on a high-stakes test can result in a score that is higher or lower than the student's true achievement level. If measurement error results in a test score that is higher than a student's true achievement level, the student may be falsely classified as needs improvement, proficient, or advanced. In technical terms, the student is a false positive. Conversely, if the test score is below the student's true achievement level, the student may be falsely classified below a cut-score. The student is a false negative. False positives and false negatives are a particular problem for students whose true achievement is close to a given cut-score.

Since all tests contain some degree of error, false positives and false negatives will always occur when cut-scores are used to sort students into discrete groups. Using a statistic called the *standard error of measurement,* it is possible to estimate how many students are likely to be misclassified as false positives or false negatives.[34] Al Beaton, a renowned psychometrician, showed that the problem of misclassification increases as a test becomes less reliable. He showed that for a test that attempted to place students into one of four performance levels, 19% of students are misclassified if the test's reliability is .95—a very high degree of reliability. Misclassification errors increase to 29% when the reliability is .90—the reliability for many state tests. For a reliability of .80, 38% of students are misclassified and misclassification errors increase dramatically as reliability drops further.[35]

When test scores and subsequent classifications are examined across large numbers of students—all students in a school, district, or state—the classification errors that naturally occur tend to balance out. That is, for each student falsely classified above a cut-score, there is one student who is falsely classified below a cut score. For this reason, false classifications tend to have little impact on the accuracy of the group performance when the number of students forming the group is large.

When test scores and subsequent classifications are examined for individual students, however, classification errors can have a profound impact on the student. Based solely on a student's test scores, important decisions are often made about such things as retention in grade, receipt of a diploma, and eligibility for a scholarship. A student who is false positive may be denied additional educational services when he really needs them or may receive a scholarship when his true achievement level is not actually among the top candidates. Conversely, a student who is a false negative may be retained in grade or denied a diploma when she has in fact acquired the expected skills and knowledge. The bottom line is that the reliance on a single test to make a critical determination will inevitably lead to inaccurate decisions that create adverse results for some individuals.

An example from baseball illustrates how an individual can be adversely affected by a false classification. In a January 2008, the Boston Red Sox's star third baseman, Mike Lowell, voiced fears over the implications for ballplayers of a false positive classification from a test for Human Growth Hormones. He argued that such a test had to be 100% accurate and reasoned that if the test is only 99% accurate there would still be seven false positives out of the 693 players tested. Worse still a 90% accurate test would generate 70 false positives—"that's 3[team] rosters." Lowell pointed out that the careers of the false positives "would be scared for life," and that Major League Baseball can't say, "Sorry we've made a mistake."[36]

While Lowell makes a compelling argument, the problem with it is that screening tests are not 100% accurate. Measurement and human error will always effect a person's score. An analogy to this problem of false classifications is captured in a recitation entitled *Cosmo The Fairly Accurate Knife Thrower.* In each verse the name of Cosmo's assistant changes.[37] High-stakes tests, like Cosmo's knife throwing, are fairly accurate, but by no means perfect. That imperfection carries with it real consequences for some students. These consequences are, themselves, a compelling reason for insisting on employing multiple, and *different* measures of the trait or condition before classifying a person.

MISCLASSIFICATIONS: MEDICINE VERSUS EDUCATION

In some fields, like medicine, false classifications are taken very seriously.[38] Doctors do not want to give treatment to someone falsely classified as having an illness, nor do doctors want to withhold treatment from someone who really needs it. For example, to screen hospital blood-bank donors for hepatitis, measures of serum enzyme are employed.[39] To set a cut-score for decisions about the blood's acceptability, pathologists plotted the distributions of the serum of healthy individuals and those with damage. The overlap area allows pathologists to estimate, for various cut-scores, the number of false positive and false negative classifications. Informed cost-benefit judgments are made about where in the overlap zone to place the cut-score to minimize either of these unavoidable misclassifications.

Unlike medicine, in education false positives receive little scrutiny. Instead of identifying and directly addressing the problems caused by misclassifications, testing programs attempt to reduce false negatives by providing students with multiple opportunities to take the same test or a very similar test. In essence, this "solution" enables advocates of high-stakes testing to discount the measurement error around the false negative classification, arguing that the student has multiple opportunities to retake the test. This assumes, of course, that the student who fails takes advantage of these opportunities. But it also assumes that the false negative classification is due to random rather than systematic error.

In the physical sciences, taking repeated measures of a trait is common practice. This practice aims to overcome the effects of error on a single measure by finding the average across repeated measures. It is important to recognize that measurement error in the physical sciences is viewed as random and that over repeated measures the random error balances out. In education, however, measurement error can occur at random or it can be systematic. As we saw earlier, culture, home background, poorly constructed items, the use or denial of computers for writing tests, and other factors cause systematic error in student performance. When measuring achievement, it is not enough to simply take repeated measures using the same instrument. Instead, multiple methods or instruments are needed to overcome the effects that systematic error may have on measures taken by any one instrument.[40] In medicine, if a person tested for an illness is flagged, he or she undergoes further testing using various techniques. All of the data are then used to make a clinical decision. This is simply not the case in education.

VALIDITY OF DECISIONS BASED ON CUT-SCORES

The necessity of employing multiple methods to measure student attainment goes beyond the issue of test reliability; it is, at its core, a validity issue. Repeating the same test may provide reliable information, but that information may not be valid for a specific decision. As an example, giving the SAT to fifth grade students multiple times will produce consistent, low scores. But, these scores cannot be used to make valid inferences about fifth grade achievement level or whether a student should be retained in grade.

Rather than simply using the same method to measure student achievement multiple times, alternate methods are often needed. For a test of reading comprehension, having the student read aloud and talk about the passage may be one alternative to multiple-choice questions. Similarly, letting the student use a computer when measuring writing instead of repeating a paper-and-pencil test, may provide a more valid measure of the student's writing ability.

Given the deep knowledge most teachers have of their students, teacher judgment can also serve as an additional source of information about a student's achievement. Teachers are the only ones who witness a student's performance over an extended period of time. Given this wealth of data collected over time, the teacher is better positioned to evaluate student achievement than a one-off high-stakes test. Unfortunately, many policy makers and critics of education distrust teacher judgments. For this reason, teacher judgments are seldom used in state testing programs in making decisions about students.

This distrust of teacher judgments in the United States contrasts sharply with the practice in Sweden. In Sweden, teacher judgments are integrated with information from standardized tests. The Swedish researcher Andres Bojörklund and his colleagues find that combining teacher judgments with standardized test results humanizes assessment, increases teacher authority, and better predicts future success.[41]

While no single solution—be it incorporating teacher judgments, repeated measures, or multiple measures—will eliminate false classifications entirely, it is important to consider the extent to which they occur within any testing program. When the stakes are high for participants—be it schools, teachers, or students—it is important to incorporate strategies to reduce the false classifications and increase the validity of any decisions that are made.

SUMMARY

While all testing programs conduct some form of a validity study that provides confirming evidence regarding the psychometric characteristics of the test, disconfirming evidence is rarely examined. In addition, the extent to which cut-scores misclassify students, the stability of these classifications, and the effects of misclassifications is under-examined in most of today's testing programs. While cut-scores are used to make "objective criterion-based" decisions about a student's performance level, the actual process of establishing cut-scores is normative and based on subjective judgments. Differences in the actual tests and the way in which cut-scores are set also make it impossible to compare student achievement across testing programs.

Collectively, the many issues explored in this and the previous chapter may create the impression that high-stakes testing programs are flawed beyond repair and should be abandoned. This is **not** the case. Tests are useful tools for learning about student achievement, identifying areas of the domain that present challenges to some students, and providing a broad picture of performance across a group of students. Nonetheless, all of the stake-holders in testing—students, teachers, school leaders, politicians, policy makers, parents, the press, and the general public—need to recognize the fallibility of testing and the multiple issues that affect the validity of inferences and decisions based on a test score. Herein lies a major paradox of testing. A test provides useful, but fallible information.

NOTES

1. The standards were developed jointly by the American Educational Research Association, the American Psychological Association, and the National Council on Measurement in Education. For a more recent treatment of validity see *Educational Researcher* Vol. 36, Number 4, November 2007. The issue is an up-to-date "Dialogue on Validity."
2. These three states were Pennsylvania, Massachusetts, and Montana.
3. Data for figures 3 & 4 were collected between December, 2005 through February, 2006. Information is based on the most recent technical report available at that time on the state's department of education website. Attempts were made to contact all states for which a technical report could be found. None of these states were able to direct us to an on-line report.
4. Dillon (2005a).
5. Russell & Abrams (2004); Wood (2005).
6. Wood (2005).
7. Markely (2004).
8. Houston Chronicle (2007).
9. Haney (2005).
10. Test experts who have advanced training in developing and analyzing the statistical properties of tests are also referred to as psychometricians.
11. This quote is taken from an August 6, 1991, memo to Lauren Resnick, et al., from Chester E. Finn Jr. It was part of a package of material that George Madaus received as a member of the Prerelease Review Panel of the evaluation of the NAGB performance categories by Stufflebeam, Jaeger, & Scriven (1991).
12. Rhoades & Madaus (2003).
13. This same advice was made by the then president of CTB/McGraw-Hill. Myers (2001) and Mathews (2000). Note that many advocates for high-stakes testing programs argue that the student must also pass all the courses needed for graduation. However, the single measure of attainment, the test, overrides all else.
14. Myers (2001, p. 1).
15. Quoted in Hayward (2001, p. 1).

16. Percy (1991, pp. 211–212, emphasis in original). In fact, education doesn't follow the scientific method described by Percy at all. The education of the individuals (albeit in a group situation) is the claimed focus of what schools should do. People in the testing community like to think they follow the scientific method and that their devices are "scientific"; users, from teachers to policy makers, do not make such claims. Further, the test developers and users often claims to be interested in what the person can do in an absolute sense, not in reference to the performance of a norm group. The word "symptoms" in the Sullivan excerpt raise the hackles of educators, since it denotes pathology. Educators do not like to think of themselves as dealing with pathology, but with the positive unfolding of an individual's "unique" potential. Nonetheless, the offending phrase could be paraphrased to read, "I am not interested in you as an individual, but only in you and your achievements insofar as they resemble other individuals and other achievements."
17. Dearing (1993, p. 42).
18. Ballou (1916a); Thorndike (1918).
19. The exceptions are Rhode Island, New Hampshire, and Vermont
20. See Fuller, Gesicki, Kang, & Wright (2006).
21. Dillon (2005b).
22. Romano (2005).
23. If 50% of seniors take the SAT and 16% of those taking the test score above 600, then 8% of all seniors have scored above 600.
24. Madaus, Clarke, & O'Leary (2003).
25. Stufflebeam, Jaeger, & Scriven (1992, pp 1, 31, emphasis in original)
26. Chelimsky (1992).
27. Commision on Behavioral and Social Sciences and education (CBASSE) (1999, p. 7).
28. Boyd, Musick, & Glode (1991). The full quote is as follows: [A] staff member of the National Education Goals Panel stated that the 1990 NAEP mathematics results, reported by achievement levels, will be the centerpiece of the Goals Panel's first annual report to the nation on the status of education. Clearly, the Goals Panel's action, representing the governors of the fifty states and the administration, and including members of Congress, indicates a consensus that the achievement levels adopted by the Board will be useful in helping the public understand whether American students are preforming [sic] well enough.
29. Bracey (2005).
30. Will (2003).
31. Raising the passing score by 2 points would mean that 78% rather than 85% of students would pass on their first try. However, the passing rate for black students would drop from 64% to 51%, and the passing rate for Hispanic students would go from 60% to 47% (Alspach, 2005).
32. Dillon (2005b).
33. For example, see the New York Times article by Staples (2005).
34. For example, on a state's 10th-grade math test, the cut-score for passing is set at 220. A student who scores 218 is thus classified as "failing." However, the standard error of measurement for this math test is 3.35 points. This standard

error of measurement indicates that the student's true score will be within 3.35 points of the reported test score 68% of the time and that the student's true score will be within 6.7 points of the reported test score 96% of the time. In other words, if the student were to take the test a second time without any additional learning occurring between test administrations, there is a 68% chance that the student's score would fall in the range 214–221, and a 95% chance that the score would be between 211 and 224. Depending upon where in these ranges the students score falls that day, the student will be classified as either failing or passing.

35. Beaton (2000).
36. Lowell is quoted in Edes (2008).
37. Barker (2006).
38. The physician Jerome Groopman offers this cogent reminder about the fallibility of diagnosis and treatment in medicine that is equally applicable, but too often ignored, in education. "There are dark corners to every clinical situation. Knowledge in medicine is imperfect. No diagnostic test is flawless. No drug is without side effects, expected or idiosyncratic. No prognosis is fully predictable" (Groopman, 2000, p. 4).
39. Colton (1974).
40. See Campbell & Fiske (1959) seminal paper "Convergent and Discriminant Validation by the Multitrait-Multimethod Matrix."
41. Bojörklund, Clark, Edin, Fredriksson, & Krueger (2005, p. 135).

CHAPTER 6

WHY IS IT IMPORTANT TO REGARD TESTING AS A TECHNOLOGY?

Testing is deeply ingrained in America's psyche. Our familiarity with testing is one reason why most Americans do not think of it as a technology. But this is precisely what high-stakes testing is—a technology with deep roots in our educational system.[1]

A common definition of technology is something put together to satisfy a pressing and immediate need to solve a problem, or serve as a means to an end.[2] Tests have long been used to solve a variety of social and educational problems. The Chinese used tests to eliminate patronage and open access to public service. Schools use tests to ensure that students acquire certain skills and to establish and maintain standards of performance. And governments use tests to hold teachers, students, and schools accountable for learning and to allocate scarce resources.

Technology is also defined as a set of *special* knowledge, activities, skills, methods, and procedures that create standardized techniques for carrying out a task or attaining a predetermined goal.[3] For every important technology, a community of experts forms and develops its own specialized vocabulary and value system.[4] Testing is no exception. Testing has it's own techniques, special knowledge, and a community of practitioners—referred to as psychometricians. This community relies on specialized techniques and

The Paradoxes of High Stakes Testing, pages 95–108

arcane algorithms, the most common of which are based on Item Response Theory, or IRT for short. Psychometricians depend on IRT for such tasks as determining which questions are included on a test and calculating the scores used to classify students.

The term "technology" often conjures up images of inventions, artifacts, machines, or devices such as cars, trains, power transformers, or computers. Although testing is not thought of this way, it also has its own "hardware." For years, test booklets, answer sheets, and optical scoring machines were used to make the testing of large numbers of people efficient and economical. Today tests are also administered on computers to increase the speed of reporting results, improve convenience, and decreases administrative and scoring costs.

Like other technologies, testing has hidden values.[5] Testing values measurement and quantification. It values objectivity over subjectivity. As we saw in Chapter 4, this value for objectivity results in ignoring the subjective and qualitative judgments used to establish quantitative cut-scores. Testing experts also believe that a single trait can be measured by a test, and that the degree to which a person has the trait explains his performance on a test. As we also saw in Chapter 4, however, the testing community places little value on the many social, cultural, and individual factors that also influence how a student performs on a test.

Neil Postman, a scholar of technology, astutely observes that technology is both a friend and an enemy. Technologies are developed to solve problems and to make human activities easier to perform. With every technology, though, there is a dark side that has serious costs.[6] In the remainder of this chapter, we explore how characteristics such as the emergence of a technical elite, specialized language, arcane algorithms, and hidden values make high-stakes testing a seductively attractive friend, yet a potentially harmful enemy for some students, teachers, and schools.

HIGH-STAKES TESTING'S TECHNICAL ELITE

In the early days of our republic, scientists and technicians spoke almost as easily to lay people as to each other. With the rise of standardization in the 19th century, specialized vocabularies evolved and highly specialized groups associated with various technologies and social techniques emerged.[7] Today, technical specialization, with its unique vocabulary and techniques, has created a barrier between lay people and technical communities.[8]

The formation of technological communities is a double-edged sword. A technical community enhances the members' accomplishments and facilitates communication, but it also isolates them from those outside the community. Ladgon Winner, a philosopher of technology, reminds us that for important technologies, "there is almost no middle ground of rational discourse, no available common language with which persons of differing backgrounds can discuss matters of technology in thoughtful, critical terms."[9]

Too often, the technical elite thinks in terms of what is useful and efficient rather than what is good or just.[10] Partly because of this way of thinking, serious criticism of a socio-technical practice meets with strong opposition or defensiveness. Winner describes what happens:

> A typical response of engineers, for example, is to announce that they are merely problem solvers. "Tell us the problem," they demand. "We will find a solution. That's our job. But you may not presume to question the nature of our solution. You are not a member of a technical profession and, therefore, know nothing of relevance. If you insist on raising questions about the appropriateness of means we devise, we can only conclude that you are anti-technology."[11]

The gulf between the community of technical elite and lay people is clearly evident for the technology of testing. The language used by testing's technical community differs from the language used by the general public. Take test bias as an example.

To a layperson, a test is often considered biased if one group of examinees performs noticeably lower than another group. As an example, if on average males perform 10 percentage points better than females on a test, many people would say the test is biased. For the general public, issues of test bias focus on systematic differences in the average score for specific groups of examinees.

For the technical community, however, bias has a very different meaning. Rather than focus on overall scores, psychometricians focus on individual items. For them, bias relates to the extent to which differences in overall scores are consistent with differences for each individual item. For example, if the average test score for males is 10 percentage points higher than that for females, and this 10 percentage point difference occurred for each individual item, the psychometrician would conclude that the test is not biased. Even though females, on average, scored lower, this lower performance is consistent across all items. For this reason, a psychometrician would argue that the items and the test are working exactly as intended—a higher percentage of examinees who score well overall also perform better on each item.[12] For the psychometrician, a test is consider biased when there are inconsistencies between average overall scores and performance on a sub-set of items.

The psychometrician's and the lay-person's conception of test bias differs dramatically. The psychometrician focuses on individual items and whether differences in performance are consistent across items. For the layperson, a test that results in females performing, on average, ten points lower is viewed as unfair, and hence biased. When a common meaning for a term such as test bias is lacking, people talk past each other. As a result, there is no communication—just frustration and recurring misunderstanding.

Beyond using terms differently, the testing community has developed a language that is *linguistically complex* and *mathematically opaque.* Without specialized training, many of the techniques and terms used by psychometricians have no meaning for lay-people. For example, psychometricians regularly use terms such as Delta Plots, a-plots, v-plots, cycles of convergence, logistic information function, differential item functioning, item discrimination, item fit statistic, and three-parameter stochastic model. These, and other terms, are arcane and shield the testing profession from scrutiny by those most directly affected by a high-stakes test—teachers, students, and parents.

DEPENDENCE ON HIDDEN ALGORITHMS

Credit checks, bank loans, the triggering of an IRS audit, econometric modeling, and census projections are all dependent on hidden algorithms and complex computer modeling.[13] Most people are not aware that hidden algorithms and assumptions that form the foundation of technologies like these have a profound affect on their lives. But they do. As just one example, consider the time and energy consumed by an individual whose name is identified by the National Security Agency as a potential threat. Based on hidden assumptions and algorithms, many law-abiding, loyal Americans have been placed on the No Fly List. This false classification has caused them considerable delays, frustration, and, at times, humiliation when they travel.[14]

Like these other technologies, testing depends heavily on hidden algorithms and computer modeling. The assumptions and decisions psychometricians make when using these algorithms and models to analyze test data produce unintended consequences. For example, item response analyses produce scores that contain decimal places (e.g., 35.5). Before reporting these scores, the psychometrician must decide whether to round them up or down. Since students can guess correct answers for multiple-choice items, psychometricians must also decide whether and how to adjust scores to account for guessing. These decisions affect student classifications and their subsequent treatment.

The effect of rounding decisions on student classifications was evident on the 2001 10th-grade math test in Massachusetts. Prior to 2001, the decision rule did not allow a student's score to be rounded up to avoid classifying a student above a cut-point when their un-rounded score was below a cut-point. As a result, a student whose score was just .01 below a cut-point was placed in the lower category. In 2001, the rule changed allowing students' scores to be rounded up. This new rule affected the classification of approximately 3% of students.[15] Depending upon whether or not scores were rounded up, the classifications for approximately 2,200 students moved up or down one category.

The classification of students is also impacted by decisions about whether to remove test items based on their difficulty and how to adjust students' scores for guessing.[16] In one case, two groups of psychometricians made independent decisions about removing items and adjusting for guessing. Both groups of analysts were conscientious, very experienced, and highly skilled. Their decisions were based in part on their considerable experience using an IRT computer program called PARSCALE, and in part by their professional judgments about the two issues.

One group decided to eliminate items based on the item's difficulty and to set the numerical correction for guessing at .22 (Analysis 1). The second group decided not to eliminate items because of their difficulty and set the correction for guessing at .20 (Analysis 2). Table 6.1 shows how these arbitrary, but not capricious, assumptions about item difficulty and student guessing led to different classifications for many students.[17]

As seen in Table 6.1, students in the Advanced classification were not affected by the decisions made by either group. But the numbers classified as Proficient, Basic, or Failing changed as a function of the decision rules. The students whose classification shifted have no way of knowing this, nor did the psychometricians when they made their decisions. Nonetheless these two examples demonstrate the affect that hidden decisions can have on student classifications. These examples also remind us of the tenuousness of classifications for students who are close to a cut-point.

TABLE 6.1 Classification of 7th Grade English/Language Arts Test

	Group A		Group B		A – B
Classifications	**% Students**	**# Students**	**% Students**	**# Students**	**# Students**
Advanced	10.0	8,000	10.0	8,000	0
Proficient	55.1	44,080	57.9	46,320	–2,240
Basic	28.1	22,480	26.9	21,520	960
Failing	6.8	5,440	5.2	4,160	1,280
Totals		80,000		80,000	

HIDDEN VALUES AND HIGH-STAKES TESTING

Technologies affect the nature of our lives and society in significant ways. Ladgon Winner observes that technologies are more than aids to human activity, they are "powerful forces acting to reshape that activity and its meaning."[18] In Winner's view, the problem with technologies lays not so much in the fact that they are shaping our lives, but that they do it in uncontrolled ways. Most people sit on the sidelines allowing this reshaping to occur without participation or even awareness of what is happening. Consider how technologies like automobiles, telephones, and television have reshaped our lives and society. Not only have they affected the way we travel, communicate, and entertain, they have created massive industries, influenced politics, and reshaped the structure of society. The many ways in which technology shapes people's lives applies to high-stakes testing.

When used as a policy tool, high-stakes testing shapes society by promoting a variety of values that include utilitarianism, economic competitiveness, technological optimism, objectivity, bureaucratic control, accountability, administrative convenience, numerical precision, efficiency, standardization, and conformity. Testing also shapes important educational values.

Using test scores to classify students and schools reshapes our conceptions of student attainment and school quality. Attainment no longer focuses primarily on skills and knowledge. School quality ceases to focus first on teaching, resources, and opportunities for learning. Instead, attainment and school quality become defined by individual and group test scores.

Testing subjects like mathematics, science, and language arts, and not testing other subjects like history, music, and art, defines the relative value of different curricular areas. High-stakes tests also reshape student-teacher relationships and define what an educated person should know, understand, and be able to do, and therefore what should be taught and learned.

While promoting certain values, high-stakes testing diminishes others. This is captured by chief inspector of schools Edmond Holmes' when he described 19th-century school examinations in Great Britain:

> Whenever the outward standard of reality (examination results) has established itself at the expense of the inward, the ease with which worth (or what passes for such) can be measured is ever tending to become in itself the chief, if not sole, measure of worth. And in proportion, as we tend to value the results of education for their measurableness, so we tend to undervalue and at last ignore those results which are too intrinsically valuable to be measured.[19]

Today, Holmes' observation is made clear with high-stakes testing. To understand what a society values in education, simply examine its important tests. The saying—What You Test Is What You Get—captures how tests come to embody social values.[20]

The predominant, often tacit, values in testing have been those of policy makers, the test sponsors, testing advocates, and the technical community. Their values have not been critically examined, nor weighed against the competing pluralistic values of teachers, test takers, parents, critics, and other concerned citizens.[21]

For example, policy-makers who mandate high-stakes testing programs place a high value on a single test score that is based on student performance on a small set of items. This value dismisses a comprehensive, holistic evaluation of a student, a teacher, a school, or a school system. The late physician, researcher, and writer, Lewis Thomas captures the problem of a narrow focus on a single measure:

> Science gets most of its information by the process of reductionism, exploring the details, and then the details of the details, until the smallest bits of the structure, or the smallest parts of the mechanism, are laid out for counting and scrutiny.... *Much of today's public anxiety about science is the apprehension that we may forever be overlooking the whole by an endless, obsessive preoccupation with the parts.*[22]

Thomas' observations about the physical sciences are equally applicable to the domination of quantitative test results and the disregard of qualitative holistic teacher assessments of students.

HIGH-STAKES TESTING AND POLITICAL POWER

Many technologies are a source of political power. Military weapons, medical technologies, transportation, farming techniques, and energy are all sources of power in the political process. High-stakes testing is no exception. The information tests provide empowers policy makers at the federal and state levels to make important decisions about our schools, educational system, and how quality is defined. At the same time, high-stakes tests empower policymakers, who control the content and form of the test, to shape what and how teachers teach and students learn.

In his book, *Discipline and Punish,* the French philosopher-historian Michel Foucault wrote intriguingly about educational tests. For Foucault a test is a technology used to regulate schools, teachers, and students. He understood that those who control a high-stakes test could use the results to control the actions of the examinees, as well as school personnel. He argues that the test exercises power over the examinee, who is perceived as an object and in turn objectified. Taking a test not only places examinees in a "field of surveillance," it also "situate[s] them in a network of writing... in a whole mass of documents that captures and fix them."[23] For Foucault, this "new technology of power" turns the examinee into a "describable, analysable object," and the test is the "ceremony of this objectification."[24] Foucault's description of tests as a mechanism of power was based on his experience with the essay form of testing used in Europe. He does not mention the ease of objectification that multiple-choice tests and high-speed scoring machines allow.

The use of a test to objectify an individual can lead to positive outcomes. As an example, test scores can be used to tailor instruction to meet the specific needs of individual students. However, a single measure does not fully capture a student's attainment. Nonetheless high-stakes testing programs use a single measure to summarize a student's performance and provide the bureaucratic mechanism to hold the student accountable.

Quantitative test scores also allow groups to be described and objectified. Test scores make it possible to classify students into groups, calculate averages, and establish norms. This ability to objectify groups provided the bureaucratic mechanism to hold teachers and schools accountable. Coupling test performance with important rewards or sanctions gives those who control a high-stakes test power over the action of students, teachers, and schools.

THE AFFECT TESTING HAS ON TEACHERS

The introduction of a technology can require "workers to take on more responsibility, use more judgment, and have a broader understanding of the total work process."[25] As an example, satellite technologies allow soldiers on the ground to participate in decision-making about an engagement with field commanders and leaders in Washington. But, technology can also deskill, routinizes, and put workers under closer supervision.[26] Unfortunately, the technology of high-stakes testing diminishes teacher judgment and decreases their responsibility, and instead routinizes instruction, deskills many teachers, and places them under closer supervision.

For some teachers, a high-stakes test simplifies their job. The test gives teachers a clear target and allows them to simply teach to the content of the test. At the same time, high-stakes testing can degrade teaching skills by reducing teaching to narrow test preparation. Rather than developing each child as an individual, focus is placed on improving tests scores. When these test scores are then compared among teachers and schools, relationships and trust among teachers is endangered. This leads some teachers to blame their colleagues in lower grade levels for poorly preparing students and humiliates others when class or school averages are displayed publicly.[27]

Focusing solely on tests scores also devalues teachers' judgments about the achievement of their students and their readiness for specific instructional treatments. Mistrust of teachers' qualitative judgments has long been a hidden value that underpins policies dictating the use of a single standardized test score to make decisions about students. Despite contradictory teacher insight about what a student knows or is able to do, decisions based solely on tests scores are often non-negotiable. A parody of this disdain for qualitative teacher judgments in favor of quantitative test scores is seen in Groucho Marx's question, "Who are you going to trust—me or your own eyes?"

While there is much talk about the need to make teaching more attractive, high-stakes testing programs treat teachers and students as passive beneficiaries, which comes at the cost of other core values. For example, in an interview, Rafe Esquith, an outstanding teacher at Hobart Elementary in a tough part of Los Angeles, was asked about enforcing standards through testing.[28] Esquith answered:

> I think standards are useful. But they've become the be all and end all of existence. When a child reads, I don't want him reading because I have to fulfill standard 27. I want him reading because when he reads John Steinbeck, he says, "My God, OF MICE AND MEN was fantastic. Rafe, what other books has Steinbeck written? I'm going to the library to check him out." Now that might not be in the local standards but it is in his best interest to have that passion for reading.[29]

When the host, David Brancaccio, followed up by asking, "So standards, in your view, [are] not the worst problem of American education. What would you identify is the worst problem?" Esquith replied:

> The worst problem in American education is [that] great teachers are crushed by a system that doesn't let them be great. There are so many good young teachers who have great ideas that they're using in their classroom, and they're being told no before they're even given a chance. And—that's a huge problem. We've made teaching so unattractive that the best and the brightest people don't become teachers.

Throughout history, policy-makers have linked test results to high-stakes to coerce the actions of teachers and students. And there is no doubt that such pressure works. The high-stakes test alters the instructional delivery system, and in turn, what and how children learn.

High-stakes testing is a minimalist technological strategy used to reform education. While these tests can provide useful information about student attainment, they do not address the deeper underlying problems that are barriers to student learning such as, student health, nutrition and living conditions, class size, and teachers' pre- and in-service training.[30] Ironically this list, however long, is one of the reasons that the technological solution of testing is so attractive. Mandating high-stakes testing allows policy-makers to sidestep difficult ideological, economic, and political issues that complicate addressing these underlying problems. Making high-stakes testing the heart of reform paves over the surface and obscures the root causes of poor attainment.

THE PARADOX OF TESTING

A prevalent attitude in society is that technology is fundamentally neutral in its moral standing. In this view, *the particular use* of a technology in *a particular context* determines its moral standing. But this belief fails to recognize that any technology produces effects apart from how it is used.[31] Moreover, the use to which a technology is put simultaneously produces both positive and negative effects. Langdon Winner, describes technology's hidden, often unintended, effects:

> [There] are instances in which the very process of technical development is so thoroughly biased in a particular direction that it regularly produces results heralded as wonderful breakthroughs by some social interests and crushing setbacks by others. In such cases it is neither correct nor insightful to say 'Someone intended to do somebody else harm.' Rather one must say that the technological deck has been stacked in advance to favor certain social interests and that some people were bound to receive a better hand than others.[32]

For the technology of testing, the entire test-development process—what we decide to measure, the cultural background and specialized training of test developers, the material chosen for inclusion, the design choice of individual items, the language and idioms used in framing test questions, the directions given to teachers and students, the acceptable or "right" answers to questions—unintentionally stacks the "deck" in favor of certain values and groups in our society. But, as we saw in Chapter 4, the technology of testing, and the ways in which a test is used, deals a weaker hand to students of certain cultural and economic backgrounds.

Like all technologies, testing creates new possibilities, but the uses to which tests are put produce unintended consequences that make high-stakes testing a paradox of good news and bad news. Unintended effects are unavoidable, but not to test comes with it's own consequences. When campaigning for, defending, or challenging a high-stakes testing program, proponents and critics must acknowledge the good news-bad news duality inherent in the technology of testing. The competing costs, and short- and long-term consequences that testing produces, must also be taken into account by proponents and critics.

SUMMARY

It is hard to imagine education without testing. Testing has achieved so much momentum and power that our society would find it very difficulty doing without it.[33] Like other technologies, our society sees testing as a solution to a problem. But, as the historian Daniel Boorstin argues, the central problem for society in dealing with technology is how to come to terms with solutions.[34] The idea that a new test design, item format, delivery platform, scoring machine, or testing program such as NCLB can improve our schools and restore our nation's competitiveness conceals many of the negative side effects produced by a technological fix. Testing can assist in reform efforts, but we cannot test our way out of our educational problems.

Often technological solutions predate the problems they are used to solve, and we accept the solutions as good because they represent progress. As Winner argues, technology often is not tailored to human needs, but instead human needs are redefined "to match what modern science and engineering happened to make available."[35] As we saw in Chapter 2, testing is an existing technology that policy-makers have repeatedly adopted to define educational problems and then solve the problems. Testing is an attractive technology because it enables students' performance and abilities to be reduced to numbers that lend themselves to statistical analyses, graphs, and comparisons. But this use of testing redefines human needs as improved test scores. This focus on test scores detracts attention from the larger social, economic, cultural, and instructional issues that pose barriers to student learning.

The use of high-stakes testing to reform education is another aspect of the paradox of testing: We need test information, but this information has reshaped our value system. What we value most about schools seems increasingly to be students' performance on standardized tests. Valuing test scores so much leads to policy decisions that are not based on theory or research, or, worse, that are contrary to research findings. As an example, the systematic use of test scores to retain students ignores a large body of research that shows that students who are retained are less likely to graduate.

Ultimately, this faith in quantitative test scores distorts reality because the tools of behavioral science are not the neutral measurement devices people assume them to be. Educational and psychological tests are not like yardsticks or scales for measuring pupils' heights and weights. Tests are more complex, less direct, less transparent, and require that the objects of the measurement accommodate themselves to the style and method of the tools.

Testing is a complex technological system with its own infrastructure akin to transportation, power, communications, computing, or manufacturing systems. Educators, policy makers, test contractors, and their clients should heed Winner's warning that our technologies are institutions in the making. Our sometimes single-minded use of technology, including the technology of testing, is pragmatic, utilitarian, economic, and instrumentalist in its view of the world and people. The danger is that technological consciousness can lead to a neglect of moral, esthetic, and artistic consciousness.[36] Chief Inspector Holmes's words echo down the decades. Testing as a social technique raises a host of value issues about who benefits or is empowered and who and what is hurt or diminished. It's essential that we confront the moral and ethical values inherent in the tests themselves and in their various uses.

NOTES

1. Thomas P. Hughes, an historian of technology, reminds us that "Americans [need to realize] that not only their remarkable achievements but many of their deep and persistent problems arise, in the name of order, system, and control, from the mechanization and systematization of life and from the sacrifice of the organic and spontaneous" (Hughes, 1989, p. 4).
2. Basalla (1988); Staudenmaier (1988).
3. Lowrance (1986); Winner (1977). In this sense, technology, or what is sometimes called *technique*, is a complex of *standardized means* for attaining a predetermined end in social, economic, administrative, and educational institutions (Ellul, 1964; Ellul, 1990; Winner, 1977). In a strict sense, technology is discourse on technique; for example, computer technologies or space technologies must be understood as techniques of communication (Ellul, 1990).
4. Staudenmaier (1985).
5. Borgmann (1984).
6. Postman (1992, p. xii).
7. Gleick (1987).
8. Ellul (1964). Also Winner points out that many fictional utopias propose government by a technical elite, and a number of works, like F. W. Taylor's 1914 *Principles of Scientific Management,* make similar arguments Taylor (1914). On examining how this literature describes ideal membership in such an elite, Winner notes that one group is excluded—the great mass who are considered to simply lack the knowledge or credentials to participate in the government of a technological society.
9. Winner (1986, p. 11).
10. Merton (1964).
11. Winner (1977, p. 11).
12. However, when females and males both perform the same on a given item, the item is said to be biased against males and in favor of females. In contrast, if males perform better than expected on a given item, the item is said to be biased against females and in favor of males.
13. For a detailed treatment of the issues surrounding the ethics of modeling, see Wallace (1994b).
14. Kroft (2007).

15. For the Grade 10 Mathematics test, it was unclear whether this rounding affected one or two raw scores (that is, raw scores of 20 and 21). Based on the distribution of scores between 7 and 20 and between 22 and 33, it would appear that two raw score points were impacted by this rounding rule.
16. If a student were to randomly guess on a four-choice multiple-choice question, he/she would be right .25 of the time. Since students generally do not randomly guess, but are able to eliminate one or more of the distracters, setting the correction for guessing at .25 would overcorrect; the analyst, therefore, must estimate the correction. The correction for guessing is known as the c-parameter in a three-parameter IRT model.
17. The data are real and come from one state's testing program. The total number of test takers was changed to disguise the state. All states that use the three-parameter IRT model would experience similar results. We chose 80,000 for our example because it approximates a state that is neither a very large or small state. Readers can change the estimated number of students taking the test to approximate their own state demographics.
18. Winner (1986, p. 6).
19. Holmes (1911, p. 128, emphasis added).
20. One of the authors first heard this acronym used by Hugh Burkhardt of the University of Nottingham.
21 For example, the use of the three-parameter item response model by several commercial vendors in designing their elementary and secondary school achievement tests embodies value judgments and assumptions about the underlying ability level and guessing behavior of the test taker. However, most educators, students and their parents have little or no knowledge of how these psychometric values and assumptions influence the derived scores of different students. In fact, most do not even know that the arcane three-parameter model is even used at all.
22. Thomas (1980, emphasis added).
23. Foucault (1979, p. 189).
24. Ibid., p. 190 & 187. Foucault saw a "new modality of power in which each individual," whom he describes as calculable man, "receives as his status his own individuality, and in which he is linked by his status to the features, the measurements, the gaps, the "marks" that characterize him and make him a case" (p.192).
25. Applebaum (1992, p. 537).
26. The movement toward standardization and conformity and deskilling began in America in about 1815, when the Army Ordnance Department drew up "a system of regulations for... the uniformity of manufacture of all arms ordnance" (Smith, 1987, p. 42). It became clear that the engineering of people was as important as the engineering of materials (Smith, 1987). The idiosyncrasy of the skilled craftsman had to yield to uniformity. Standard work rules replaced the village mode of negotiation over working conditions (Staudenmaier, 1989). Over several decades, the Ordnance Department developed the administrative, communication, inspection, accounting, bureaucratic and mechanical techniques that fostered conformity and resulted in the technol-

ogy of interchangeable parts and the eventual manufacture of a host of mass-produced products in the 20th century (Smith, 1987).

27. Booher-Jennings (2005).
28. The website for *NOW* (http://www.pbs.org/now/archive_transcripts.html) describes Rafe Esquith this way:

> Rafe Esquith grew up in Los Angeles and attended the city's public schools. A 1981 graduate of UCLA, Esquith has taught fifth grade at Hobart Boulevard Elementary in L.A. for over 20 years. His efforts to give disadvantaged kids a better chance at the American dream have earned him the Walt Disney American Teacher Award for National Teacher of the Year, *Parents* Magazine's As You Grow Award, and Oprah Winfrey's Use Your Life Award. He has donated his award money to the nonprofit fund he has established to support the work of the Hobart Shakespeareans. In 2003, he received the National Medal of Arts. He is the author of THERE ARE NO SHORTCUTS: CHANGING THE WORLD ONE KID AT A TIME, and is currently working with the NEA to help put Shakespeare in 10,000 American classrooms.

29. Brancaccio (2005).
30. Kellaghan (2000).
31. Ellul (1990, p. 35).
32. Winner (1986, p. 25). Bijker & Law make very a similar observation to that of Winner's:

> Most of the time, most of us take our technologies for granted. These work more or less adequately, so we don't inquire about why or how it is they work. We don't inquire about the design decisions that shape our artifacts. We don't think very much about the ways in which professional, political, or economic factors may have given form to those designs—or the way in which they were implemented in practice. And even when our technologies do go wrong, typically our first instinct is to call the repair person. There are routine methods for putting them right: it doesn't occur to us to inquire deep into their provenance (Bijker & Law, 1992, p. 2).

33. Staudenmaier (1989, p. 125).
34. Boorstin (1978, p. 39).
35. Winner (1986, p. 170).
36. Madaus & Greaney (1985); Vandenberg (1983).

CHAPTER 7

WHY IS THE HISTORY OF TESTING IMPORTANT?[1]

What has been is what will be, and what has been done is what will be done; and there is nothing new under the sun.

—Ecclesiastes 1:9

Each of us is familiar with testing through our own experiences. Testing, however, has a long and rich history that provides deeper insight into the paradoxes of high-stakes testing. The British historian G. R. Elton reminds us, "a knowledge of the past should arm [people] against surrendering to the panaceas peddled by too many myth makers."[2] Unfortunately, the history of testing is too often either cavalierly dismissed with assertions that "times have changed" or, worse yet, overlooked completely.[3] While history may not repeat itself, the ways in which past testing programs have solved problems, been corrupted, and helped some while dealing a weaker hand to others, provides a cautionary tale for contemporary debates about how best to craft high-stakes testing programs.

This chapter examines the history of testing and unveils three important lessons for today's high-stakes testing programs. First, we will see that testing has been embraced across cultures and time as an important social technology. Second, the technology of testing has evolved to meet new demands and integrate new technologies. Third, tests have always been used as a tool to address political, social, educational, and economic concerns of the power elite.

The Paradoxes of High Stakes Testing, pages 109–138

Our history begins with the earliest of tests, those of authenticity or character. We then trace the evolution of testing through China, the Qumran community, Europe, and finally the United States. As we trace this history, we visit themes such as the transition in Europe from a qualitative to a quantitative world view; linking teachers' salaries to student test performance; the influence of testing on beliefs about whether all students can learn if properly taught; and the emergence of intelligence testing.

Throughout this chapter we highlight changes in the technology of testing. The historian of technology Thomas Hughes uses the metaphor of a reverse salient to explain how most technologies evolve.[4] As he explains, a reverse salient occurs when a military advance along a battle line becomes uneven. Before a general advance can continue any reverse bulge, or salient, in the front line must be eliminated. Like a military advance along a battlefront, all technological systems develop unevenly. As a technology is put to new uses, or the environment in which the technology is used changes, some of its components function less efficiently and act as a drag on the entire system by malfunctioning, or adding disproportionately to costs.[5] A technology advances by overcoming each new reverse salient. As we will see, testing has evolved by eliminating a number of reverse salients that were drags on the technology.

EARLY FORMS OF TESTING

Tests of Character and Authenticity

Pre-industrial societies placed high value on a person's character. To assess character, they employed what are known as "authenticity tests."[6] For example, the Dead Sea Scrolls describe the physical characteristics associated first with wickedness, and then with virtue:

1. His teeth are of uneven length . . . His fingers are thick, and his thighs are thick and very hairy . . .
2. His eyes are black and glowing . . . His voice is gentle. His teeth are fine and well aligned. He is neither too tall nor short. And his fingers are thin and long. And his thighs are smooth.[7]

Although they seem ridiculous today, authenticity tests were popular during the 19th century. Examining the shape and presence of bumps on a person's head, phrenologists believed that intellectual aptitudes and personality traits could be identified.[8] Vestiges of "authenticity testing" are still alive. An article on admissions to elite colleges recounts how physical characteristics played a role as late as the 1980s:

> When the Office of Civil Rights at the federal education department investigated Harvard in the nineteen-eighties, they found handwritten notes scribbled in the margins of various candidates' files... One application—and at this point you can almost hear it going to the bottom of the pile—was notated, 'Short with big ears.'[9]

Authenticity tests are important, not for what or how they measured various traits, but because they offer a window on the distinctive characteristics of all tests.[10] The anthropologist F. Arthur Hanson reminds us that the intended purpose of all testing is to "reveal the truth about some purely objective, independently existing state of affairs."[11]All tests are representational techniques crafted to uncover information of which the test itself is but a sample or representation. The test's score is "the signifier," while the "signified" is the trait, characteristic, or construct about which information is sought.

For all tests, what counts as representational is a matter of social convention. As we saw in Chapter 4, tests provide us with "reality" as constructed by culture. In present-day high-stakes testing programs, what society defines as the "signifier" is the student's score on the test. The "signified" is student "achievement."

Ancient tests, like all tests, "act to transform, mold, and even create what they supposedly measure."[12] Take, for example, tests for witches. People believed that there were witches and they had certain properties. A test for witches revealed that unfortunate people possessed those properties, and therefore were witches. The test, then, provided proof that witches existed.[13] Although they are unlike the tests we are familiar with today, tests of authenticity demonstrate the power a test has to shape what is valued by society, how those values are measured, and subsequently how those measures are applied to foster those values.

The same power is seen with the more familiar cognitive tests used by societies to classify, describe, diagnose, certify, and select individuals and groups. In Chapter 6, for example, Chief Inspector Holmes explains that educational high-stakes tests were used to provide an external measure of worth. Over time, the tests became the sole measure of worth and transformed what teachers taught, students learned, and ultimately what society valued.

Let us turn now to these more familiar tests of cognition.

The Chinese Civil Service Examinations

The Chinese system of civil service examinations is arguably the first example of employing testing, as we know it today, as a national administrative technique.[14] Faced with the need to consolidate government, lessen patronage and select men of merit for government office, the Han Dynasty (206 BCE–230 CE) took the first steps to recruit civil servants on the basis of merit.[15] Before civil service examinations were introduced, the central government relied on recommendations by local officials to identify "men of talent" who then had to pass an oral exam before being assigned a position.

However, the shear number of recommended candidates that had to be screened and a lack of standardization in oral examining became a drag on the selection process. The invention of paper by Cai Lun in 105 CE, eliminated this drag on the process of selecting candidates based on merit.[16] The paper-based Chinese civil service exam, which was administered simultaneously to many candidates and lasted for several days allowed the emperor to quickly narrow the large body of candidates down to a select few. The 2% who passed the written exam then had to pass the oral exam. The written exam standardized the initial screening process, clearly defined the skills and knowledge required to enter civil service, and produced a paper trail for each examinee.[17]

At its pinnacle during the Sung Dynasty (960–1279 CE), candidates wishing to join the civil ranks took examinations in a number of disciplines.[18] Most highly prized was the Letters examination whose domain was the Confucian classics.[19] The skills were assessed using supply-type questions that included completing passages from memory, summarizing the meanings of the classics, composing a discussion, a poetic description and a piece of poetry, and demonstrating reasoning ability by discussing five (apparent) conflicts within the classics.[20]

The demonstration on reasoning ability—called higher-order thinking skills today–became another drag on the system. Government officials became worried that the scoring of these questions was too subjective, so they included only those questions that required rote responses and had a single correct answer.

The Chinese civil service exam system lasted until the beginning of the 20th century. In the end, the exam system failed because its emphasis on memory of the Confucian classics produced civil servants who mastered the classics but were unable to respond to practical issues of western technology and modernization.[21]

The Qumran Community

Like the Chinese's use of tests to select people of merit for civil service positions, other ancient cultures used tests to screen people for study and eventual admission into closed communities. An example of this practice is found in the Dead Sea Scrolls. The leader and men of the Qumran community made formal observations and administered a series of oral examinations in order to verify their preparedness following a period of study and to admit them into the community.[22] The Qumran Manual of Discipline describes the procedures:[23]

> As for everyone from Israel who would freely pledge himself to join the council of the community, the Deputy [or Examiner] at the head of the Many shall examine him concerning his understanding and his deeds. If he passes muster for the discipline, he will admit him into the Covenant, in order to turn to the truth and to turn from all iniquity. He shall instruct him in all the regulations of the community. Later, when he comes to stand before the Many, they shall inquire about everything concerning his affairs. As the decision is made according to the council of the Many, he shall enter or withdraw.... On his completion of a year, the Many shall make inquiry about his affairs, about his understanding and his observance of the Law.... On his completion of his second year, they shall examine him. According to the word of the Many, if the decision favors him to enter the community, they will inscribe him in the order of his rank among his brothers in what concerns the Law, [merit] equity, [justice] the Purity [i.e., the common meal], and the mingling of his property.[24]

The first of the three exams, for admission to study, is roughly analogous to taking a college entrance exam. It involved observing the applicant in his daily routines, (e.g., how he interacted with people) and asking him questions about his interpretation of common aspects of the Law (the test domain).[25] If the postulant passed muster, he was admitted for instruction. At the completion of a year, he was examined a second time, similar to taking a graduate-school entrance exam. At the end of two years, the final examination, somewhat comparable to a certification exam like the bar exam or medical boards, determined if he should be given full admission into the community. This final certification decision was based on the examinee's grasp of the Law and of justice, and was determined by a vote by the entire community.

There are four noteworthy aspects to these Qumran examinations that are common with the high-stakes tests used today. First, as there is today, there was a perceived need to screen applicants and eventually certify them or not. Second, like the tests mandated by No Child Left Behind, the final two Qumran exams were measures of attainment following instruction. Third, like all tests, the Qumran Community's exams derived their power from the social organization that mandated them. Later in European history, religious denominations or orders developed and administered tests for selection into the priesthood and for certification of a person's knowledge of the catechism. Fourth, the community determined what constituted a "correct" answer. The Pharisees, for example, might have a different "right" answer than that of the Essenes. As we explore next, reliance on oral exams and qualitative judgments of an examinee's performance were features of the Qumran examinations that became drags on testing and which forced the technology to evolve.

THE MIDDLE AGES INTO THE 19TH CENTURY

From the Middle Ages into the 19th century, testing was put to a wide variety of uses. During this period, population explosions and social, cultural, and commercial developments forced testing to evolve. As the worldview shifted from a qualitative to quantitative perspective, testing also shifted from relying on qualitative judgments to producing quantitative scores. As the number of examinees increased, the oral examination fell out of favor. As in China, this drag on testing was resolved by introducing written exams.

Efforts to link commercial interests and education also required information about student achievement that tests readily provided. This expanded the importance of testing in education. Linking education and commercial interests also produced notions of educational accountability. The first form of this accountability was the payment by results movement that held teachers accountable for student achievement.

From a Qualitative to a Quantitative Worldview

In Europe, until the middle of the 13th century, those educated enough to count and measure saw little need for quantification. They were qualitative people living in an oral-aural culture, superstitious about numbers, alchemy, the heavens, and natural forces. They viewed the world almost entirely from a qualitative perspective and used numbers for "effect not accuracy."[26]

Several developments led to a gradual, yet relentless, shift toward a quantitative worldview. A population explosion, the Crusades, a dramatic increase in trade with distant lands, a new breed of wealthy merchants, lawyers, traders, and money changers, all conspired to increase the need for quantification.[27] During this time, mechanical clocks began to appear, first to signal monks to prayer, then workers to work.[28]As commerce grew, money and its exchange became vital, and the cost of an item quantified its worth. As trade increased, the importance of rigor and standardized measures also increased throughout Europe.[29] Weights and measures were created for nearly every traded good including such things as land, grain, bread, wine, and precious metals.[30]

As the world of commerce became dependent on standardized measures, testing also gradually embraced quantification. As we see below, the quantification of testing began as oral exams were replaced by written exams and expanded as holistic judgments about student's abilities were replaced by rankings based on quality of performances. The importance of quantifiable test scores expanded further with early efforts to link teacher performance to pay.

It is important to recognize that not everyone fully embraced this transition to quantification. As an example, in her book *Shakespeare and the Mismeasure of Renaissance Man,* Paula Blank recounts how Shakespeare was deeply concerned with attempts "to quantify personal, social, and political aspects of human experience."[31] For Shakespeare:

> The mind's true measure is beyond our capacity, beyond our place and time. *Yet even so, for Shakespeare, what's left to us is still worth knowing—the range of the rules we apply, the contrariety of measures we mete, in our ceaseless efforts to find it.*[32]

Shakespeare seemed to recognize the need to measure even though the measure does not provide a full and accurate representation of the trait of interest.

Despite reservations by some, the quantitative score gradually replaced qualitative evaluations of examiners and became the basis for ranking students. This quantification of test performance helped to create, and then strengthen, the impression that test results are significant, absolutely rational, objective, definitive, and right.

The need to quantify assessment would accelerate throughout the 19th century, spurred by concepts of efficiency and standardization in manufacturing. Quantification of testing reached its pinnacle in the 20th century with the introduction of the multiple-choice item and electronic scanners. Let us briefly trace these changes, which begin with the oral exam.

The Viva Voce Examination[33]

In the Middle Ages and Renaissance, academic education was oral-aural in nature. In the late 12th century, the University of Paris and the University of Bologna were the first to introduce "examinations" as we know them.[34] They were theological oral—*viva voce*—disputations in Latin in which students were examined on their knowledge of a fixed canon.[35]

The apprentice scholar demonstrated his mastery of a traditional form of rhetoric by responding to a set of known questions.[36] As the historian Keith Hoskins explains, the student's "ability to remember... knowledge [and] present it in eloquent form, and a tacit conformity to orthodoxy, educational and social" were *qualitatively* evaluated by the moderator.[37] Students were not trained to be "objective," but only how to "take a stand and defend it and how to attack the defense of others who were taking stands."[38]

The popularity of oral exams was due in part to the scarcity of paper, an expensive commodity at the time. While students did use writing to learn Latin, once Latin was mastered, all further learning and testing was entirely oral.[39] It wasn't until the 18th century, when paper became more readily available, that written exams became more common in Europe.

In the 16th century, the Jesuits used classroom competition as both a learning device and a means of assessing performance. Students were required to memorize large amounts of information, often without emphasis on reasoning. Each week, students were divided into groups for oral disputations on the grammatical, rhetorical, poetic, and historical aspects of the week's lessons. The prefects and teachers judged the winners of these competitions, and prizes were awarded accordingly.[40]

Arguably, the catechism was the first widespread, formal technique to assess a child's attainment of a fixed body of knowledge.[41] For very pragmatic reasons, Luther and his fellow reformers, counter-reformers like Canisius and Bellarmine, and Jewish rabbis used the oral catechistic approach to educate and assess young children in aspects of the faith.[42] This oral presentation of short questions, which were known in advance, was to assure the transmission of religious orthodoxy. Answers were evaluated as factually right or wrong.

Unlike today's high-stakes tests, the catechistic approach to learning seamlessly melded instruction and testing in an ongoing formative way. The instructor immediately knew whether a student had mastered the material or whether he needed additional instruction. This instruction, however, was based on a transmissionist view of learning and instruction; an instructor stood before students and recited the information students were expected to learn. The domain of knowledge students were expected to master was fixed, narrow, and finite.

The Rise of the Written Exam and the Invention of the Mark

With the introduction of Mathematics into the curriculum at Cambridge University during the mid-18th century, it was soon apparent that the oral mode of examining was inappropriate for measuring mathematical skills. To overcome this limitation of the oral exam, a written exam was introduced.

Named after the three-legged stool the candidates sat on while being examined, the *Mathematical Tripos* contained an oral and written component. Initially, qualitative judgments based on a holistic impression of both performances were used to rank students. Toward the end of the 18th century, concerns were raised about the subjectivity and partiality of the qualitatively-based rankings.

To remove the influence of qualitative judgments, in 1792 William Farish introduced the innovation of *quantitative marks*. Quality was now quantified, and qualitative judgments were replaced by seemingly precise quantitative marks.[43] To simplify the process of quantifying performance, questions with one correct answer and those designed to measure technical competence in specific subject areas replaced questions aimed at assessing rhetorical style.[44]

During the mid nineteenth century, the replacement of the oral exam with written exams and the emerging value of quantitative scores began to influence practices in American schools. As Secretary of the Massachusetts Board of Education, Horrace Mann was faced with two major challenges in measuring the attainment of students in the Boston public schools. First, was the growth in the number of student that had to be tested. Second, was his desire to standardize testing in order to rank and compare students. To address these problems, Mann replaced the oral exam with printed essay tests that yielded quantitative scores.[45] Mann recognized that a written exam could pose an *identical* set of questions *simultaneously*, under *similar conditions*, in *much less time*, to a *large number* of students, thereby producing comparable scores.[46] By his own account, Mann predicted that "the mode of examination *by printed questions and written answers*... will constitute a new era in the history of... schools."[47] He was correct. The practice quickly spread throughout the country.

The adoption of a written exam administered and scored under standardized conditions occurred during a larger movement toward standardization and interchangeable parts that began at the federal Armory in Springfield, MA. Standardization was becoming a hallmark of clock-making, machine shops, and textile mills throughout New England. Mann's adoption of written exams paralleled industrial capitalism's developing commitment to *uniformity, standardization, precision, clarity, quantification, and rational tactics.*[48]

Bureaucratic and Political Impacts of Quantification

The emergence of quantitative test scores soon provided policy makers with a powerful new bureaucratic tool. Quantitative scores were easy to accumulate, aggregate, organize, and rank. Using quantitative scores, students could be efficiently classified and sorted into categories. Group averages could be calculated, and used to describe and objectify groups of students. Quantitative scores allowed individuals and groups to be described relative to others in a population. Normative comparisons then become possible. Using test scores in these ways opened an entirely new technique for program and school-level accountability, and was the necessary first step in the development of the field of psychometrics. As Foucault described, the creation of quantitative scores was "the beginning of a pedagogy that functions as a science."[49]

Mann's adoption of the written exam was the first clear example in the United States of using examination results for bureaucratic, policy, and political purposes. Boston's headmasters were resisting Mann's attempt to abolish corporal punishment. Mann and his confidant Samuel Gridley Howe recognized that school-by-school test results gave them political leverage over the recalcitrant headmasters. As Mann explained:

> Some pieces should be immediately written for the [news]papers, containing so much of an analysis of the answers, as will show that the pupils answered common and memoriter [from memory] questions far better than they did questions involving a principle; and it should be set forth most pointedly, that in the former case, the merit belongs to the scholars, in the latter the demerit belongs to the master. All those abominable blunders... [in] orthography, punctuation, capitalizing and grammar are the direct result of imperfect teaching. *Children will not learn such things by instinct. They will not fail to learn them, under proper instruction*.... One very important and pervading fact in proof of this view of the case is the great difference existing between schools, on the same subject, showing that children could learn, if teachers had taught.[50]

Mann's reasoning has a very contemporary ring. He called for the publication in the newspapers of school-by-school rankings. He wanted to hold teachers and administrators accountable for poor results, and the rankings gave him leverage. He highlighted the importance of what today is called higher order thinking skills. And, echoing a belief prevalent at the time, Mann argued that given "proper instruction," "students will not fail to learn."[51]

The Link Between Commerce and Education

For centuries there has been a lasting relationship between the worlds of education and commerce, and testing has been a key element in that relationship. Commercial practices have been put fourth as a model for education. The commercial world sees education as a source of an "educated" work force and a key contributor to the nation's competitiveness. Emulating the commercial practice of using outcomes, such as profitability and production goals to evaluate and reward employees, student test scores have long be used to evaluate, motivate, and reward teachers financially.

During the 16th century, the French mathematician Peter Ramus and his followers laid the foundation of the factory model of schooling. They introduced an approach to education that had, as its controlling method, a kind of intellectual commercialism.[52] The Ramist curriculum was built around the knowledge and skills congenial to the commercial, merchandising views of artisans and burghers who hired schoolmasters to educate their children.[53] The Ramists saw knowledge in terms of "intake," "output," and "consumption"—"terms which were not familiar to the commercial world in Ramus' day... but which [did] refer to realities present within that world."[54]

In Europe linking high-stakes national examinations, to global competitiveness dates back, at least, to the 19th century. As an example, a German professor argued that Britain needed to introduce an external high-stakes exam system in order to increase its economic competitiveness with Germany (perceived to be ahead of Britain at the time). He opined, "If no examination is introduced the best schemes will fail, and will produce no effect: introduce the examination, and all the rest [competitiveness] follows of itself."[55] As we will see below, this argument resonated with the British.

Attempts to model schools on commercial practices also emerged during the 19th century in the United States. David Tyack, a historian of education, describes what has come to be known as the factory model of education: "Like the manager of a cotton mill, the superintendent of schools could supervise employees, keep the enterprise technically up to date, and monitor the uniformity and quality of the product."[56] In fact, the factory model with its techniques of conformity and dressage "by location, confinement, surveillance, the perpetual supervision of behavior and tasks" continued to be embraced by educators well into the 20th century.[57] Presently business and commercial terms such as accountability, outputs, bottom line, deregulate, competition, and free-market forces pervade today's calls for educational reform.

Payment by Results[58]

For more than 500 years, financial incentives have been used as a tool to motivate and hold teachers accountable for student learning. This strategy became known as payment-by-results and places the blame for student achievement or failure squarely on the shoulders of teachers.

The 1444 contract between the town fathers of Treviso, Italy, and its schoolmaster is perhaps the earliest effort to link teacher accountability to student attainment.[59] By contract, a schoolmaster's salary varied according to the level of attainment of his students on the grammar curriculum of the time. There were four levels of reward that ranged from a half ducat—about a 10th of an ounce of gold—for proficiency in the alphabet to two ducats for proficiency in stylistic exercises or rhetoric.[60]

In 1799 the concept of payment by results appeared in the Irish Parliament when a Select Committee recommended that payment of teachers should be based partly on a fixed salary and partly on their students' exam performance.[61] Although the recommendation was not implemented, fifty years later school funding in England and Ireland was linked to students' performance on a series of written and oral examinations in reading, writing, and arithmetic.[62] Robert Lowe, a strong advocate for the payment by results system, justified the need for teacher accountability in terms that have very contemporary overtones:

> ... the results come out in this rather mortifying form, that of the children that are in the schools which the grants... are intended to assist, only one-ninth get the benefit of a really good education... There shall be some collateral and independent proof that such teachers do their duty. And that I think... is only found in a system of individual examination.[63]

Like those who advocate today for payment by results systems, Lowe argued that the schools of his day were failing to provide a solid education for too many students and, that tests were required to determine whether or not teachers were doing their "duty" to educate students.[64]

In addition to the programs introduced in Ireland and England, during the 19th century, payment-by-results policies were also implemented in Australia and Jamaica.[65] Many of the legislators and civil servants in the British Empire were themselves products of the civil service competitive examination system. So it is not at all strange that they proposed using examination results to define effective instruction and teaching, and to allocate public funds for education.[66] *The Newcastle Commission* of 1858, for example, concluded, "[I]n the face of expenditures for [the Crimean] war education was regard as a suitable field for economics. At any rate, value for the money should be received."[67]

During this time, it was not only teachers who received awards for student performance, but also students. In an attempt to encourage middle-class youth to matriculate to the university, the English rural gentry awarded cash prizes and books to students based on their examination results.[68]

In general, student-reward systems have three goals: motivating students, providing their parents information to identify effective teachers, and giving teachers the incentive to improve. In 1857, Sir Henry Acland extolled the benefits of the English program: "The one thing that is offered to the middle class" by a group of interested citizens who have provided the prize money "is an examination which shall test the education given... and thus at once *give parents the power of discriminating efficient teachers, and teachers the opportunity of proving their own skill.*"[69] One can infer from Acland's description that if students did well or poorly, teachers were the reason—a commonly held belief.

In the United States, variations of payment-by-results are abundant. For example, the performance contracting movement of the 1960s based payment to firms on the delivery of a given level of student performance as measured by a standardized test. In the 1980s, merit pay for teachers was linked to student test performance.[70] When first introduced, Edison, the largest educational-management company in the United States, linked teacher bonuses to student test scores.[71] In 2006, the Houston Board of Education enacted the largest merit pay system in the country, rewarding teachers up to $3,000, and administrators up to $25,000 annually, depending on student performance on standardized tests.[72] Most recently, New York City undertook an experiment that examined the use of student test scores to award teacher bonuses and make decisions about teacher tenure.[73] NYC also implemented a program in which students are paid up to $50 for earning high test scores and teachers can earn up to $3000 for their student's test performances.[74]

Why do people who introduce payment by results believe that linking financial rewards with students' performance on tests will increase numeracy and literacy and, at the same time, improve teacher efficiency? Part of the answer is that principles of competition, free enterprise, utilitarianism, and self-help influence how they view the world. These reformers also accept testing as a practical technological tool that can bring efficiency and bureaucratic control to the educational system. They believe that tests will provide concrete evidence of success or failure and that the competitive spirit in teachers and schools will lead them to work harder to improve student learning.

But what does the history of student achievement as measured by examination results tell us about the workings of payment-by- results? An analysis of indices from the *Annual Reports of the Intermediate Education Board for Ireland* during the 19th century indicates that exam standards and rewards were systematically manipulated.[75] As the percentage of students passing the exam increased, expenditures on performance rewards to teachers grew. When the pass rate became too high, and thus too costly, the tests were made more difficult and the standards for passing were increased in order to reduce pass rates. This manipulation of pass rates assured there was no significant upward or downward trend in the percentage of students passing during the results era.[76] Efforts to manipulate the score required to pass Irish exams is similar to current practices, except that today states either make tests easier or *lower* cut-scores in order to increase the percentage of students passing their state tests.[77]

DEVELOPMENTS IN THE UNITED STATES DURING THE 19TH AND 20TH CENTURIES

A key assumption underlying payment-by-results programs was that all students would learn if properly taught. This belief was evident in Treviso and in the thinking of, among others, Horrace Mann, Henry Acland, and Robert Lowe. Matthew Arnold articulated this belief when he observed that the curriculum "is well within a child's power . . . and if children are not fit [to be promoted], unless there is some special reason, *the teaching has not been right.*"[78]

The belief that all students could learn if properly taught began to erode in the latter part of the 19th century, when compulsory attendance and the abolition of child labor forced educators to work with a more diverse student body. Two developments in testing also helped undermine the belief that all students could learn if properly taught: the invention of the IQ test and the movement from an absolute to a normative standard of student attainment. In turn, these developments paved the way for the relatively inexpensive and efficient current testing programs that rely heavily on multiple-choice items and computer-based technologies.

The Invention of the IQ Test

Until the end of the 19th century, educational tests were what we now call "achievement" tests. They measured skills and knowledge required for a craft or listed in a syllabus or curriculum. In the late 19th century, however, a new type of test emerged. With the importance of quantification firmly established in the industrial world, those interested in psychology, undertook efforts to formally measure and quantify intelligence.[79]

These efforts began in England in 1860 with Francis Galton's study of individual and racial differences. As the famous evolutionary biologist Stephen Jay Gould recounts, Galton "believed that, with sufficient labor and ingenuity, anything might be measured, and that measurement is the primary criterion of a scientific study."[80] Galton spent much of his time quantifying just about everything imaginable. He counted the number of steps people took to travel a specific distance, undertook studies to quantify boredom, attempted to measure the efficacy of prayer, and even measured the "beauty" of woman in British towns and cities.

Then, in 1883, Galton began dabbling in eugenics—the study of the conditions under which men of "high type" are produced. He undertook a series of studies that explored ways to measure the worth of people. Galton's fascination with worth led him to believe that innate qualities were responsible for the social behavior of individuals. This dual fascination with quantification and innate qualities led Galton to focus specifically on the measurement of mental abilities. Initially, he collected measures of skulls and body parts and used them to explain differences in intelligence. A student of Galton, James McKeen Cattell, who became one of the founding fathers of American psychology, then developed a series of sensory and motor measures he called "mental tests."[81] These early attempts by Galton and Cattell however, sampled the wrong domains—physical traits and sensory motor skills—rather than the appropriate domain of cognitive skills.

Through his attempts to "measure" intelligence, Galton introduced important statistical concepts used today. He developed a method for displaying data that divided people into different categories—quartiles, quintiles, and percentile ranks. He showed that even within homogenous populations, variation exists. Therefore, qualities such as talent or "genius" could be assigned a value on a statistical scale. For the first time, Galton used the normal curve to rank order individuals, thereby making distinctions between individuals within a homogenous population. This method of analysis became the dominant approach to scaling psychological tests and it gave rise to several types of scores used to report test results, like percentile ranks and standard scores.[82]

In 1905, the French psychologists Alfred Binet and Theodore Simon rejected Galton and Cattell's efforts to use measures of physical traits and sensory motor skills as proxies for intelligence. Instead, Binet and Simon developed tests that provided more direct measures of verbal ability, judgment, adaptation, and self-criticism. Within a decade, Binet's work was adapted in the United States by Lewis Terman who introduced the *Stanford Revision of the Binet-Simon Scale*. Better known as the *Stanford-Binet* scale, this test offered a new technology for placing and grouping students within school systems based on "scientific" measures and meritocracy.

The general public widely accepted claims that testing could do more than assess what people learned: it could also measure their underlying mental abilities or intelligence. The belief that "intelligence" test scores reflected innate ability ignored the fact that Binet had developed his tests to measure *developed* ability, rather than innate ability. Binet developed his test *to identify students in need of specialized instruction*. As the Stanford psychologist Richard Snow put it, "to interpret [Binet's test] as measures of 'general intelligence' was a flagrant over generalization."[83] This overgeneralization, however, has persisted since its inception a century ago.

Intelligence test scores were used as "quantified evidence" that the innate ability of some students was "low." Low innate ability became an explanation for why some students performed poorly in school. This challenged the belief that all students could learn if properly taught.[84] For example, in 1918 Charles H. Judd, director of the School of Education at the University of Chicago, argued that poor performance in school was the product of a child's innate ability and home background.[85]

Intelligence test scores enabled educators to shift the explanation for poor attainment from teaching to a lack of a student's "ability" to learn. Intelligence test scores were also used to sort students into different tracks based on student "ability" level. Each track was then exposed to a different curriculum—often with disastrous consequences for minorities and non-English speakers.[86]

Absolute Proficiency Replaced By Normative Standards

A second factor that contributed to the collapse of the belief that all children will learn if properly taught was a shift away from an absolute standard of proficiency to normative standards. For centuries, people believed in an absolute standard of proficiency. This belief was predicated on the assumption that if teachers properly taught the content of a domain, all students would master it. Therefore, when tested, all students should earn a score that represents mastery.

As educational testing developed in the early 20th century, normative descriptions of student performance emerged. A norm-referenced score told teachers, parents, and students how a student performed relative to a larger group. The median score—the score that separates the top half of students in a group from the bottom half—became the standard of acceptable attainment. As an example, during the first decade of the 20th century, the Boston Public Schools reported the district's median test score to teachers, who then used the score to determine whether each student and their class as a whole was above or below the standard for the city.[87]

While both absolute and normative standards rely on a test score to classify students, a normative standard is based on the relative performance of a group of students who comprise the norm group. For this reason, the standard for performance varies across classrooms, schools, and districts and is dependent on the group to which a student's performance is compared. Unlike absolute performance standards, for which all students have the opportunity to succeed, using the median score to define a normative standard forces half of the students to fall below that standard. In this way, normative standards guarantee that large numbers of students will not meet a standard.

The use of normative data was a major contributor to the popularity of early standardized tests.[88] These early uses of norm referencing foreshadowed the development of nationally normed-referenced commercial achievement tests that appeared soon after World War I. Commercial achievement tests allow people to compare student or group performance to national, state, and district norm groups, as well as to public, private, religious, urban, rural, and suburban school norm groups.

Extolling the virtues of "scientific" measurement, Charles Judd linked "intelligence" to a normative criterion of student performance:

> With the theoretical ideal of perfection overthrown, there is now an opportunity to set up rational demands. We can venture to tell parents with assurance that their children in the fifth grade are as good as the average if they misspell fifty percent of a certain list of words. We know this just as well as we know that a certain automobile engine cannot draw a ton of weight up a certain hill. No one has a right to make unscientific demand of the automobile or of the school.[89]

As we learned from Walker Percy in Chapter 5, all interpretations and descriptions in science are normative. Judd, however, goes beyond normative descriptions. His "rational demands" create an upper limit for a student's performance, and implies that what schools can do for a student is bounded by the student's immutable "intelligence."

The idea that all students could learn if properly taught remained dormant until the work of John Carroll, Jerome Bruner, and Benjamin Bloom revived it in the 1960s. In the late '70s, the idea became a tenet of the school effectiveness movement that maintained that all students are expected to learn. Today, No Child Left Behind makes the same claim and re-embraces the notion of absolute proficiency.

The Rise of the Short-Answer Question

The essay exam that swept the country after being introduced in Boston in 1845 came under criticism early in the 20th century. In two historic studies Daniel Starch and Edward Elliot showed that a student's grade on an essay test varied substantially depending on who read the exam.[90] One marker might be more lenient or severe than another. Further, they showed marks varied even when read by the same person on different occasions.[91]

Subjectivity once again reared its troubling head. This time requiring students to answer test questions by supplying a word, number, or short phrase, allayed concerns about subjectivity. Responses to short answer items were easier to score objectively.

During the first decade of the 20th century, the short answer item facilitated the use of testing by administrators to aid efficiency, supervision, and bureaucratic control.[92] However, like all changes in the technology of testing, the introduction of the short answer item produced unintended negative consequences. There was a loss of depth and richness in students' responses, less focus on more complex writing skills, and an emphasis on parts of the curriculum that lent themselves to short, factual, "right" answers. The short answer item continues to be used in many of today's state-testing programs.

The Rise of the Multiple-Choice Item

The large influx of immigrants into the United States at the turn of the century raised competing social and political issues. To help new immigrants adapt to the American economy and culture, many people saw schools as an effective vehicle for "Americanizing" immigrant children. Others, however, advocated policies to limit immigration and argued that the arrivals were intellectually inferior. For both groups, Binet's IQ tests became popular. Yet Binet's approach to testing had a major shortcoming. His test required that a specially trained administrator work individually with each examinee when presenting a large series of tasks. Simply put, the test was inefficient—it did not lend itself to widespread use for screening and grouping large numbers of individuals.

To increase the efficiency of testing large numbers of examinees and assure objective scoring, Frederick J. Kelly introduced the multiple-choice item in 1914.[93] He specified that the test items should "(1) . . . be subject to only one interpretation (2) . . . call for but one thing . . . wholly right or wholly wrong, and not partly right and partly wrong."[94] With the introduction of the multiple-choice item, tests could now be administered *en masse* with many more questions answered in the same time period. The multiple-choice item also allowed tests to be scored quickly and objectively by unskilled clerks.

Arthur Otis, a student of Terman, set out to develop a more efficient version of Binet's IQ test using Kelly's multiple-choice format along with true-false questions from extant reading tests.[95] With the entry of the United States into World War I, there was a pressing need to screen recruits for officer training. Terman was on a committee to develop such a test for the U.S. Army and recommended Otis's test, which the committee accepted.[96] The test became known as the Army Alpha, the first large scale group-administered multiple-choice test.[97] The Army Alpha was administered to over 2 million recruits before the end of World War I, although the classification of recruits based on their test score was of questionable validity because of language and other cultural problems.

The multiple-choice item was widely adopted by the fledgling test-publishing industry that emerged in the 1920s, and has since evolved into a billion-dollar enterprise. Test publishers made most of their profit from selling answer sheets and scoring services, not from the sale of the reusable test booklets—a version of "give them the razor, sell them the blades."[98] By

1920, more than 100 different multiple choice achievement tests existed, with World Book publishing nearly half a million tests a year. By 1930, over 2 million copies of the Stanford Achievement Test and the Stanford-Binet Intelligence Test were sold.[99]

Among established testing programs that embraced the multiple-choice item was the College Entrance Examination Board. In 1926, the Board began using multiple-choice questions in addition to one written essay for a test administered to students seeking college admission. Eleven years later, the board dropped the essay test, and the admission test was composed solely of multiple-choice items.[100]

During the 1920s, state educational agencies and educational researchers increased their dependence on the use of multiple-choice tests to monitor schools and examine the impact of various educational reforms. During the 1920s, New York introduced the multiple-choice item to the Regents exam that was administered to thousands of high school students each year. In 1929, the University of Iowa launched its statewide testing program using multiple-choice questions. Similarly, researchers like Ben Wood and evaluators like Ralph Tyler undertook studies that included the testing of thousands of students.[101] In one such study, Wood and his colleague William Learned tested approximately 20,000 students in 1928, 1930, and 1932.[102] These large-scale testing programs were made possible by group-administered multiple-choice tests.

The paradoxical costs associated with the spread of the multiple-choice item—to improve efficiency and ease of scoring as the numbers of students swelled—were substantial. Samelson tells us that as early as 1922, one member of the educational measurement elite boasted that "most of the tests [on] the market, unless measuring handwriting, do not call for written answers."[103] In *The Bonfire of the Vanities,* Tom Wolfe, describes how the multiple-choice test became an end in itself: "'Let me ask you this. How does he do on his written work?' Mr. Rifkind let out a whoop. 'Written work? There hasn't been any written work at Rupert High for fifteen years! Maybe twenty! They take tests.'"[104]

Unfortunately, the multiple-choice item is like a sound bite that strips depth and context from a question and a student's answer. They also promote accepted social values of efficiency, standardization, conformity, and accountability. Chief Inspector Holmes' concern about valuing something for its "measurableness" is echoed in Samelson's description of multiple-choice items:

> [Multiple-choice items do] not place the emphasis on the production of coherent ideas... but on the... recognition of small pieces of mostly factual, and often trivial information. Intolerant of idiosyncrasy and individuality, it carried the latent message that the goal of learning [is] the identification of

the one "wholly right" answer as defined by seemingly impersonal, "objective," yet often quite arbitrary authority.[105]

New Technologies and Testing

The multiple choice item eliminated the drawbacks associated with the older essay exams—subjective scoring, limited efficiency, small samples of items, and lower test reliability. Nonetheless, answers to each of the multiple choice items still had to be scored by hand. For large scale testing programs manual scoring decreased efficiency, administrative convenience, and increased costs. Early attempts to address this drawback involved the use of templates superimposed on an examinee's answer sheet. Teachers or clerks simply counted the number of pencil marks showing through the holes in the template.[106]

In the late 1920s, Ben Wood of Columbia University saw the need to automate scoring and piqued the interest of Thomas J. Watson, Sr., president of International Business Machine (IBM) Corporation.[107] Wood began working with IBM engineers to enable their punch card tabulator to score the *Strong Vocational Interest Blank*, an inventory used by counselors to help guide youth into a profession aligned with their interests. At the time, it cost roughly $5 to administer and score the inventory, largely because each student's response pattern had to be compared to the response patterns of 39 different professions. Using the modified tabulator dropped the cost to 50 cents. Machine scoring of multiple-choice tests was born.

With the help of Reynold Johnson, a high school science teacher, Wood and the IBM engineers built a machine that could detect the number of correct answers by recording the amount of electricity that flowed through the graphite left by pencil marks on an answer space. Scoring the New York Regents exam in 1936 was the first large-scale use of the graphite-reading machine. That same year, the machine also rescued Connecticut's testing program. Having nearly exhausted its budget after printing only 5,000 copies of its test, the state was able to print enough machine scannable answer sheets to test nearly 50,000 students with the 5,000 reusable test booklets.[108]

It took several years for IBM to make its machine affordable, but even then it was relatively slow because the operator had to insert each individual answer sheet into a slot, press a knob, and record the number of correct answers from the graphite reading appearing on a window dial. That number later had to be converted by hand to a percentile or standard score. Even so, by the early 1950s, the electronic scoring of tests was commonplace and was being used in conjunction with a variety of specialized computing and tabulating machines to improve the efficiency of testing.[109]

In 1955, E. F. Lindquist, a University of Iowa professor of measurement, made a significant advance in the scoring of multiple-choice answer sheets. Rather than relying on electrical impulses of graphite, Lindquist developed a mechanism to optically score specially designed answer sheets fed into the machine automatically at great speed. His innovation maximized the efficiency of scoring multiple-choice tests. The cost savings brought about by the optical scanner made it economically feasible to mount large-scale district and state multiple-choice test programs in the 1960s, '70s, '80s, and '90s.[110]

As with many uses of testing, Lindquist's machine produced unintended consequences. These problems were recognized early on by several developers of automated scoring machines.[111] For example, the 1953 Invitational Conference on Testing Problems, sponsored by the Educational Testing Service (ETS), had seven lectures related to automatic scoring machines grouped under the heading "Impact of Machines and Devices on Developments in Testing and Related Fields."[112] All of the lectures emphasized the importance of machines in the field of testing, but there were reservations. For example, Arthur Traxler of the Education Records Bureau offered this prophetic assessment of the conundrum associated with machine scoring:

> The use of the kind of answer sheet required by the fixed response-position and the fixed fields of the scoring machine has tended to force objective testing into a kind of strait jacket... The four- or five-choice, discrete test item has become virtually standard so that, except for differences in content, the parts of many of our standard tests are almost as interchangeable as the housing units in Levittown.[113]

He also noted that crafting discrete test items accompanied by four or five options occasionally led to the development of "an unnatural test situation."[114] As an example, he said, "an exercise in punctuation is forced into the multiple-choice IBM answer sheet form in such a way that a considerable percent of the junior high school pupils simply do not understand what is to be done."[115]

In yet another prescient observation, mirroring today's criticism of standardized multiple-choice tests, Traxler expressed the concerns by some teachers about:

> the multiple-choice mind... uncomfortable over the thought that regardless of the resourcefulness, skill, imagination, and stimulation to thinking that they bring to their teaching, in the end the achievement of their students, and indirectly their own success, is going to be judged largely by how well their students respond to a single type of test item.[116]

The efficiency and speed of scoring "objective" answer sheets came with another downside. It changed the teachers' relationship with the test, thereby decreasing its instructional value. One test publisher put it this way:

> [Before machine scoring] most standardized tests were hand-scored by the teachers....Under that system, tests corrected and scored by the teacher provided opportunity for careful pupil analysis by the teachers....As the machine-scoring movement grew, the activities related to testing changed. Certainly, the scoring activity left the classroom and often as not the school system itself. Test results moved increasingly into the hands of administrative staff...the hands-on dimension for teachers receded and in due course disappeared almost entirely.[117]

Finally, and perhaps most significantly, "the invention of the optical scanner had consequences that [Lindquist] perhaps did not fully anticipate. It made scoring multiple-choice items so easy, fast, and inexpensive that, in most contexts, no other testing modality could compete."[118] The widespread use of multiple-choice exams ended up limiting what could be assessed:

> [F]rom the earliest days of application of these technologies, critics lamented the loss of richness in detail that had been a feature of open-ended questions scored by human judges, and contended that machine-scored tests encouraged memorization of unrelated facts, guessing, and other distortions in teaching and learning.[119]

In the '80s and '90s, concerns about the dominance of multiple-choice tests sparked a movement called "authentic assessment" or "Beyond the Bubble."[120] The movement generated great interest in reviving supply items and performance modes of testing. However, in their attempts to replace multiple-choice tests with "authentic" assessments, proponents overlooked the very features of performance-based assessment that historically led to the adoption of multiple-choice items.

With the advent of affordable desktop computers during the 1980s, the technology of testing began to take another step towards increased efficiency. Rather than having examinees mark answers on paper that was then scanned, computer-based testing enabled answers to be recorded and scored simultaneously. In addition, test developers became aware that since a paper copy of a test was no longer needed, it was also no longer necessary to present all examinees with the same set of items. Instead, algorithms could be used to tailor the items presented to each examinee so that those that are too easy or too hard for a given examinee are avoided. By some estimates, this new approach to testing (known as computer adaptive testing) cuts in half the amount of testing time need to obtain a reliable test score.

Initially, the military and large-scale testing programs like the Graduate Record Examination (GRE) were the first to begin using computer-based tests. Today, however, several states are either using or are experimenting with the use of computer-based tests for their state testing programs.[121] But, as we will see in Chapter 9, we have just begun to scratch the surface of the many ways in which computer-based technologies will dramatically alter the ways we test students.

CONCLUSION

What lessons does history tell us about using high-stakes testing to solve perceived problems in our schools? The first is that society's need to test is immutable. Testing is an enduring technology that has been used for more than 2,000 years to address a variety of social, political, and religious issues. Testing has been and continues to be used to open doors of opportunity and eliminate patronage, select people for admission to an organization, identify talent, certify the successful completion of a given course of instruction, hold teachers accountable for student learning, and document the outcomes of schooling.

Second, as tests have been used to solve new problems, the technology of testing has been forced to evolve. This evolution altered testing from an oral to written mode, from extended responses to multiple-choice items, from hand scoring to machine scoring, and most recently from paper to computer.

Third, the history of testing reveals that well-intentioned uses of testing produce paradoxes. We have seen how the use of tests to evaluate teaching narrows and controls the curriculum. We have seen how high-stakes tests come to dictate what is "important" in schools. We have also seen how the type of items used on a test—supply, selection, oral written, or product—influences teaching and learning.

Finally, lessons from the past make clear that policy makers and the general public should not treat testing ahistorically nor deny that what happened centuries or decades ago is not relevant today. If we are not to stumble forward into yesterday, policy makers must come to grips with the lessons from history about the limitations and challenges of high-stakes testing. As we detail in the next chapter, however, today's high-stakes testing programs are producing many of the same paradoxical effects seen throughout history.

NOTES

1. This chapter draws heavily on the following work: Madaus & Greaney (1985); Madaus (1993); Madaus (1994); Madaus, Clarke, & O'Leary (2003); Madaus & Kellaghan (1992); Madaus & O'Dwyer (1999).
2. Elton (1991, pp. 72–73).
3. A historical example of this ahistorical view of educational measurement can be seen in the following 1918 quote from Leonard Ayres of the Russell Sage foundation: "Measurements in education are fifty years old if we count from the oldest beginnings of which we have record" (1918, p. 9).
4. Hughes (1989).
5. Hughes points out that most people don't realize that inventors such as Edison, the Wright brothers, Bell and Sperry concentrated their efforts on eliminating reverse salients impeding the advance of *already existing* technologies.
6. Hanson (1993).
7. Vermes (2004, p. 371).
8. See Paul (2004) for a detailed treatment of phrenology and other measures such as personality tests and the negative consequence associated with their use.
9. Gladwell (2005, p. 83).
10. For example, Hanson points out that character was often tested in folklore by asking the candidate to solve riddles. This practice calls to mind riddle songs in folk music such as "The Devil's Nine Questions." In the song the devil poses riddles to a person (e.g., "What is whiter than the milk, and what is softer than the silk?" The correct responses are snow and down). After nine successful answers, the devil tells the antagonist, "You have answered questions nine. You are God's; you're none of mine." While answering "riddles nine" may indicate a godly character—an authenticity test—it strikes us that the person scored high on a forerunner of the *Miller's Analogies Test,* a cognitive qualifying test. Nonetheless, this apparent contradiction in fact supports Hanson's argument that constructs are culturally defined. In the pre-scientific world, solving riddles was a signifier of the construct "character"; "intelligence" is a much later construct.
11. Hanson (1993, p. 44).
12. Hanson (1993, p. 52).
13. Op. cit.
14. Loewe (1986).
15. Meskill (1963).
16. While archeologists have discovered ancient paper relics of the Western Han Dynasty (206 BCE–CE 25), Cai Lun is credited with inventing paper as we have come to know it. He improved the earlier papermaking techniques—eliminating a reverse salient—thereby making paper more available and usable. (See Franklin Institute at tp://sln.fi.edu/tfi/info/current/inventions.html, and China.org.cn at http://www.china.org.cn/english/2002/May/33019.htm.)
17. Jesuits brought the idea of the Chinese technique back to France, influencing the development of the French civil service exam system on which our own was modeled (Webber, 1989).

18. In addition to selecting civil servants, there was a separate exam to select military officers. According to Miyazaki (1976, p. 102), graduates of the military examinations were "neglected and disdained."
19. Franke (1963). Candidates who studied for and passed the Letters examination progressed more rapidly within the ranks of the Civil Service than those choosing to sit for Law, History, Rituals or Classical Studies.
20. Kracke (1953). The military examinations were also supply/performance type tests. Candidates had to perform a set of three tasks in marksmanship, military talent and scholarship, which in today's testing parlance would be labeled "job related." Marksmanship, both on foot and on horseback, was assessed against fixed criteria. For example, examinees had to shoot three arrows from a horse at a man-shaped target 5-1/4 feet high. Three hits received an "excellent" score, two was a "good" score, one hit was a "pass" and zero hits meant elimination. Having candidates draw a bow into the shape of a full moon, brandish a sword without touching the ground, and lift weights assessed military talent. Finally, and least important, scholarship was assessed by having candidates write out several hundred characters from three of the seven military classics they were required to memorize. This was the only indoor examination.
21. Franke (1963); Kracke (1953); Nivison (1963).
22. Iamblichus (c. 240 AD), in his treatise *On The Pythagorean Way of Life,* described a similar series of examinations for entrance into the Pythagorean community: "[W]hen young people came and wished to study with him, he did not immediately agree until he examined and tested them." (From a translation by Dillon & Hershbell (1991, p. 97). Professor Yonder Moynihan Gillihan of the Boston College Theology Department was of great assistance in interpreting the Qumran excerpt and in pointing out the similarity to Pythagorean testing.
23. Fitzmyer (1992).
24. Quoted in Fitzmyer (1992, from IQS 6:13–23).
25. For example, if there is a basin of impure water and a pitcher of pure water and you pour from the pitcher into the basin, does the water in the pitcher become impure? (For the Essenes, the "correct" answer was yes. The impurity traveled up the stream of the water coming from the pitcher.)
26. Crosby (1997, p. 41).
27. Porter (1995).
28. Boorstin (1989); Boorstin (1985).
29. Porter (1995).
30. Kula (1986).
31. Blank (2006).
32. Ibid., p. 197. emphasis added
33. We are indebted to Professor Stephen Brown, Professor of Medieval Philosophy, Boston College, for his help in locating and translating documents.
34. In addition to these academic exams, there were performance exams to certify guild members who worked with their hands. The medieval guilds used the production mode of examining apprentices. To become a master in the golden era of the Middle Ages, "it sufficed to have served an apprenticeship,

[and] to undergo an examination (the so-called masterpiece) which was then both simple and practical." While we could not find explicit descriptions of the criteria used to evaluate the "masterpiece," we believe that the process must have been close to what Eliot Eisner calls connoisseurship evaluation a qualitative assessment. That is, connoisseurs appreciate what they encounter; they possess an awareness and an understanding of what they have experienced, which provides the basis for their judgment about an object. A modern example of the type of "masterpiece" produced by an apprentice is the "Apprentice Bowl" created by those finishing their training at Waterford Crystal in Ireland.

35. The canon was made up of *Thomas Aquinas's Summa Theologiae*, Peter the Lombard's *Sententiae* (The Sentences), the Bible, and Comestor's the *Historia Scholastica*. The teachers or *magisters* read texts and their related commentaries repeatedly so that all students could follow along (textbooks were not available for all the students). *The Sentences* by Peter the Lombard is considered the first official textbook; it was introduced in 1231 (Graves, 1920).
36. This type of examination system was also popular at both Oxford and Cambridge from the 12th century onwards (Webber, 1989).
37. Hoskins (1968, p. 68).
38. Ong (1977, p. 241).
39. Ibid.
40. Graves (1920).
41. Tynan (1985). In 1529, Luther also produced a catechism for adults (Graves, 1920).
42. Lewy (1996) uses the example of the catechism used by a 16th-century Italian Jewish scholar. Students learned the doctrines of the Jewish faith by learning set responses to religious questions. For example:

    Rabbi: For what purpose did God create the man in this worthy form?

    Pupil: He created everything for His Glory's sake, and I was created to serve my Master, and to love him and fear His Glory, and to give him pleasure without any anticipation of reward.

    The oral questioning was often a precursor to further discussion between instructor and pupil.
43. Hoskins (1968).
44. Ibid.
45. The idea was Samuel Gridley Howe's, Mann's friend and confidant, who consciously modeled it after written examinations used in Europe at the time.
46. The examinations that were set were of the short-answer or essay variety and many of the questions were geared to what today would be termed behavioral objectives.
47. Mann (1845, p. 243, emphasis added).
48. Staudenmaier (1988); Staudenmaier (1985); Staudenmaier (1989). The movement toward standardization and conformity began in America in about 1815 when the Army Ordnance Department drew up "a system of regulations for... the uniformity of manufacture of all arms ordnance" (quoted in Smith,

1987, p. 42). The idiosyncrasy of the skilled craftsman had to yield to uniformity. Standard work rules replaced the village mode of negotiation over working conditions (Staudenmaier, 1989). Over several decades the Ordnance Department developed the administrative, communication, inspection, accounting, bureaucratic and mechanical techniques that fostered conformity and resulted in the technology of interchangeable parts and the eventual manufacture of a host of mass-produced products in the 20th century (Smith, 1987).

49. Foucault (1979, p. 187).
50. Mann (1845, emphasis added). We are indebted to the late Edward Riedy, who researched this document while a graduate student at Boston College.
51. Madaus & Kellaghan (1992).
52. Ong (1971).
53. Aries (1962); Ong (1971).
54. Ong (1971, pp. 173–174).
55. Quoted in Foden (1989, p. 74).
56. Tyack (1974, p. 41). The factory model of education that emerged in the United States in the late 19th century was related in part to industry's need for literate workers and the desire to teach punctuality, regular attendance, and other useful job-related attitudes (Parenti, 1978).
57. Kritzman (1990, p. 107). A 1991 service advertisement in *The Atlantic Monthly* proposed replacing the "dumbed down" assembly line of the past where teachers perform routine repetitive acts, with a new kind of factory metaphor: the "high tech assembly line," in which teachers trouble-shoot and problem-solve (Doyle, 1991).
58. Ong (1971, pp. 173–174).
59. For a full discussion of the Treviso contract and a translation of it, see Bowler (1983).
60. The curriculum of the time comprised the *Donat* and Alexandre de Vaillediey' *Doctrinal*. See Madaus & Kellaghan (1992).
61. This bill did not survive the 1800 Act of Union, which removed educational responsibility for Ireland to the Parliament at Westminster. However, the idea lived on, emerging in various forms in 1820, 1846 and 1856.
62. Rafferty (1985, p. 13) describes the payment-by-results system this way:

    By 1862, with Robert Lowe's adaptation of the Newcastle Commission's recommendations in the famous Revised Code of that year, examinations were being spread to the widest possible constituency in the form of "Payment by Results." Thus, while diversity characterized the examinations in the few and scattered secondary grammar schools, draconian uniformity was the hallmark of this state-sponsored, centralized system of assessment for elementary schools. Detailed requirements were laid down as to what was necessary to pass at each standard of the school, and so by the subtle metamorphosis of language, the standard, rather than the age group or form ("grade") in American usage, became the unit within the school. Inspectors were instructed on the use of examinations and their results to allocate money to schools. Few items of legislation were to harness the energies of teachers and students so inexorably to an examination treadmill.

63. Hansard's Parliamentary Debates a, (cols. 198–199-16, emphasis added).
64. Lowe had a second, perhaps stronger motive for mandating a results-based reward system; a desire to maintain a balanced budget and spend funds efficiently. As Lowe justified the program to Parliament, "[I cannot] promise that this system will be an economical one, and I cannot promise that it will be an efficient one, but I can promise that it will be one or the other. If it is not cheap, it will be efficient; if it is not efficient, it shall be cheap." Tacit in this justification is the direct relationship between budgetary constraints and the desire to reward or punish teachers for student attainment or lack thereof.
65. For 18th-century Ireland, see Burton (1979). For 19th-century Great Britain, see Montgomery (1967); Sutherland (1973). For Ireland, see Bowler (1983); Coolahan (1975); Madaus (1979). For Australia, see Hearn (1872). And for Jamaica, see Gordon (1968).
66. For an excellent treatment of payment by results in the British Isles, see Rapple (1994).
67. Quoted in Barnard (1961, p. 110).
68. The strategy of rewarding students for good test performance also surfaced in 20th century America, see Hughes (1979); Laffer (1982). More recently, in the 21st century, students in Baltimore were offered $110 for improved scores on the state test. See Neufeld (2007).
69. Acland (1857, p. 6, emphasis added).
70. Levine (1971); Shanker (1986).
71. Saltman (2005).
72. Blumenthal (2006).
73. Medina (2008).
74. Ibid.
75. Madaus, Ryan, Kellaghan, & Airasian (1987). Data included financial statements, rule changes, passing criteria, amount of results fees, and the total percentage of students passing examinations at the three levels on a year-by-year basis. The analysis was twofold: a regression analysis in which finances, passing criteria, and the like were used to predict percentage passing from year to year; and a time series analysis comparing the "drift" in percentage of passing during and after the results era. For full details, see Madaus, et al., (1987).
76. In contemporary financial incentive programs, the contractors have fixed but known passing criteria (standardized test results) and can manipulate finances through negotiations. The incentives offered students also could be altered. This means that the contractors soon know with a very high probability how many students can be brought to the passing criteria for a given expenditure. If the money offered in the contract is not sufficient to make the venture profitable, renegotiations or withdrawal from bidding are options. Both systems have been tailored for the lowest achievers and potential dropouts and both tend to foster "teaching for the test" by explicitly stating criterion skills of behavior. At payoff time, school boards can argue—just as the Board of Governors in Ireland did—that since no funds were spent for children who failed

to attain the criterion, the school budget had been wisely managed. But this, then and now, affords little comfort for those who haven't learned.

77. See for example, Bracey (2005); Fuller, Gesicki, Kang, & Wright (2006); Neill (2005). Interestingly, research in industrial settings indicates that the use of incentive pay systems can be easily corrupted and that it is better to focus on process rather than product. See Fisher (1992) for a decryption of problems with incentive pay systems in Sear's Auto Centers and Zimmerman (1990) for similar problems in Nordstrom. Also see Prescico (1990). Howe argued that the belief that external rewards can be motivational, at least in the work place, is wrong. Also see Deming (1982) who focused on process and was against ranking people and pay for performance.
78. Royal Commission on Education (Great Britain) (1886, p. 211, emphasis added).
79. For detailed history of psychological testing from 1890 to 1930, see Sokal (1987). For details of the origins in the United States, see Zenderland (1998).
80. Gould (1981, p.107).
81. Cattell was the founder of the Psychological Corporation that developed a number of psychological tests.
82. Stigler (1986).
83. Snow (1982, p. 505).
84. Nineteenth-century educational theorists such as Pestalozzi, Hebart, Froebel, Emerson, Parker and Dewey in the 20th century believed that intelligence, while absolute, was educable (Snow, 1982).
85. Judd (1918, p. 152, emphasis added).
86. Madaus & Kellaghan (1993).
87. Ballou (1916).
88. Tyack & Hansot (1982).
89. Judd (1918, p. 153, emphasis added).
90. Starch & Elliot (1912); Starch & Elliot (1913).
91. This finding has been replicated many times since (e.g., Hartog & Rhodes, 1935; Madaus & Macnamara, 1970).
92. Travers (1983). Also see Callaghan (1962) for a description of the "efficiency movement."
93. Thorndike & Lohman (1990) credit the Chinese with the development and use of the selection/multiple-choice item type. Nonetheless, Samelson (1987) names Frederick Kelley the inventor.
94. Quoted in Samelson (1987, p. 119).
95. Samelson (1987).
96. Reed (1987).
97. A version of the Army Beta was also developed to be used with illiterate or non-English-speaking recruits.
98. Haney, Madaus, & Lyons (1993); Lyman (1989).
99. U.S. Congress Office of Technology Assessment (1992).
100. Angoff & Dyer (1971).
101. For more information on Tyler's groundbreaking work, see Madaus (2004); Madaus & Stufflebeam (1989); Smith & Tyler (1942).

102. Downey (1965).
103. Quoted in, Samelson (1987, p. 12).
104. Wolfe (1987, pp. 130–131).
105. Samelson (1987, pp. 123–124).
106. This procedure was still being used in the '50s when one of the authors began his teaching career.
107. See www.columbia.edu/acis/history/benwood.html.
108. Downey (1965).
109. See Educational Testing Service (1954) for details.
110. Baker (1971).
111. For a discussion of these downsides, see U.S. Congress Office of Technology Assessment (1992).
112. Educational Testing Service (1954). Among the lecturers were representatives of companies that had recently developed scoring and computing devices, faculty who were heading computing and scoring centers within their universities, members of the U.S. Department of Army Personnel Research Branch, and a representative of ETS.
113. Traxler (1954, p. 140).
114. Ibid., p. 140.
115. Ibid.
116. Ibid., p. 141. Seven years later, Arthur Adams of the American Council on Education echoed Traxler's concerns: "With the pace of technical advance having reached the point where from three to six thousand test papers can be scanned by a machine in an hour, one could become beguiled with the marvelous efficiency of such a process and at least momentarily forget the hopes, the aspirations and the future of the individual human being tied up in every one of those papers" (Adams, 1961, p. 80).
117. Cited in U.S. Congress Office of Technology Assessment (1992, p. 255, emphasis added).
118. Brennan (2004, p. 15, emphasis added).
119. U.S. Congress Office of Technology Assessment (1992, p. 253).
120. A reference to the bubbles on answer sheets students fill in when answering a multiple choice item.
121. Bennett et al. (2008).

CHAPTER 8

WHAT ARE THE PARADOXICAL CONSEQUENCES OF HIGH-STAKES TESTING?

Across the centuries and over continents, high-stakes testing has been used for both symbolic and practical purposes. Mandating a high-stakes testing program sends a symbolic message that policy-makers are serious about reforming education. The numeric scores produced by these programs have an objective, scientific, almost magical persuasiveness about them. The policy makers and the general public accept these scores as a symbol of educational quality and, in turn, use scores to make decisions about school choice, hiring and firing of school administrators, restructuring of schools, and even home buying.

Beyond symbolism, high-stakes testing programs provide policy-makers with a powerful tool that directs what is taught, how it is taught, what is learned, and how it is learned. This power was evident when test directors across 40 states with high-stakes testing programs were interviewed in 1990. When asked whether they believe "teachers spend more time teaching the specific objectives on the test(s) than they would if the tests were not required," the answer was a nearly unanimous yes. While shaping teaching and learning is well intended and sometimes beneficial, it also produces unintended negative consequences. These negative consequences were cited by about a third of the state test directors who viewed the practice of

The Paradoxes of High Stakes Testing, pages 139–174

spending more time teaching the test's specific objectives negatively. As one director put it, "There are some real potential problems there.... *Basically the tests do drive the curriculum.*" [1]

It is the combination of positive intended outcomes and unintended negative consequences that makes high-stakes testing paradoxical. In this chapter, we examine the unintended negative consequences that make high-stakes testing paradoxical. These consequences fall into four broad categories encompassing effects on teaching and learning, retention and dropouts, the test itself, and students and families.

HIGH-STAKES TESTING DRIVES TEACHING AND LEARNING

A score on a high-stakes test triggers a reward, such as a diploma, financial award, admission to a program, or a sanction, such as the denial of diploma, retention in grade, being fired, or placing a school in receivership. High-stakes testing is a form of Pavlovian conditioning; rewards and sanctions direct teacher and student behavior. There are positive effects associated with this scenario. Consequences provide motivation for some. Consequences focus instruction and provide administrators, teachers, and students with clear goals and useful information. They also can help facilitate change to an otherwise moribund curriculum.[2]

Benefits of testing have been recognized for centuries. In 1612, the Oxford English Dictionary included its first reference to an academic examination, stating, "Which worke of continual examination is a notable quickner and nourisher of all good learning."[3] In the same century, Philip Melancthon, a German professor argued, "no academical exercise can be more useful than that of examination. It whets the desire for learning, it enhances the solicitude of study while it animates the attention to whatever is taught."[4] In the 19th century, John Stuart Mill and Adam Smith reasoned that the publication of test results engenders competition, which motivates change in the behavior of school personnel and affects parents' attitudes about schools.

In the late 20th century, a movement called Measurement Driven Instruction embraced the idea that high-stakes tests *should* drive instruction. Three characteristics of Measurement Driven Instruction were viewed as working together to improve students' learning. These characteristics include a clear concept of educational goals, a test that measures the goals, and high-stakes associated with the results that act as a motivating force on teachers and students.[5] Each of these characteristics is found in No Child Left Behind (NCLB).

In the 21st century, proponents of high-stakes testing openly acknowledged that tests drive teaching and learning. They argue that if the *right kinds of tests are used*—ones that go beyond the multiple choice format and the measurement of facts and lower order skills—then it is perfectly acceptable for such tests to drive the curriculum and teaching. While there is some truth to these claims, proponents disregard a number of problems. These "right" kinds of tests are more costly, time consuming, and difficult to administer and score.[6] But even if these administrative drawbacks could be overcome, significant problems persist when a test is used to drive the curriculum.

There are three predictable ways that a high-stakes test, even one that employs the "right" kinds of tests, adversely affects teaching and learning. First, teachers give greater attention to tested content and decrease emphasis on non-tested content. This narrows the content and skills taught and learned *within a discipline.* Second, a high-stakes test preempts time and coverage from disciplines not tested. This narrows the curriculum *across subject fields.* Third, there is a "trickle down" effect. The content and skills covered on the high-stakes tests at the upper grades displaces the content and skills of non-tested lower grades, altering the curriculum *across grades.* As we examine next, each of these effects is well documented by historical evidence, literary accounts, surveys, interviews, and classroom observations.

Narrowing What Is Taught and Learned Within a Discipline

A 1990 report by The National Commission on Testing and Public Policy describes how pressure to improve scores on reading and math tests can narrow teaching to test preparation. The Commission warned that the high-stakes attached to test use, "... is driving schools and teachers away from instructional practices that would help to produce critical thinkers and active learners."[7] As one example, the report described how "[i]nstead of reading books, students in many classrooms read isolated paragraphs and practice answering multiple-choice questions about them."[8]

This unintended consequence of a high-stakes testing is not unique to the United States. The same undesired outcome was recently documented in England. As an English department head in a British secondary school describes, it is possible to obtain a top grade on a national exit exam without ever reading any book in its entirety.

Because the exam asks student to write detailed linguistic analyses of extracts, it is perfectly possible to show pupils the film of the set novel and play, provide a synopsis, and encourage them to look at selected passages rather than demand that they read the whole book. As a result, most students never learn to read independently and are never actually required to.[9]

The problem described by the department head and the National Commission is not unique to today's high-stakes tests. In fact, they are ageless.

Historical Evidence

Examining 1,298 years of official and unofficial records, Hoi Suen and Lan Yu uncovered several negative effects of China's high-stakes civil service testing program. Their article, *Chronic Consequences of High-Stakes Testing? Lessons from the Chinese Civil Service Exam,* documents several unintended consequences which included targeting test-specific content, students memorizing and reproducing model answers to essay questions without understanding the content, students focusing on test taking skills, the emergence of a commercial tutoring system and large-scale commercial publishing of successful essays from previous exams, and elaborate cheating.[10]

As Suen and Yu document, repeated attempts to introduce changes in the Chinese civil service exam to overcome these negative consequences were unsuccessful. Students and tutors simply developed new test taking tactics to beat any new requirement.

Europe's long history with high-stakes tests also offers numerous examples of narrowing the curriculum within a discipline. Naturally, the stakes associated with European exams made students want to do well on the tests. This led to the development of *cramming books,* analogous to today's *Barron's* or *Princeton Review* guides. The first such book was an anonymous manuscript written for students by a master in the Arts Faculty at the University of Paris between 1230 and 1240. It listed the questions most frequently asked during oral examinations and succinct answers to them. While it is unknown whether cramming books narrowed the curriculum teachers covered, they certainly narrowed students' coverage of the curriculum.[11] Likewise, during the seventeenth century at Oxford, books containing previous exam questions became available to students.

Evidence of narrowing the curriculum in response to testing is also evident in literary works. In China, Suen and Yu recount several literary works that satirized the Civil Service Exam, described intense preparation for it, and the psychological and physical toll it took on those who failed.

Wilfred Sheed's 1982 literary description in *Transatlantic Blues* satirizes test preparation establishments. He tells the story of a student who was sent to a Jenkins Tutorial establishment in London.

Their only texts were examination papers:

> Within six months, I was able to pass London matriculation [exam] without knowing any of the subjects involved; and by applying Jenkins method later,

> to pass every exam that ever came my way afterwards. Hence, I remain a profoundly uneducated man.[12]

Metaphors about high-stakes tests abound in English and Irish literature.[13] The examination is depicted as a grinding machine and success a form of divine election, with Oxbridge as the heavenly Jerusalem. When the stakes are high, teachers and students do not worry about the niceities of a well-rounded education. The exam is portrayed as the common enemy and any strategy used by teachers or students to cope with it is justified. Prevelant in this literature is a frank admission that what was memorized, regurgitated on the exam, and then quickly forgotten is irrelevant in life after school.[14]

Writing in 1892, H. G. Wells, captures the power that attaching high-stakes to test performance can exert on teachers, "The examiner pipes and the teacher must dance... If the educational reformers really wish the dance altered they must turn their attention from the dancers to the musicians."[15]

There are other historical, non-literary strands of evidence from England and Ireland illustrating the effect of testing on the curriculum. For example, in 1868, the Taunton Commission in England appointed to examine secondary education concluded that "the examination dictates the curriculum and cannot do otherwise."[16] When test results were linked to teacher's pay during the payment by results era, Matthew Arnold, then a school inspector, rendered the following timeless indictment of attaching high-stakes to student test performance. He described teaching under these pressures as:

> a game of mechanical contrivance in which teachers will and must learn how to beat us. It is found possible by ingenious preparation, to get children through the... examination in reading, writing and ciphering, without their really knowing how to read, write and cipher.[17]

Arnold's observation illustrates how high-stakes tests can deeply influence teacher and student behavior.[18] The exam exercised prescriptive authority, delimited and eventually defined what and how things are taught and learned.[19] As one Irish researcher summarized, "draconian uniformity was the hallmark of this state-sponsored, centralized system of assessment for elementary schools."[20]

Similar concerns were raised in America in the 19th century. In 1888, the Superintendent of Schools in Cincinnati complained that when essay tests were used for promotion decisions, teachers:

> ...shut their eyes to the needs of the pupils and put their strength into what will 'count' in the examinations,... [the retention requirement] perverted the best efforts of teachers, and narrowed and grooved their instruction; they have occasioned and made well-neigh imperative the use of mechanical and

> rote methods of teaching; [the requirements] have occasioned cramming and the most vicious habits of study; they have caused much of the overpressure charged upon schools, some of which is real; they have tempted both teachers and pupils to dishonesty; and last but not least, they have permitted a mechanical method of schools supervision.[21]

A 1938 evaluation of the New York State Regents exam raised similar concerns. It reported that teachers disregarded the objectives in local curriculum guides in favor of objectives tested by the Regents' examinations.[22] During the 1930s, movements towards statewide testing in several states were criticized on the grounds they would lead to a standardization of the curriculum and destroy programs that might cater to local needs.[23] Ironically, today's critics of proposals to develop a national test no longer mention local needs, but instead raise concerns that a national test would destroy statewide programs.

Findings From Research

Over the past forty years, surveys of American teachers about testing document the effects of high-stakes tests on the practices and attitudes of teachers. Across a range of state testing programs, large percentages of teachers report:

- Considerable attention and time given over to material covered by a high-stakes test at the expense of non-tested content and skills;
- More classroom time spent preparing students specifically for the test;
- A decrease in teacher morale and increased stress on teachers.[24]

Not surprisingly, the stakes linked to a testing program influence teachers' responses to survey questions. For example, the results from a 2001 national survey of over 4,000 teachers found large differences between those teaching in high-stakes situations and those teaching where the stakes are not as high.[25] The differences included:[26]

- 80% of teachers in high stakes states reported that there is so much pressure for high scores on the test that they have little time to teach anything not on the test; in contrast only 56% of teachers in lower stakes states felt this way.
- 85% of teachers in high stakes states reported teaching test-taking skills to prepare students for the test while only 67% of teachers in lower stakes states reported doing so.

- 43% of teachers in high stakes states reported that they greatly increased time spent on instruction in tested areas. In contrast, only 17% of teachers in lower stakes states reported greatly increasing time on tested areas.
- 63% of teachers in high-stakes states reported using test preparation materials developed commercially or by the state and 44% used items from the state test to prepare students. In contrast, only 19% of teachers in lower stakes states reported engaging in this type of test preparation.
- 70% of teachers in high stakes states also indicated that they prepared students for the test throughout the year as compared to only 43% in lower stakes states.

In addition to the influences that high-stakes have on instructional practices, the survey also revealed that more than 80% of respondents felt that scores on state-mandated tests do not accurately reflect the quality of the education students receive. Similar percentages of teachers believe that their state-mandated test is not as accurate a measure of student achievement as the teacher's own judgment.

Beyond impacting what is taught, preparation for state tests also affects the methods of teaching and learning. As an example, instructional use of computers is affected in at least three ways due to test preparation. First, to help students become accustomed to writing an essay for a paper-and-pencil state test, approximately thirty percent of teachers nationwide report that they either decreased the amount of time or did not allow students to use word processors in the classroom. This reduction occurred despite a large body of research showing that regular use of word processors improves the quality of student writing.[27]

Second, in hopes of increasing student test scores, many schools make use of computer-based test preparation materials that are widely available. However, this practice displaces the use of computers for writing, research, creating presentations, and exploring data.

Third, high-stakes tests also lead teachers to shift the focus of computer use from developing higher-level skills to acquiring discrete pieces of knowledge of names, places, and events likely to be on the test. During a study of computer usage in schools, a teacher described how computer use changed in her classroom since the implementation of a high-stakes testing program. Prior to the test, students web-searches took the form of complex problem solving in which they had to find information, interpret that information, and reach a decision. As an example, students were told that a kangaroo from Australia wanted to relocate to the United States. The animal was thinking of living in Wyoming, Arizona, or Vermont. Students were asked to research the habitat of the kangaroo and the habitats in each of the three states. Students were then required to use the information they found to make a recommendation to the kangaroo.

After the state test was introduced, the web-quests took the form of worksheets that contained incomplete sentences about important historical figures and events. Students used the Internet to find information left out of sentences in order to fill in the blanks. Boring busy work.[28]

These effects on how and what is taught in the classroom were evident in interviews with 360 educators in urban, suburban, and rural settings across three states.[29] The following responses offer a flavor of how teachers see the test narrowing the curriculum:

- [Guidelines for] the state test came out earlier this year. We had to chop the middle of our social studies curriculum in half so we could teach Kansas history, because the state decided to test Kansas history [a grade earlier than we usually teach it]. So our students have had to stop what they're learning in . . . Western hemisphere geography and cultures . . . to learn Kansas history instead. (Middle School Special Education Teacher in a Low-Stakes State)
- When I teach, I put a lot of things into my lessons that will prepare students for the tests, and I remove a lot of the project-type activities such as writing plays, writing poetry, performance activities. Now we don't do a lot of that because we're concentrating on preparing for the tests. (Eighth-Grade English Teacher in a Moderate-Stakes State)
- If I didn't have the MCAS hanging over my head, and if the kids didn't . . . I could teach [the] material more in-depth. I could take these frameworks and really explain the connections [in the] content. The MCAS is such a constraint on my time that I can't always get my students to see the deep connections, even though I try to show them and approach the topic [in] different ways. The framework strands would absolutely support in-depth teaching; however, the test doesn't allow [that]. (Middle/High School Mathematics Teacher in a High-Stakes State)

These three vignettes are but a small sample of teachers' reflections on their state test.[30] Across the three states, many teachers reported paradoxical effects on curriculum and instruction. On the positive side, teachers saw the state-testing program adding new important topics, removing unneeded content, and emphasizing important content and student writing.

While supportive of the state frameworks, teachers also reported that the state test narrowed the curriculum by overemphasizing certain topics at the expense of others, reduced teaching creativity, and infringed on the time they can dedicate to helping students develop the skills and knowledge specified in the frameworks. Teachers also reported increased test preparation, a focus on breath rather than depth in content coverage, and a pace of instruction that was inappropriate for some students. It's important to note, the extent to which teachers discussed these effects varied by the stakes associated with their state's test. Compared to their peers in moderate- and low-stakes states, respondents in the high-stakes state were twice as apt to report such effects, while moderate-stakes respondents reported them more than did those in the low-stakes state.

Not only do the effects of state testing programs on the curriculum and instruction vary by the stakes associated with the test, they also vary by classroom demographics. A 1992 nation-wide survey of more than 2,000 teachers, funded by the National Science Foundation (NSF), examined the effects of high-stakes tests on math and science instruction. The survey compared the responses of teachers in classrooms with high-minority enrollments versus low-minority enrollments.[31] When compared to their colleagues in low-minority classrooms, the study found that a higher percentage of teachers in high minority classrooms reported:

- The state-testing program influenced their instructional practices
- High-stakes standardized tests caused them to spend more time in whole-group group instruction, developing basic skills, and solving problems likely to be on the test
- The state test made them gear their instruction to the test
- The test led them to teach in ways that go beyond their own ideals of good educational practice
- Their districts pressured them to improve test scores[32]

Why are classroom demographics important in understanding test performance? After all, one-size fits all high-stakes tests are meant to improve and document the achievement levels of all children regardless of the school they attend. The answer can be found in the observations of the psychologist Robert Sternberg, Tufts University's Dean of Arts and Sciences. When a reporter interviewing him asked, "How well can we measure a student's intelligence through such standardized testing?" Sternberg's reply illuminates the importance of classroom demographics in understanding the performance of an individual student or groups of students on high-stakes achievement tests:

> If you grow up in . . . [affluent] Weston or Wellesley, for most of the kids the tests are fairly good measures of the analytical part of intelligence. If you grow up in [not so affluent] Roxbury, chances are it's not going to tell you the same things as it does a kid from Weston. And the reason is that kids grow up with different challenges. Kids who grow up in middle-class, mostly white suburbs have the luxury of developing memory and analytical skills, *which is*

> *what these tests, and to a large extent schools under the current administration, very much value.* If you grow up in a more challenging environment, then you kind of have to develop creative and practical skills because every day can be a real challenge.[33]

In essence, the types of skills and knowledge included on most state achievement tests are aligned with the skills of students from more affluent areas. This gives them a head start over their less affluent peers who have developed other, important, but non-tested, skills. To overcome these differences, teachers in high minority schools feel they must make more modifications to their instruction to prepare their students for the state test.

Narrowing What Is Taught and Learned Across the Curriculum

Cuckoo birds have developed an interesting strategy for survival. Mother cuckoo birds lay their eggs in the nest of other birds. When the cuckoo egg hatches, the nesting mother bird attends to the cuckoo chick. As the cuckoo chick grows, it throws the nesting mother's chicks and eggs from the nest and becomes the primary focus of the mother.

An analogous phenomenon occurs when a high-stakes test is introduced. Like the nesting mother, teachers gradually spend more time attending to tested subject areas. Given that there is a limited amount of time in the school day, this increased attention squeezes out time for other school subjects and activities.[34]

In addition to this squeezing effect, the focus on preparing students for tests diminishes the development of other valued talents.[35] As Robert Sternberg puts it, "[the] increasingly massive and far-reaching use of conventional standardized tests is one of the most effective, if unintentional, vehicles this country has created for suppressing creativity."[36] The negative consequences that high-stakes tests have for non-tested subject areas, activities, and the development of valued talents are well documented in history, literature, and recent research.[37]

Historical Evidence

Disregarding things not tested was apparent in China as long ago as 1043. A critic of the civil service exams complained that because the examinations did not assess imagination and studies of practical utility these areas were neglected.[38] Nearly a millennium later, the newly introduced Chinese tertiary entrance examination system was also criticized for dominating teaching and learning in secondary schools at the expense of things not examined.[39]

Similar complaints were registered in Europe during the 19th century. Auberon Herbert collected an array of testimony from teachers and other academics. Their testimony showed that tested subjects were given prominence in the classroom to the neglect of untested subjects. They also reported that rote methods and cramming flourished.[40] During debates prior to the enactment of payment-by-results in Great Britain, Sir James Kay-Shuttleworth offered this prophetic concern:

> [There will be] a strong motive to limit the instruction more and more to the three elementary subjects. The largest amount of [reward] can be obtained by sacrificing the moral and religious instruction, the intellectual training and general information, and restricting the instruction to mechanical drill in the reading, writing and arithmetic.[41]

His prediction came to pass. Teachers did limit their instruction to what they sarcastically nicknamed the "paying subjects."[42] Thomas Huxley explained what happened: "The Revised Code did not compel any schoolmaster to leave off teaching anything; But, by the very process of refusing to pay for many kinds of teaching, it has practically put an end to them."[43]

Literary sources also speak to a high-stake test's corrupting effect on things not tested. George Orwell's reminiscence on his school experience is a good example:

> Subjects which lacked examination value, such as geography, were almost completely neglected, mathematics was also neglected if you were a "classical," science was not taught in any form... and even the books you were encouraged to read in your spare time were chosen with one eye on the English paper.[44]

Findings from Research

Contemporary evidence supports the historical and literary testimony that high-stakes tests adversely affect non-tested subjects. In addition, contemporary evidence shows that high-stakes testing impinges on ancillary enrichment programs, field trips, and even cuts recess time.

A 2001 national survey asked teachers about the effect of high-stakes testing on non-tested subjects and other activities. About 80% of the teachers reported increasing time spent on subject areas that are tested and nearly 50% said they decrease time on subjects that are not tested, such as fine arts, physical education, foreign languages, and industrial/vocational education. In addition, teachers reported that testing decreased the amount of time spent on activities not directly related to specific subject areas such as field trips and other enrichment activities. In general, the influence of state testing programs on teachers' instructional practices is stronger where the stakes are high for both schools and students than in settings where the stakes are lower. The impact of testing programs is also generally stronger in elementary and middle schools than in high schools.[45]

During interviews, educators tell how courses or projects not covered by the test are diminished:[46]

- I felt I was a math teacher from January until spring break. We had to drop other curriculum areas because of this—spelling, writing....We couldn't drop science because we had a science assessment coming up at the same time. (Fourth-Grade Teacher in a Low-Stakes State)
- In ninth grade [the students would] take a survival course, so we would actually... teach them how to build survival shelters and things....We're very rural, so survival skills are important. That course is gone. We had 'Our Town' where we... actually integrated history and research techniques with the communities around here, so that when the kids moved out they really understood their roots. We had 'Troubled Times' for freshmen, which... helped students deal with adolescent issues, you know, drug abuse, sex, all those things. The course is gone... We had some wonderful, wonderful programs....These are the things that MCAS has killed. (Middle/High School English Department Chairperson in a High-Stakes State)

A more recent study by the Center on Educational Policy, which should be required reading for policy makers, documents the effect of high-stakes tests on non-tested subjects.[47] They found that 71% of school districts reduced time in at least one subject to expand time for reading and math. More specifically, 33% of districts reduced time for social studies, 29% reduced time for science, and 22% reduced time for art and music.[48] The study also found that in some districts the amount of time struggling students spent on tested subjects doubled, at times causing them to miss other subjects altogether.[49]

The Center on Educational Policy also reported that some school leaders viewed this extra time for reading and math as a necessary trade off to help low-achieving students catch up. Other officials, however, felt that the extra time for reading and math shortchanged students "from learning important subjects, squelched creativity in teaching and learning, or diminished activities that might keep children interested in school."[50]

A 2007 Gallup Poll reveals that the public is aware of the negative effects that high-stakes testing has on non-tested subjects. Fifty-two percent of respondents believe that school curriculum is being narrowed as a result of high-stakes testing. Ninety-three percent of these respondents also said they were very or somewhat concerned about reduced emphasis on non-tested subjects.[51]

Shortchanging time is not limited to non-tested subjects but also extends to recess. To provide more time for reading and mathematics, schools across the nation are cutting back on recess time. In 2006, encroachment on recess time prompted the National Parent Teachers Association (PTA) to launch a *Rescuing Recess* campaign. As the PTA put it:

> ... [N]early 40 percent of American elementary schools have either eliminated or are considering eliminating recess. Due to school budget cuts and *an increased focus on academic standards,* millions of American schoolchildren may miss out on unstructured play with their peers including hopscotch, tag, kickball or jump rope.[52]

Narrowing Teaching and Learning Across Grades

The demands of high-stakes tests do not only affect what is and what is not taught within test grades, but trickle down to non-tested lower grades. To better prepare students for high-stakes tests given in the upper grades, the curriculum in kindergarten and first grade is altered. More emphasis is placed on academic skills at the expense of social, emotional, and physical goals for children.[53]

At the same time, some school districts have started to "red shirt" kindergarten students. In athletics, red shirting refers to the practice of holding back a scholarship athlete from playing for a year to let him/her develop further in the given sport. In elementary schools, red shirting occurs when a student is either not allowed to enter kindergarten despite meeting the age requirement or is retained once in kindergarten. Red shirting attempts to capitalize on the cognitive growth that occurs as students get older. By delaying the start of kindergarten or first grade, the hope is that test scores will be higher down the road if for no other reason than red shirted students are a year older when they take a high-stakes test.[54]

Gearing Instruction to the Type of Questions on a High-Stakes Test

As we have seen so far, high-stakes testing leads to a narrowing of the curriculum within a discipline, across disciplines, and across grades. But the effects do not end here. Beyond changing the content that is taught, high-stakes tests also change the way in which the content is taught. This influence on instruction has positive and negative effects.

On the positive side, high-stakes tests that include essays and open-response items lead teachers to increase emphasis on writing and communication skills. Several studies of state tests that require students to supply written responses to questions rather than answering a multiple-choice question show increased emphasis on teaching writing and higher-level thinking skills.[55] In Kentucky, for example, 80% of teachers surveyed indicated that they had increased their instructional emphasis on problem solving and writing as a result of requiring students to submit multiple writing samples as part of the state test.[56]

On the negative side, teachers narrow the focus on their instruction so that students respond to only the item types found on the test. This is particularly problematic when a test includes only multiple-choice items. Deborah Meier, a highly regarded principal in Manhattan, describes how students in reading classes were required to read dozens of short paragraphs about which they then answered multiple choice questions that resembled the tests given each spring. She also recounted that when synonyms and antonyms were dropped from the test, teachers promptly stopped using worksheets on synonyms and antonyms.[57]

More recent studies of teachers found that many teachers have decreased the use of time intensive instructional strategies and more lengthy enrichment activities and increased the use of problems and questions similar to those on the high-stakes test.[58] As we saw above, the use of computers to teach writing is also jeopardized by the paper-and-pencil format of a high-stakes test.[59]

Triaging "Bubble-Kids"

A 1993 study conducted by researchers at Leeds University identified another way in which teachers narrow the focus of their instruction; they concentrate their efforts on those students who are most likely to succeed on the *Standardized Assessment Tasks.*[60] These students are often referred to as "Bubble Kids" because they are on the bubble of passing the test or of moving up to the next performance level. Other researchers have found that teachers concentrate instruction on those most likely to succeed, to the detriment of those not expected to do well.[61]

In the United States, the 2001 national survey of teachers found that about 25% of teachers in states with high stakes-testing reported that they targeted students on the border of passing compared to 5% of teachers in states with low-stakes tests. Additionally nearly 20% of teachers in high-stakes situations targeted students on the border of moving to the next performance level compared to 5% of teachers in low-stakes situations.[62]

Jennifer Booher-Jennings investigated the treatment of "bubble" kid" in the Texas high-stakes testing program. A teacher in her study describes the "bubble" kids this way, "The ones who miss by one or two points—they just need a little extra help to pass so we concentrate our attention on that group. The bubbles are the ones who can make it."[63] Booher-Jennings calls this emphasis on bubble kids "educational triage." She reports that bubble kids receive a variety of benefits. These benefits include more teacher attention, more class time and extra help to prepare them for the test, individual attention or small group instruction, help from literacy teachers, after school and Saturday tutoring, and test preparation from music, gym, and library teachers instead of instruction in those non-tested subjects. She also found that referring bubble kids for special education exempted them from the accountability requirements of the test, thereby improving the school's accountability rating.

It is important to recognize that educational triage has historical precedent. Brendan Rappel, a historian at Boston College, found evidence of "educational triage" during the 19th century payment by results era. As he reports, many teachers concentrated on those pupils most likely to gain the full monetary reward for them.[64]

Recently, the practice of "educational triage" has caught the attention of the press.[65] Joshua Benton of the Dallas Morning News describes the downside of this triage approach this way: "But what if you're one of the "remedial" kids—everyone below the bubble?. . . .You get the shaft. Teachers aren't stupid. They realize they're going to be judged on how many of their kids pass—not how much improvement they can squeeze out of their weakest kids. So they go after the low-hanging fruit: the bubble kids."[66]

A TRADITION OF PAST TESTS DEFINES WHAT IN THE CURRICULUM IS TAUGHT

History shows that whenever a high-stakes testing program is put in place, a tradition of past tests quickly develops. Teachers see the kinds of content and intellectual activities that previous test questions required, and then prepare students to meet these demands. Soon afterwards, the test becomes the de facto curriculum.

Advocates of high-stakes testing argue this tradition of past tests defines and maintains standards. This tradition also gives teachers and students a clear and consistent target to aim at. But the paradox is that teachers and students often spend inordinate time simply on test preparation. And, as described above, this coaching comes at the expense of subjects, content, and skills not tested.

The tradition of past test questions lead some teachers to ingrain mnemonics to help students remember important information that appeared on past tests. For example, George Orwell describes how a tradition of asking students to list the Battle of the Roses, led him and his classmates to rely on a memorized mnemonic. Orwell writes: "Did you know . . . that the initial letters of 'a black negress was my aunt; here's her house behind the barn' were also the initial letters of battles in the Wars of the Roses?"[67] Another example comes from one of the author's daughters who was taught the mnemonic "A Rat In Tom's House Must Eat Tom's Ice Cream." Unlike her father, she has never misspelled arithmetic since. The example in Chapter 4 of essays from the Irish Primary Certificate exam provides another example of the tradition of the test shaping the delivered curriculum—rather than teaching students to be strong writers, the teachers required students to memorize canned opening, transition, and closing paragraphs to regurgitate on the exam.

Like their teachers, students develop an appreciation for the tradition of an important test. Garrison Keillor, in *Lake Wobegon Days* provides a fictional account of how students adjust to the tradition of a test:

> For years, students of the senior class were required to read ["Phileopolis "] and answer questions about its meaning. . . . The test was the same from year to year, and once the seniors found the answers and passed them on to the juniors, nobody read 'Phileopolis' anymore.[68]

A final example of how the tradition of past tests influences students comes from a colleague who was visiting a classroom of a former student, now a professor in India. To show his mentor that he was keeping abreast of new developments in the field, the professor departed from his prepared lecture notes. Almost immediately his students drowned him out with the chant: "N-O-E! N-O-E! N-O-E!" The outburst was a forceful statement that the material was Not On the Exam, and hence, irrelevant.[69]

The effects of this tradition of past tests extend beyond students and teachers. When high-stakes are attached to a test, a commercial industry develops to prepare students for it. This happened in China and Europe where whole industries of private coaching schools called "crammers" developed. In Japan it is common for parents to enroll their children in special extra-study schools known as *juku*. In the United States there are commercial firms in every major city selling coaching services to students for the SAT, ACT, and more recently for state mandated tests. Whether in China, Europe, Japan, or the United States, these coaching schools capitalize on the tradition of past tests.

HIGH STAKES CORRUPT THE TEST

In economics and sociology, experts acknowledge that the act of measurement distorts what is being measured. Charles Goodhart, a Bank of England monetary advisor, tells us that every measure that becomes a target, ceases to be a good measure.[70] In the social sphere, Donald Campbell notes that when a quantitative indicator is used for social decision-making, it distorts and corrupts the indicator itself and the social process it was intended to monitor.[71] The same corrupting effect results when educational tests are used as social indicators and targets for accountability.

When the stakes are high, students and educators alter their practices, and at times try to game or beat the system. Teachers in the 2001 national survey acknowledged this gaming. Forty percent of teachers reported that colleagues found ways to raise state-mandated test scores without really improving student learning.[72] When this happens, the test scores increase, but the validity of the scores diminishes. A test is supposed to serve as a representative sample of achievement within a broader domain. Focusing only on the content of past tests narrows coverage of the entire domain. As a result, test scores are no longer useful for making inferences about student achievement across the broader domain.

As a crude analogy of how test scores can corrupt the process of teaching and learning, consider the National Football League's combine. As part of the scouting process, candidates complete a series of activities that include such things as running a 40-yard dash, weight lifting, agility exercises, and an aptitude test. Based on the performance on measures such as these, a combine score is calculated. The score is used to make inferences about a candidate's potential to be a strong NFL player. However, if a candidate dedicated his senior year to training for these tests—in essence becoming faster, stronger, and more agile—it would be possible to score higher on the combines without improving as a player. The targeted preparation deliberately distorts the measure and undermines the validity of the inference about the candidate's potential to be a strong NFL player.

The same holds when instruction is reduced to narrow test preparation. Focusing on test preparation corrupts the score and the test no longer measures what a student knows and is able to do within the broader domain.

A legendary example of wide spread test corruption was exposed in 1987 by John Cannell, a West Virginia pediatrician. Cannell collected standardized test results from states and school districts across the country. He found that most states and districts were reporting above average scores. Cannell's study—nicknamed the *Lake Wobegon Report*, after Garrison Keillor's mythical town where "the women are strong, the men are good-looking, and all the children are above average"—concluded that these results were implausible and misleading.[73] One of the explanations for the above average results was that schools routinely taught directly to the test, and even to specific test questions.[74]

Similar effects of teaching to the test on test scores were found in a 2002 study by Audrey Amerin and David Berliner, researchers at the University of Arizona. After studying high-stakes testing programs in 18 states, they concluded, "While a state's high-stakes test may show increased scores, there is little support... that such increases are anything but the result of test preparation and/or the exclusion of students from the testing programs."[75] Cannell's and Amerin and Berliner' findings demonstrate that emphasis on test preparation distorts the test's ability to validly portray the "true" achievement level of many students.

A similar conclusion was voiced in a New York Times editorial. After supporting high-stakes testing in its editorials for several years, the Times reported on a study that found too much attention placed on test preparation in Chicago's schools came at the expense of high-quality classroom instruction. The editorial's final two lines revealed an important paradox of high-stakes testing—testing is the only way to measure student learning, yet teaching to the test so that students earn high scores is self-defeating.[76]

THE AGENCY THAT CONTROLS A HIGH-STAKES TEST CONTROLS THE CURRICULUM

When a state mandates a high-stakes test, control over the curriculum shifts from local school districts to the state department of education. This shift in power affects a variety of school policies that directly affect individual students and their families, such as entry into kindergarten, retention in grade, summer school programs, length and start of school years, and awarding high school diplomas. An example of a state's high-stakes test controlling local policies comes from Falmouth, Massachusetts. In 2003, the Falmouth school committee decided to continue the practice of awarding a diploma to special needs students who met all the course requirements established by the school district. The state, however, mandated that students had to also pass the state test. Under the threat of losing state funding and the licensure of the school principal and superintendent, the School Committee reluctantly complied with the state policy. This shift in control of the district's graduation policy shattered the hopes of a special needs student seeking admittance to a non-academic culinary degree program.[77]

Three years later, the mayor and school committee of neighboring New Bedford also sought to award diplomas to students who met all local course requirements, regardless of their performance on the state test. When the Governor threatened to withhold $103 million in state funding, this district reversed its decision.[78]

Policies regarding the use of tests established by the federal government also infringe on the states' and the local school districts' control over the curriculum. By mandating which grades and subjects are tested and linking funding to performance on these tests, federal policies drive which areas of the curriculum and grade levels receive more or less attention. These federal policies produce tension between states and the federal government over control of testing and the curriculum and lead to the states filing lawsuits challenging these policies. As an example, Connecticut challenged the policy to administer reading tests at each grade from 3–8, arguing that such testing interferes with their current assessment system without adding additional value.[79]

To be clear, we are not suggesting that a shift in control of the curriculum and educational policies from the district to the state or from the state to the federal government is either desirable or undesirable—that is an ideological, political judgment. It is clear, however, that mandating a high-stakes testing program shifts power to those who establish and control the testing program.

OTHER EFFECTS OF HIGH-STAKES TESTING

Beyond driving teaching and learning, corrupting the test itself, and shifting power, there are at least three other unintended consequences associated with high-stakes testing programs. These consequences include effects on dropout rates, impact on student motivation, and effects on students and their families.

Retention, Dropouts, and High School Completion Rates

A number of studies document the links between high-stakes testing, retention in grade, dropping out of school, and, consequently, high school completion rates. For example, between 1943 and 1967, sixth graders in Ireland were required to sit for a high-stakes test called the Primary Certificate Examination, which certified the successful completion of primary school. Teachers employed a policy of not promoting weaker pupils in order to control the potential failure rate on the sixth grade Primary Cert Exam. Higher retention rates occurred in grades 3 and 5. At that time in Ireland, a pupil held back at one or both points was old enough to leave school before reaching the sixth grade. These school dropouts reduced the number of over age, and often low performing, students taking the Primary Certificate Examination.[80] In 2002, a study of Chicago's high-stakes testing program also revealed higher retention rates in grades other than those in which the test results were used to make promotion decisions.[81]

This influence of high-stakes tests on retention occurs across the United States. In a national survey, 30% of US teachers in states with high-stakes tests reported that state test results were used to promote or retain students in grade.[82] In contrast, only 5% of teachers in states without high-stakes tests reported such practices.

These findings are important given a solid body of research documenting that the negative effects outweigh the intended benefits of retention. For many students, grade retention does not help them improve academically and eats away at their sense of academic worth. Students who are retained once have a higher chance of being retained in grade again. And, most importantly, students who are retained in grade are more likely to drop out of school.[83]

In the United States, research consistently shows that there is a high correlation between high stakes testing programs and higher dropout rates.[84] A study conducted in the 1980s compared ten states that had the highest dropout rates to ten states with the lowest rates. The study found a strong correlation between the use of high-stakes tests and dropout rates.[85] Five states with the lowest dropout rates did not have high-stakes testing programs while the other five states with low dropout rates had testing programs with relatively low stakes.[86] None of the ten low dropout states used tests to make decisions about graduation or grade promotion. In contrast, nine states with the highest drop rates used test results to make decisions about high school graduation and four used test results to make decisions about grade-to-grade promotion.[87]

Another study that examined national data collected between 1988 and 1990 compared drop out rates for students who had to pass one or more high-stakes test in eighth grade versus those who did not have to take a high-stakes test. In schools with high stakes tests, the dropout rates were 4 to 6 percentage points higher than in schools with similar demographics but without a high-stakes test.[88] A 2005 study also found that as pressure exerted by high-stakes testing increases, retention and dropout rates also increase.[89] Studies that focused on high-stakes testing programs in Florida and Texas also found links between graduation tests and dropping out of school.[90] For example, a 2008 study in Texas found that "more than 135,000 youth are lost from the state's high schools every year."[91]

Finally, using data collected over the past 30 years for each state and the nation as a whole, another study tracked cohorts of students as they progressed from kindergarten through grade 12.[92] Funded by the Ford Foundation, the study found a growing bulge of students in the 9th grade, significantly fewer students reaching 10th grade, and major declines in high school completion rates, especially in some of the nation's largest states.[93]

These increases were associated with three reforms—minimum competency testing in the 1970s, standards-based testing in the 1980s, and the high-stakes testing from the 1990s onward. Collectively, these studies show a relationship between the use of high-stakes tests and increased retention and dropout rates.

High-Stakes Tests and Motivation[94]

Proponents of high-stakes testing assert that if test performance is tied to important consequences, fear of a low score will motivate lazy, recalcitrant, or otherwise unmotivated students to work harder and learn more.[95] They also maintain that motivated students will increase our nation's productivity and contribute to the restoration of our global competitiveness.[96]

There is little doubt that attaching high stakes to students' performance will motivate some students to work for good test results. However, the link between high stakes tests and student motivation raises two questions. Why are some students motivated and others not? And, what are students motivated to do?[97]

Why Are Some Students Motivated and Others Not?

Research supports the view that motivation is an important determinant of learning and achievement.[98] Motivation is particularly crucial during adolescence, when students can become increasingly involved in nonacademic activities at the expense of academic work.[99] But the assumption that students who are currently unmotivated will suddenly become motivated by a high-stakes test is an oversimplification.[100] A ninth grade English teacher in an urban school describes that the effect a high-stakes tests has on some students is very different than what is promised by proponents:

> Some of these kids are so upset really... it doesn't motivate them. The legislators don't have a clue. Clearly, whoever thinks that has never been in the classroom. They get upset over it, and they don't try any harder; if anything it becomes a defeatist mentality, especially in a school like this, where they don't get motivated from a challenge, they back down.[101]

For high-stakes tests to increase motivation, students must believe that the rewards attached to test performance are important and realistically within reach. When students believe this, they are more likely to accept the challenge and expend effort to do well on the test. On the other hand, students who perceive their ability to be low tend to avoid challenge, behave helplessly, and have little persistence.

Still other students may believe they have the ability to be successful, but are not motivated to do well on the test. These students do not equate test performance with improved job or college prospects due to the scarcity of jobs or lack of relevance of college in their family and community settings. For them, the rewards for passing the test are illusory. Students who are not motivated by high-stakes testing are more likely to become alienated, not only from the tests but from the entire educational process. These students may react by avoiding academic challenges, quitting school, or just not learning in order to protect their self-esteem.[102]

What Are Students Motivated to Do?

What students are motivated to do is often very different from what proponents assume will happen. As predicted, some students do work hard to pass high-stakes tests. They study harder and some develop intrinsic interest in subjects covered by the tests. Others, however, are extrinsically motivated to pass. Rather than mastering subject matter and honing lasting competencies, they focus on strategies to help them game the test and pay for tutoring and test-preparation courses.

Worse yet, some students cheat. The author Colman McCarthy describes the reaction of high-school students to questions about cheating:

> . . . I asked the students: If during a test the opportunity came to cheat, with no fear of being caught, would you? A majority of hands went up. A few students dismissed the question as naive. Not cheat if you could get away with it? Get real. When speaking at high school assemblies, I ask students how many can raise their hands and say with total honesty that they never cheated in school. Few hands go up. If some brave souls do confess to honesty, they are greeted with jeers or calls of "yeah, right."[103]

While there is not solid data on how much cheating occurs, the pressure exerted by high-stakes tests motivates some students to cheat.

The argument that high-stakes tests motivate unmotivated students is simplistic. For too many students, a high-stakes test simply is unimportant and a non-motivating factor in their lives. For other students, high-stakes tests do motivate them to work harder. Unfortunately, many of them attend schools that reduce the curriculum to what is contained on the high-stakes test. The paradox is that while these students may study harder, their education is narrowed.

Emotional Toll of High-Stakes Test: A Literary Perspective

So far, we have explored historical evidence and findings from recent research that document the many unintended consequences of high-stakes tests on teaching, learning, and schools. Although high-stakes tests are intended to motivate students, the pressure to perform well on these tests also exerts an unintended emotional toll on students and their families. While no one that we are aware of has attempted to quantify this emotional toll, these effects are pervasive throughout literature.

Our late colleague and friend Martin Rafferty chronicled how authors across different literary genres depict testing.[104] One of his findings was that authors—both religious and agnostic—use prayer, religious diction, allusion, and imagery to illuminate the importance of major tests in the lives of students and their families, and show the power of tests to instill anxiety.

An example of prayer is seen in *Malone Dies* where Samuel Beckett describes Mrs. Saposcat praying for [her son's] success on an exam, "Oh God grant he pass, grant he pass, grant he scrape through."[105] Similarly, the Irish novelist John McGahern recounts the prayer of a student facing a university matriculation exam:

> Please God may I not fail.
> Please God may I get over sixty per cent.
> Please God may I get a high place.
> Please God may all those likely to beat me get killed in road accidents and may they die roaring.

Here, the prayer not only focuses on the test taker, but spills over to ill wishes for his fellow classmates. Prayers, however, are not always answered—thankfully in the case of McGahern's student. H. G. Wells recalls his own formal rejection of such pieties at the age of twelve.

> I would pray when I was losing a race, or in trouble in an examination room, or frightened. I expected prompt attention. In my first book-keeping examination . . . I could not get my accounts to balance. I prayed furiously. The bell rang . . . "All right, God," I said, "catch me praying again."[106]

Many of us remember praying for divine intersession before, during, and after important tests. This is an ancient practice. In China, during the 12-century reign of the civil service exam, examinees prayed to specialized exam gods; today in Taiwan those taking the college entrance exams pray to them still.[107] Prayer in the face of a test is such a pervasive practice that Ronald Reagan is purported to have said: "As long as there are exams there will be prayer in school!"

Beyond influencing one's prayer, literature also depicts how high-stakes tests impact one's hopes and aspirations for the future, often employing Biblical metaphors. For example, V.S. Naipaul describes the potential impact of a scholarship exam: "[The winners] were the *elect*, the *anointed*. . . We all knew who among them were *the candidates for glory*. . . I too would be *immortalized* and become *an object of veneration* to succeeding generations."[108]

Conversely, A. A. Milne describes how his poor exam performance evoked the Biblical gesture of doomed resignation from his father: "When he read [the results], father turned his face to the wall, and abandoned hope."[109] John McGahern views the three-hour test as having its parallel with three hours on the Cross.[110]

In addition to religious imagery, Rafferty describes how authors used other metaphors of sport, animals, war, nature, machines, commerce, and the law to express students' and their families' experiences with high-stakes tests. Rafferty recounts how some literary works depict the testing system as a series of obstacles or an elaborate race that sifts out "successful" candidates and fails others.[111] For example, in her book, *That's how it was,* Maureen Duffy portrays tests as a series of hurdles in a race. For some, these hurdles are so high that they are unable to complete the course:

> I thought how it was like *a long-distance run* I'd started on, with people *dropping out* all along the way at the higher and higher *examination hurdles,* until out of sixty-odd children who'd started with me in infants [kindergarten] maybe only *two would ever get all the way* to university.[112]

Other authors employ animal metaphors. In his poem *The Reading Lesson,* Richard Murphy describes a routine classroom examination where the teacher looks at the child and wonders at the contrast between the "natural" world the child instinctively inhabits and the constraining world that schooling and examinations impose:

> Fourteen years old, learning the alphabet,
> He finds letters harder to catch than hares
> Without a greyhound. Can't I give him a dog
> To track them down, or put them in a cage?
> He's caught in a trap, until I let him go....
> He looks at a page as a mule balks at a gap
> From which a goat may hobble out and bleat.
> His eyes jink from a sentence like a flushed snipe Escaping shot.[113]

Rafferty sums up Murphy's analogy, "The animal world is alive and vigorously 'real'; the world of schooling and examinations is alien and constraining: the boy who was the natural 'trapper' is now himself 'caught in a trap'; the hunter has become the hunted."[114]

Still other authors use factory metaphors. Philip Larkin in his book *Jill* describes his scholarship coach relishing the sensation of "manipulating a powerful and delicate machine" (p. 77),... but soon finds that his prize student has become "a mechanical man he had painfully constructed".[115] And Lewis Carroll in *Sylvie and Bruno* uses the metaphor of a machine to describe competitive examinations that "pumped our wells dry before they were quarter full" and "stripped our orchards while the apples are still in blossom."[116]

Rafferty concludes there is, "little doubt that the metaphors and images reecho a prevailing sense of the examination as the unique testing time of youth, their parents, and teachers. Some few students may glory in the challenge, most feel demeaned and used by a system that casts a shadow over schooling and leaves the student as prey to forces he still resents. A fact of life? Perhaps, but certainly not one of adolescence's more pleasant memories."[117]

Today's classroom teachers echo many of the emotional effects of high-stakes tests found throughout literature. Ask any teacher and they can recount the emotional stress high-stakes tests can have on some students. As an example, a fourth-grade teacher in a large urban district recounts the emotional toll of a high-stakes test on her students.

For them to sit in the testing situation for that length of time, they're exhausted... They do very well at the beginning [but] they're so tired at the end that you see a drop off in the test scores... I've seen kids break down: "I'm not doing this." Crying. Complete frustration. I've seen kids get sick to their stomach... a lot of physical things that are responses to stress. And I've also seen kids do the reverse. Kids who didn't do so well during the year who really shine on the test.[118]

A teacher in a suburban elementary school describes the severe reaction one student had while taking a high-stakes test.

> We had one little boy who had an accommodation to work on the computer [for] the long compositions... and what normally took children anywhere from two [to three] hours... took this poor child two days. And by... the second day, he wet his pants he was so nervous and so upset.[119]

A principal in a rural elementary school describes students' anticipation of and reaction to high-stakes tests:

> There were kids in tears over [the test], and there have been for the last two years. Kids who didn't want to come to school. Kids that had stomachaches they never had before, who would just put down their pencils in frustration.[120]

Finally, a middle school teacher in a small urban district describes how students anticipate failure on a high-stakes test they will take in two years and how they wonder what will happen to them as a consequence:

> The students will say to me... 'You know, I've gotten B's and B-pluses, and I've done well all year. Suppose I fail the test in high school, does that mean I don't go anywhere, does that mean that all of these years of work have been no good?' That's their big fear.[121]

These teacher descriptions attest to the fact that many children, motivated or not, experience unintended negative effects when subjected to the pressures of a high-stakes test.

CONCLUSION

The term *iatrogenic* refers to doctor induced illness—that is a negative, unanticipated effect on a patient of a well-intended treatment by a physician.[122] The paradox of high-stakes testing might well be called *peiragenics,* that is the negative, unanticipated effects on students, teachers, and schools of well-intended testing policies.[123]

As we have seen, the negative effects are many. They include narrowing the curriculum, decreasing attention on non-tested subjects, changing pre-school and kindergarten curricula, narrow test preparation, corruption of test results, cheating, triaging "bubble" students, retaining students in grade, increased dropout rates, and increasing student stress and anxiety. All of these paradoxical negative consequences of high-stakes testing are chronic, predictable, and well documented over centuries and across continents.

It is important to recognize, however, that it is not the test per se that causes these disorders. Instead, it is the *stakes* associated with test scores that drive teachers, pupils, and other stakeholders into behavior that results in the many paradoxical unintended outcomes discussed in this chapter. The conundrum in this paradox is that the stakes attached to test results are the driving force of the reform policy. The stakes produce both the salutary effects and the unintended negative consequences.

The debate over the use of tests in policy is really a debate over what we want from our schools. It is a debate over educational values, competing educational philosophies, and is about means and ends. It is not a debate on technical matters related to testing. In fact, if testing is the answer, then we have done a poor job of stating the question. By merely focusing on the tests results we side-step the more crucial question of the proper role of testing.

Medicine offers another apt analogy, namely the systematic evaluation of the impact of new medical technologies or treatments.[124] One such study offered the following advice:

Good decisions cannot be made without an adequate assessment of the relevant facts . . . This evaluation should *assess the likelihood of a favorable outcome and the benefits and burdens to the patient of all possible outcomes. Further, there should be candor not only about what is known, but also about what is unknown.*[125]

This mentality is generally absent in discussions about high-stakes testing programs. Despite the fact that the advantages and disadvantages of such testing programs—for different kinds of students, at different grades and ages, in different kinds of educational settings—are predictable before implementation, too often policy makers ignore them.

This does not mean that we must wait for the "perfect" test—there is no such thing. Nor does it mean that when we find harmful effects—and we will—the program must be scrapped. Medical technology is not perfect; there are potentially harmful side effects associated with treatments determined to be *generally* safe and efficacious. However, we should know the nature and extent of harmful side effects before adopting a high-stakes testing program.

Equally important we need to know how the infrastructures of a high-stakes testing program will change our schools and other social systems. We have to satisfy ourselves that the benefits of the test and its accompanying infrastructures will clearly outweigh the harms before implementation. If we then proceed, we need to monitor effects to see that the benefits continue to outweigh the harms, and to identify any unanticipated negative side effects.

NOTES

1. Shepard (1990, p. 19, emphasis added).
2. In Australia the rigidity of the exams was blamed for a lack of change in the chemistry curriculum for almost 70 years. When the exam was changed the chemistry curriculum changed (Morris, 1969).
3. Oxford English Dictionary (1993).
4. In *De Studiis Adolescentum*, quoted in Hamilton (1853, p. 769).
5. See Popham (1983); Popham (1987); Popham, Cruse, Rankin, Sandifer, & Williams (1985).
6. See Madaus & Kellaghan (1993) for a description of the difficulties of using these kinds of assessments in England. Michael Winerip (2006) writing in the New York Times cited Thomas Toch's research that showed it costs a test company 50 cents to $5 to score an essay, compared with pennies for each multiple-choice question. Lynn Olson (2005) reported on a study by the Government Accountability Office that estimated in 2003 that it would cost states $1.9 billion to meet the testing requirements of NCLB if they used machine scorable multiple-choice questions; $3.9 billion if they used multiple-choice and open-ended items; and up to $5.3 billion if the tests required hand-scored, written responses.
7. National Commission on Testing and Public Policy (1990, p. 19).
8. In a paper prepared for the *National Commission on Testing and Public Policy,* Edward Haertel of Stanford University describes how high-stakes testing can undermine effective instructional practices and narrow the curriculum:

> There has been a subtle shift ... toward instructional activities resembling objective test formats. This shift reflects not only of good student performance, but also the effect of specifying intended learning outcomes in the language of measurable behavioral objectives. Classroom discussion, simulations and small group activities, and extended writing opportunities will do less to improve test scores than will worksheets requiring students to answer brief, isolated questions by filling in blanks or selecting fixed choices. Of course teachers use such activities not primarily to improve test scores, but to foster student learning. *Nonetheless, their use of worksheets and practice tests is likely to increase if they accept objective tests as valid measures of most important learning outcomes. If teachers believe the goal of schooling is to shape a certain behavioral repertoire then worksheets and practice tests are the kinds of instructional activities that make sense* (National Commission on Testing and Public Policy, 1990, pp 20–21, emphasis added). For the entire commissioned paper see Haertel (1989).

9. Gilbert (2008).
10. Cheating was common despite unrelenting measures to prevent it or tough punishment for those caught. From the program's beginning in 606 CE, cheating on the exam that included bribery of officials, the use of hired substitutes to sit the exam, communicated with outside accomplices, and concealed cheat sheets and notes hidden in pockets or sown in the linings of clothing and undergarments or in hollowed out shoe heals or pens. A 2006 news article reported on the discovery of 40 miniature-cheating books from the Qing Dynasty. See The Epoch Times (2006) for details. For a picture of a silk cheating jacket and details of an exhibit on cheating held at Shanghai Museum of Chinese Keju (Imperial Examination) System see China Culture at www.chinaculture.org/gb/en_newupdate/2006-02/23/content_79628.htm.
11. Brown S., Professor of Medieval Philosophy, Boston College, translation, June 1998. The following is an extract from Dr. Brown's translation:

> Recognizing the hard challenge of the many questions and the difficulty in dealing with them, which is especially commonplace in the examinations, because these questions are exceedingly diverse and derived from many different disciplines that have no order or continuity among them, we thought it worthwhile to treat in a certain compendium the questions of the sort that show up along with their solutions and to present them in a certain order and with a certain interconnection to the degree that we are better able to do so, starting first with philosophy, which is the common name given to all these disciplines (Grabmann 1927, translated by Brown).

12. Sheed (1982, p. 117). Today's cramming tactics have expanded beyond books and tutorial establishments to computer programs and Web sites.
13. Fiction, biography, poetry, drama, even the lowly detective novel, all contain a large corpus of information directly from authors who have been through an external examination system and have been eminently successful in later life. This body of evidence comes from the work of our late colleague and friend Martin Rafferty (1985).

14. There is ironic comment on the high-stakes exam's ability to predict future "success." In Ted Allbeury's novel, *The alpha list,* an affluent alumnus who had failed the exam returns to his old grammar school to be greeted by the school-porter with the laconic observation: "It's always the same... Them what was top of the class is working in the library for three quid [English pounds] a week. And the cheeky buggers like you are driving around in Jaguars" (Allbeury, 1979, p. 145), from Rafferty (1985). He also has a similar observation from an Irish author: "The leaving certificate marks a beginning as well as an end, and though the boys at the top of the list start off with a good handicap the boys at the bottom often finish up with bigger cars" (Sheridan, 1949, pp. 86–87).
15. Wells (1892, p. 382).
16. quoted in Kelly (1989, p. 152).
17. Arnold (1867–1868, p. 297).
18. Joshua Fitch (1864–65) similarly charged that the Revised Code "tend[ed] to formalize the work of elementary schools, and to render it in some degree lifeless, inelastic and mechanical. Too many teachers narrow their sense of duty to the six Standards, or what they sometimes call the paying subjects."
19. A Mr. Grove leveled a very similar indictment in 1879; "Upon what is the salary, nay reputation of a teacher made to depend? Upon his ability to turn out so many yards of reading, writing, and arithmetic from his human machines at 3[s] per yard (quoted in Christian, 1922, p. 119). Other commentators on the English system have noted similar effects (e.g., Bell & Grant, 1974; Broadfoot, 1984; Gordon & Lawton, 1978; Holmes, 1911; Morris, 1961).
20. Rafferty (1985, p. 13).
21. White (1888, p. 518). White called for a plan of promoting pupils on the judgment of teachers, approved by the principal. The judgment for promotion would be based on monthly estimates of the "the pupil's fidelity and success in school work" and the ten separate judgments formed the basis for promotion. He argued that "the test, oral and written, is made an element of teaching – not the basis of promotion" (p 519).
22. Spaulding (1938).
23. Travers (1983, p. 143) notes that professors of pedagogy "saw that statewide testing programs had the effect of casting the curriculum into a rigid mold. The professors also realized that testing programs in England had had a disastrous effect on teaching practices."
24. The review was by Abrams, Pedulla, & Madaus (2003). The surveys reviewed were by Corbett & Wilson (1999); Jones, Jones, Hardin, Chapman, & Yarbough (1999); Koretz, Barron, Mitchell, & Keith (1996); McMillan, Myran, & Workman (1999); Pedulla et al. (2003); Romberg, Zarinia, & Willams (1989); Smith (1991); Stecher, Barron, Chun, & Ross (2000). Gipps et al (1991) also found increased stress and decreased teacher morale in their survey of British teachers working in a high-stakes testing situations. Teacher stress ranged from reported "general pressure" to manifestations of temper, tension, tiredness, and tears to stress related illness and absence. It was likely there was even more stress beneath the surface, brought on by continuous focused efforts of concentration needed to observe pupils perform the same exercises over and

over again. For more details on high-stakes testing's impact on British teachers see Madaus & Kellaghan (1993).

25. For details see Pedulla et al. (2003). Differences were statistically significant (alpha < .001).
26. Teachers' response to the statement "The state-mandated testing program leads some teachers in my school to teach in ways that contradict their own ideas of good educational practice" is also very interesting. While 76% of teachers in high-stakes states reported that they taught in ways that contradict notions of good educational practice, a surprising 63% of teachers in states with low or moderate stakes agreed. Regardless of the stakes associated with a state test, just having a state mandated test influences how teachers teach. One possible explanation is that local officials use the results of a state test in ways that teachers perceive have serious consequences for students – retention in grade—or for themselves—financial incentives or evaluations.
27. Russell & Abrams (2004).
28. Field work notes from USEIT study, see Russell, O'Dwyer, Bebell, & Miranda (2004).
29. See Clarke et al. (2003) for details.
30. The reader is urged to look at the entire range of educator comments contained in Clarke et al. (2003). It is much richer than any sample can hope to convey.
31. See Madaus, West, Harmon, Lomax, & Viator (1992) for details and methodology. High-minority classrooms contained 60% or more minority students. Low-minority classrooms had 10% or fewer minority students.
32. See Lomax, West, Harmon, Viator, & Madaus (1996).
33. See DeMarco (2005, emphasis added).
34. National Research Council (2007).
35. For insight into how important the arts can be in the lives of 5th graders see *Mad Hot Ballroom,* a documentary film on ballroom dancing taught in the New York City schools.
36. Sternberg (2006).
37. While it may seem obvious that increasing focus on tested subjects must decrease focus on non-tested subjects, policy-makers and public leaders seem unaware of this conundrum. An example is found in an Op-Ed piece by former Supreme Court Justice Sandra Day O'Connor and Roy Romer, former Governor of Colorado, and Superintendent of the Los Angeles Unified School District. They acknowledge the need to improve math and science education and early literacy, but go on to recommend more classes on government, law, history, and current events (O'Connor & Romer, 2006). Given finite time in the school day, it is not feasible to continue the amount of time dedicated to math, science, and early literacy while also increasing time for government, law, history, and current events.

    Interestingly, two years later, O'Connor recognized that an unintended affect of the No Child Left Behind Act was that it squeezed out Civics education because it was not tested (Schiesel (2008).
38. Little (1993).
39. Meng (1993).

40. Herbet concluded:

> What is learnt is learnt in the wrong way. It is learnt to produce at a certain moment and then thrown away. It has well been called a vast jumble of information that, like a ship's cargo is packed, labeled and laded, and then having reached its destination is unladed, consigned, and done with ... The men, who are not fitted to gain prizes, suffer. There is generally real power of a certain kind in these men, possibilities of interest and successful devotion to work, but these things are not discovered in them by others under our present system, nor are they allowed to discover them for themselves (Herbert, 1889, pp. 176–178).

41. Quoted in Smith (1931, p. 254, emphasis added).
42. Smith (1931, p. 263). In a similar vein in 1872 the political economist William Hearn, observed that because the examinations concentrated on reading, writing and arithmetic instruction found its level and "higher branches of instruction" were neglected.
43. Huxley (1870, p. 4). We are indebted to Brendan Rappel of Boston College for this quote.
44. Orwell (1968, p. 336).
45. Pedulla et al. (2003).
46. Clarke et al. (2003).
47. Center on Educational Policy (2006a); Center on Educational Policy (2006b). When published in March of 2006, the CEP study was the most comprehensive national investigation of the impact of NCLB; it included a survey of education officials in 50 states, a nationally representative survey of 299 school districts, and in-depth case studies in 38 geographically diverse districts and 42 individual schools. Another 2006 survey, that of Vermont teachers found that 46% reported that "enriching activities" are less possible and 50% reported that such activities were "much less possible." See Rapp (2006).
48. Center on Educational Policy (2006b, p. 11).
49. Center on Educational Policy (2006a, p. 2).
50. Center on Educational Policy (2006a, p. 2). A spate of 21st century news stories also highlight the negative impact high-stakes tests have on non-tested subjects. See for example, Dillon (2006); MacPherson (2004); Peristein (2004).
51. Rose & Gallup (2007).
52. National PTA (2006).
53. See Kellaghan & Greaney (1992) for data in how this happened in African schools; for American data see Cunningham (1989); Kamii (1990); Koretz (1995); Meisels (1989); Shepard & Smith (1986); Shepard & Smith (1988); Shepard & Smith (1989); Smith & Shepard (1988).
54. Shepard & Smith (1988).
55. Abrams & Madaus (2003); Koretz et al. (1996); Stecher, Barron, Kaganoff, & Goodwin (1998); Taylor, Shepard, Kinner, & Rosenthal (2003).
56. Koretz et al. (1996).
57. National Institute of Education (1981).
58. Pedulla et al. (2003); Taylor et al. (2003).

59. This is a classic trait/method measurement problem that states, for the most part, have ignored; the method you use to measure a trait or skill differentially affects how different students perform.
60. See Shorrocks, Daniels, Stainton, & Ring (1993) for details. The study also showed that student demographics and performance on a high-stakes test were strongly related. Seven-year old pupils from advantaged backgrounds were twice as likely to score above average marks in high-stakes British *Standardized Assessment Tasks* (SATs), than those from poorer areas. In mathematics the difference was five times greater. Also see Madaus & Kellaghan (1993) for further findings on the SATs in Great Britain.
61. See Kellaghan & Greaney (1992) for a more on this aspect of high-stakes testing; also see Little (1982); Lomax et al. (1996); Madaus & Greaney (1985); Madaus (1988); Madaus & Kellaghan (1992); West & Viator (1992).
62. Pedulla et al. (2003).
63. Booher-Jennings (2005, p. 241). It should be noted that these students falling 1–2 points below the cut score could easily be "false negatives" given the measurement error of the test (cf Chapters 3 & 4).
64. Rapple (2004).
65. For example, a 2004 article by Los Angeles Times reporter Joel Rubin described California teachers' use of this practice in response to the demands of NCLB. He writes:

    > [E]ducation experts and school officials say they are paying increasing attention to the middle-of-the-road students who have fallen just short of test requirements... This new focus on so-called "cusp" or "bubble" students, many experts say, is an unintended consequence of a law that emphasizes test scores and defines success in narrow terms.

    For further details see Rubin (2004).
66. Benton (2005).
67. Orwell (1968, p. 337). It is interesting that the first letters of each word describe most but not all the battles.
68. Keillor (1985, p. 29).
69. This account was provided by the late professor of measurement at the University of Chicago, Benjamin Bloom.
70. Goodhart's Law is named for the economist Charles Goodhart, a Bank of England monetary adviser for seventeen years who became Chief Advisor in 1980. His law first stated in 1975 is the economist's version of the Heisenberg Uncertainty Principle in quantum mechanics. For a detailed history and treatment of the Law see Chrystal & Mizen (2001).
71. Campbell (1975).
72. Pedulla et al. (2003). Two corporate examples reinforce this corrupting effect and have important implications for current attempts to link teacher compensation to student test performance. First, early in the 21st century the country learned of erroneous profit statements by some companies. These bogus profit statements resulted from two related forces; during the market boom of the 1990s investors paid attention to sales growth, which became crucially linked to rising stock prices; executives stood to benefit personally by higher revenue

figures because of the way their compensation package was calculated. These factors lead to quantitative profit statements being corrupted through dubious accounting procedures (Morgenson, 2002). Second, in 1992, Sears Auto Centers eliminated its commission-based pay structure after it was charged with systematically defrauding customers with unnecessary repairs. Sears' chairman admitted that the incentive compensation program and sales goals created an environment where mistakes occurred (Fisher, 1992).

73. The Lake Wobegon effect seems to be alive and well today in Connecticut. On September 28, 2007, a headline in the New London Day read, "Waterford Sophomores Are Above Average In All Categories in the CAPT Test." The CAPT is the state test used in Connecticut.
74. Cannell (1987); Cannell (1989). Cannell's conclusion was strongly attacked by test publishers and other critics. Nonetheless, a study funded by the U.S. Department of Education, confirmed Cannell's basic finding that test results across the nation were inflated (See Koretz, 1988; Linn, Graue, & Sanders, 1990). Another study found that the conditions producing that inflation, such as important rewards and sanctions directly linked to test results, efforts to align curricula with the tests, and direct teaching to the tests, existed in virtually all the states (Shepard, 1990).
75. Amerin & Berliner (2002).
76. *New York Times* editorial (2008, June 19).
77. Myers (2003).
78. Lang (2006).
79. Another example is from Nebraska, which allows each of its 254 local school districts to develop its own assessments of student achievement (Reutter, 2006). The federal government, however, argues that these local assessments provide inadequate technical information. In an effort to force Nebraska to adopt a single statewide test, the federal government designated Nebraska's assessment system as "not approved"—a status that could have lead to withholding federal funding. In September of 2006, after considerable negotiation, Nebraska's Commissioner of Education announced that the federal government reversed its earlier decision. Nebraska educators as well as national assessment experts will visit all 254 school districts to review how schools assess students on state reading and mathematic standards. The results of those reviews will help districts assess student learning and also meet the U.S. Department of Education's documentation requirements.
80. For details see Madaus & Greaney (1985).
81. Jacob (2002).
82. The wording of the survey question does not allow us to separate state policies regarding promotion and local school or district policies regarding the use of test results for promotion.
83. See Darling-Hammond & Falk (1997); Hauser (2000); Jimerson, Anderson, & Whipple (2002); National Research Council (2001); Shepard & Smith (1988); Shepard & Smith (1989b); Shepard & Smith (1990); Shepard & Smith (1989a).
84. This section comes from a review by Clarke, Haney, & Madaus (2000).
85. See Kreitzer, Haney, & Madaus (1989).

86. Four used the tests to decide about remediation; only one used them for accountability.
87. These correlational studies do not necessarily mean that high stakes testing programs caused the higher dropout rates; one cannot infer causality from correlational data.
88. See Reardon (1996).
89. Nichols, Glass, & Berliner (2005).
90. See Griffin & Heidorn (1996) for data from Florida. See Fassold (1996); Haney (2001a); Haney (2001b) for Texas data.
91. McNeil, Coppola, Radigan, & Heilig (2008).
92. These data do not permit the tracking of individual students. A longitudinal study at the individual level is badly needed.
93. Mortality, migration, private school enrollment, and home schooling cannot explain the 9th grade bulge nor the broad trends in public school enrollment and graduation. For details see Haney et al. (2004).
94. Material for this section comes from Clarke et al. (2003); Kellaghan & Madaus (1993); Kellaghan, Madaus, & Raczek (1996).
95. For examples of this rhetoric see Kellaghan & Madaus (1993); Kellaghan et al. (1996). These contemporary declarations about the motivational efficacy of high-stake tests are strikingly similar to those the utilitarians made in support of the introduction of high-stakes examinations in 19th century Britain: self interest is the main motive for study, and since study involves drudgery it is necessary to link important rewards or sanctions to successful test performance. The arguments in support of external examinations also seem at times to be heavily influenced by behavioral psychology's assertion that important behaviors are governed by their consequences—the reinforcers and punishers that follow in a given situation. See Skinner (1953).
96. Jeannie Oakes succinctly summed up the reasoning inherent in such arguments: A national examination and certification system will pressure schools to improve; entice students to put forth more effort, and, thereby, raise student achievement. These changes, in turn, will lead to a more skilled, productive, and competitive workforce; and [here she quotes John Scully, then chair of the National Center for Education and the Economy, in a letter to the editor of *The Atlantic*, May 1991] ultimately guarantee the quality of life for us and future generations (Oakes, 1991, p. 17).
97. Kellaghan (1996).
98. Lens (1994).
99. Anderman & Maehr (1994).
100. In industrial settings, some motivational models are predicated on the belief that external rewards lead to improved performance and productivity. However, another belief is that while financial incentives are a powerful motivator, nothing will motivate some workers (Prescico, 1990; Staw, 1976). For example, Howell (1991) concluded that "80% to 85% of employees are willing to put forth the *effort* to do a good job . . . 10% of the people have to be constantly *managed* into doing an acceptable job, and 5% aren't going to work regardless" (p. 20, emphasis in original). In this context, it is of interest that the 1995 National Employer Survey, administered by the Bureau of the Cen-

sus, found that employers reported that just over 80% of their workers were entirely proficient in their current jobs. The 20% judged to be not fully proficient either lacked necessary skills or the skill requirements for the job had increased (National Center on the Educational Quality of the Workforce & Bureau of the Census, 1995). Nonetheless, these percentages are not directly applicable to education. Kellaghan & Madaus (1993) found that the use of extrinsic motivation techniques in industry seem to have little relevance for examinations. In the industrial situation, skills have already been acquired, feedback mechanisms are well developed and relatively immediate, rewards are tangible and also immediate, and serve to reinforce and direct behavior. None of these conditions holds for external examinations. While no-pass no-play or no-pass no-drive programs are closer to the examination situation than industrial analogs, they do not seem to work very well, even though they are more immediate and real in their consequences for many students than examinations.

101. Clarke et al. (2003, p. 85).
102. A student's age is another important factor that limits the motivational effect of a high-stakes test. Even when the importance of a test is communicated to students, if it is remote in time—months and perhaps several grades away—one has to question the relevance for young children.
103. McCarthy (2006, p. A21). For additional examples of contemporary instances of cheating world wide see the excellent website Caveon Test Security at http://www.caveon.com/.
104. Rafferty (1985).
105. Beckett (1956, p. 35).
106. Wells (1934, p. 71).
107. Suen & Yu (2006).
108. Naipaul (1984, pp. 66–67, emphasis added).
109. Milne (1930, p. 112).
110. McGahern (1977).
111. Rafferty (1985, p. 268).
112. Duffy (1962, p. 210, emphasis added).
113. Murphy (1975, p. 43).
114. Rafferty (1985, p. 277).
115. Larkin (1947, p. 77 & p. 83).
116. Carroll (1982, p. 564).
117. Rafferty (1985, p. 302).
118. Clarke et al. (2003, p. 84).
119. Op sit, page 83.
120. Op sit, page 82.
121. Op sit, page 82.
122. Another example comes from the environmentalists. Removing "air-borne pollutants" such as fine particles, mercury, and sulphur dioxide will make coal cleaner and hence be more acceptable to countries with growing environmental concerns. But, paradoxically, it will hasten globe warming "because pollution by particles and sulphur dioxide are key elements of "global dimming," which, by blocking sunlight, acts strongly to cool our planet." Further,

"cleaning" coal itself requires energy that will come from burning more coal. "Thus, paradoxically, 'clean coal' will exacerbate climate change" (Flannery, 2006, p. 24).

123. The Reverend Simon Clyne CM, a friend and colleague, and former president of St. Patrick's Training College, Dublin, Ireland coined this term while working on a project with one of the authors.
124. There are, of course, differences between education and medicine that will affect how this evaluation will be undertaken. Education is a social system in many ways more complex than that of medicine. It is not possible to run limited, controlled experiments to monitor the effects of a new national high-stakes testing program before widespread introduction. There is no independent agency *analogous* to the Food and Drug Administration whose sole job it is to assess the safety and efficacy of new educational technologies or treatments. Finally, the criteria to evaluate the impact of educational technologies are not as straightforward as they are in medicine.
125. LORAN Commission (1988, p. 27, emphasis added).

CHAPTER 9

WHAT IS THE FUTURE OF TESTING?

In economics, the principle of opportunity cost states that a scarcity of resources forces a choice of one action over others.[1] For every action selected, limited resources means that we must forgo alternative actions. As an example, investing $1000 in IBM stock means those funds are no longer available to be invested in Apple Computers or placed in a savings account. Depending on how well IBM stock does relative to alternative investments, the opportunity cost may be very high or insignificant.

In the field of testing, opportunity costs occur when a decision is made to invest financial and human resources in one approach to measuring student learning instead of others. In recent years, federal policy has required state testing programs to invest tax-payer dollars in standards-based high-stakes testing. This policy decision has led testing companies to invest their energy and resources to meet this high-stakes testing demand. These actions by the federal government, state testing programs, and the testing industry have produced opportunity costs. As a nation, we have invested in large-scale, primarily paper-based, high-stakes tests administered to students as a one-time, annual, culminating event. This investment has created an opportunity cost that has stifled enhancements to the technology of testing that will result by merging testing with computer-based technologies.

In 2001, Randy Elliott Bennett, a research scientist for the Educational Testing Service, predicted that computer-based testing would pass through

The Paradoxes of High Stakes Testing, pages 175–196

three evolutionary stages before reaching its full potential. First, Bennett predicted that computers will be used to increase the efficiency of testing. Second, multi-media will be integrated into tests to increase the authenticity of items and tasks presented to students. Finally, computers will be used to deliver tests anywhere and at any time, so that testing becomes more integrated with instruction.

To date, the few testing programs that have embraced computer-based testing have done so solely to increase efficiency. Their goals are quite simple—improve the efficiency with which tests are distributed, decrease the time required to score multiple-choice answers, and increase the speed with which results are reported. While achieving these goals saves time and money, they do not harvest the full benefits of computer-based testing.

In this chapter, we explore five ways in which computer-based technologies could be applied to advance the technology of testing. First, we describe how adaptive testing and automated essay scoring allow testing programs to fully capitalize on the efficiency offered by computer-based technologies. Second, we discuss how computer-based tests can improve validity by applying a concept called universal design—widely used in architecture and civil engineering to improve access for people with physical disabilities. Third, we explore how computers can be used to improve the integration of student assessment with instruction. Fourth, we show how computer-based testing can provide unique, diagnostic information about why some students struggle with a concept or skill. Finally, we describe how computer-based technologies can be used to create interactive simulations that require students to demonstrate skills and knowledge. Before exploring each of these opportunities, we briefly trace the rise of computers in our schools to show that most schools are well-positioned to capitalize on the many advantages offered by computer-based tests—at least as we see them.

THE RISE OF COMPUTERS IN OUR SCHOOLS

Computer-based technologies have had a dramatic impact on our society. They have changed how we conduct business, communicate with friends and family, find information, and entertain ourselves. Computers have also altered the way our automobiles and appliances function, how new products are developed and manufactured, and how money is invested. Although there are some sectors of our society that have managed to remain insulated from the impacts of computers, it is not an overstatement to say that computer-based technologies have had a larger impact in a shorter amount of time than the introduction of any other technology in history.

While computers have not yet had a major impact on education, their availability in schools has changed dramatically over the last three decades.[2]

On average, schools in 1983 had only one computer for every 125 students. In 2006, there was one computer for every four students and more than 1000 schools had implemented programs that provide a laptop for every student and teacher. In addition, nearly every school across the nation had a high-speed connection that provides students and teachers with easy access to the Internet.[3]

The presence of computers in our schools creates valuable opportunities to support educational testing. In fact, according to a 2008 report titled America's Digital Schools, many schools are relying increasingly on computer-based programs to prepare students for testing.[4] According to the report, more than thirty percent of districts across the nation invested in on-line test practice programs in 2007, a dramatic increase from previous years.

In addition, many states are actively exploring or have begun to transition their testing programs to computer. In fact, in 2007, 23 states delivered at least one of their tests on computer.[5] In each case, however, the computer-based test replicated the paper-based testing experience. The same multiple-choice and short answer test items were simply presented on a computer instead of paper. And instead of bubbling in circles, students clicked to record their answer. While using computers to mimic paper-based testing increases efficiency, it does little to advance the technology of testing—at least as we see the potential.

COMPUTER ADAPTIVE TESTING AND AUTOMATED ESSAY SCORING

Advances in psychometric techniques have produced two cutting edge approaches to testing. The first, called computer adaptive testing, increases the efficiency of testing by tailoring the items presented to an individual based on how previous items were answered. The second, called automated essay scoring, employs text analysis techniques to score written responses. As you will see, both techniques hold potential to further improve the efficiency of current approaches to computer-based testing.

Computer Adaptive Testing

A traditional test requires all students to answer the same set of items. On an adaptive test, each item presented to a student is tailored according to answers on previous items. Tailoring items presented to each examinee is a more efficient method for locating a student's achievement level.

The way an adaptive test works is analogous to the way a blood-hound tracks a person. The hound is given a scent and asked to find the person.

Initially, the dog moves quickly through an area taking in samples of odors. When it catches a trace of the targeted scent, it takes finer samples. When it passes the target, it doubles back, covers a smaller area and takes even finer samples. Each time it misses the target, it doubles back, takes finer samples, and further restricts the search area. Finally, it locates the person.

Similarly, an adaptive test begins by presenting items that range widely in difficulty. This initial sample of items is used to acquire a general sense of a student's achievement level. If a student answers most of the first set of items correctly, the student is presented with an item that requires a higher level of achievement to solve. If the student answers that item incorrectly, an item that requires a slightly lower level of achievement is presented. Depending on how the student performs on that item, the next item will require a slightly higher or lower level of achievement.

For a student who answers only a few of the initial set of items correctly, the test adapts and presents an item that requires a lower level of achievement to answer correctly. If the student misses that item, the test adapts to present an item that is less difficult. If the student then answers that item correctly, a slightly more difficult item is presented. This iterative procedure is repeated for each individual student until a stable estimate of the student's achievement level is reached.

Not requiring students with a high achievement level to answer very easy items and not requiring a student with a lower achievement level to answer very difficult items increases the test's efficiency. This increased efficiency allows an adaptive test to produce a reliable estimate of a student's achievement using half the number of items required by a traditional test.[6]

Realizing the value of this increase in efficiency, in 2002 four states began to implement adaptive testing. Federal officials, however, ruled that states could not use adaptive tests to meet the requirement of No Child Left Behind for two reasons. First, they felt that comparisons among students would not be comparable unless all students took the same set of items. Second, they feared that an adaptive test might present low achieving students with items that were below their current grade level.[7]

This ruling sparked a debate lasting nearly four years. After it was shown that an adaptive test could be designed to prevent below grade level testing and that tailoring items produced comparable scores, federal officials reversed their ruling. But it was too late. States had already signed multi-year contracts with test vendors to produce traditional tests. While some high-stakes testing programs may eventually re-embrace adaptive testing, the ruling by federal officials has severely curtailed the adoption of adaptive testing—an opportunity cost that decreases the efficiency of today's high-stakes tests.

Automated Essay Scoring

The thought of a computer scoring an essay is discomforting for many people. Judging the quality of writing is subjective. Writing, after all, is more than merely putting words on paper—it is about expressing thoughts, feelings, desires, and ideas with creativity and style. How can a computer differentiate great writing from good? The simple answer is, it cannot. High-stakes tests, however, do not measure a student's ability to write creatively or with style. Instead, today's writing prompts ask students to create either informative or persuasive essays.

Informative essays require students to communicate their understanding of a given topic. On a social studies test, the topic might include the causes of the American Revolution or the Civil War, the long-term effects of Jim Crow laws or American Imperialism, or the relationship between the Cold War and McCarthyism. For a science test, students may be asked to describe the carbon or water cycles, the concept of heredity, the law of conservation of energy, or how to determine whether a substance is acidic or basic. An English test may ask students to compare and contrast the conflict in two novels, describe how an author employed foreshadowing, or describe how the setting affected the mood of a scene.

Persuasive essays typically present students with an issue, require them to take a side, and present an argument to convince the reader that their position is correct. Students may be asked to write a letter to a school principal or political leader about a controversial topic. They might be asked to write an opinion column for their school or local newspaper about a specific topic. Or students may be asked to interpret a passage or poem, form an argument, and persuade the reader that their position is correct.

Both informative and persuasive essays limit the focus of student writing by requiring them to address a specific topic. Focusing students on a specific topic is designed to produce objective scores. Training readers to apply very specific criteria when scoring an essay further increases objectivity. The scoring criteria are designed to focus readers on specific aspects of the essay and thereby decrease the relevance of other characteristics such as style and creativity. In fact, readers are not allowed to score essays until they demonstrate that they have narrowed their focus to the specific criteria. Once trained, a cadre of readers then scores thousands of essays.

Having humans apply specific criteria to score thousands of essays is time consuming and expensive. Capitalizing on the objectivity instilled in readers during training procedures, automated essay scoring holds promise to greatly reduce the time and cost of scoring essays while producing equally objective scores.

Today, there are several different computer algorithms used to score essays. Each follows the same four steps. First, a small number of human readers are trained and then score a relatively small set of essays.

Second, a computer-based scoring model is developed. To develop a scoring model, a sample of essays along with the scores awarded by human readers is analyzed. This analysis quantifies several features of the essays including the frequency of specific words, word combinations, phrases, grammar errors, spelling errors, and other semantic characteristics. These frequencies are used to create a model that predicts the human score, which generally ranges from 1 to 4 or 1 to 6. In reality, the computer algorithm does not actually award a score to an essay, but instead predicts the score that a human reader is likely to award the essay given the presence of the identified features.

Third, to check the accuracy of the scoring model, a second set of essays scored by human readers is entered into the system. The scoring model calculates a score for each essay, and the scores awarded by the human readers and the scoring model are compared. In many cases, the level of agreement between the human reader and the model exceeds 95%.[8] This level of agreement is often the same or higher than the level of agreement that occurs when two human readers are used to score the same set of essays.

Fourth, when high levels of agreement result, the scoring model is applied to the full set of essays. If agreement is unacceptable, the model is adjusted until a satisfactory level of agreement is reach. Once reached, scores for thousands of students are produced in a matter of hours instead of weeks and costs are reduced dramatically.

Beyond improving the efficiency with which essays are scored, automated essay scoring also has potential to increase the authenticity of writing tests. Most high-stakes writing tests require students to produce an essay working independently for a relatively short period of time. Most writing created outside of a testing situation, however, is produced over an extended period of time, during which authors share their work with others, receive feedback, and make revisions. In a testing situation, however, an automated essay scoring algorithm could help mimic this writing process by providing preliminary feedback to students about their initial draft.

After working on an essay for a given period of time, a student could submit their essay for a preliminary score. Depending on the algorithm used, the student might receive several scores, one focusing on English conventions, another on content, and another on structural elements. Based on this information, the student would have an opportunity to reflect on his writing, make revisions, and then submit it for a formal score. Regardless of whether the final score is awarded by a human reader or a computer algorithm, allowing students to receive preliminary feedback and then revise their writing provides a better representation of the writing process and may result in more valid measures of student writing abilities.

While automated essay scoring has proven effective for persuasive and informative essays, it is highly unlikely that it would be useful for tests that attempt to measure creative writing or style. Nonetheless, for today's high-stakes tests which focus primarily on informative and persuasive writing, automated essay scoring holds promise to increase the efficiency of scoring and improving the authenticity of the writing process employed during testing.

UNIVERSALLY DESIGNED TESTS

In the field of electrical engineering, the ratio of signal to noise is an important measure of the quality of a product. Whether the product produces sound, video images, or power, engineers maximize the signal and minimize noise. In testing, the concept of signal to noise is also important. In chapter 3, we learned that a test provides a sample of behavior from a given domain and that a test score is used to make an inference about a student's achievement within that domain. We also learned that every test score contains error. In essence, the inference made based on a test score is the signal that represents the student's performance within a domain. Error is noise that distorts the signal. As error (noise) is reduced, the inference (signal) is strengthened.

According to test developers, the error associated with a student's test score is supposed to be random. Feeling ill, being momentarily distracted by noise or movement in the room, mis-marking an answer sheet, and guessing correctly on an item are all random events that may affect a student's test score. These random events produce random error.

Some error, however, is not random, but occurs systematically due to specific attributes of an individual student. The design of a test often causes these attributes to limit the student's ability to demonstrate what he or she actually knows or can do. For example, a student with dyslexia struggles to read word problems on a mathematics test, and has trouble understanding what is being asked in the problem or does not have time to complete all problems on the test. A student with impaired vision has difficulty reading graphs or figures that contain fine lines or tightly packed information, and consistently makes errors or skips the items entirely. Another student with an information processing disorder becomes over-stimulated when working on an item that contains a narrative, images, multiple answer options, requires the use of a formula sheet and a calculator. All of these students may have a firm grasp of the concept being measured, but each student has difficulty demonstrating their knowledge or ability due to the design of the test items.

In each of these examples, error occurs systematically due to an attribute unrelated to what the test is trying to measure. Dyslexia negatively affects a student's ability to decode text, but the test is measuring mathematics ability. Vision and information processing are important, but mathematics tests are not designed to measure these attributes.

To decrease the affect that these attributes—decoding, vision, information processing, etc.—have on test performance, students are provided with test accommodations. A test accommodation involves changing the setting, presentation, or delivery of the test, or the way in which a student responds to items. For students with dyslexia, reading aloud text on a mathematics, science, or history test is a common accommodation. Reading aloud text decreases the noise caused by dyslexia. A large print or Braille version of the test decreases noise caused by low vision. A student with an information processing disorder is provided with just one item on each page and is allowed to use sheets of paper to mask or hide portions of an item on which he is not currently focusing. Accommodations are designed to decrease noise and maximize the strength of an inference based on a student's test score. Without accommodations, many students are at a disadvantage in demonstrating what they actually know and can do.

Unfortunately, there is ample evidence that high-stakes testing programs struggle to provide appropriate accommodations for students with disabilities and special needs. For example, in February of 2002 a Federal District Court placed a temporary injunction that halted the administration of California's High School Exit Exam to students with disabilities and special needs because there was compelling evidence that appropriate accommodations were not being provided to students.[9]

A separate study examined the quality with which items were read aloud to visually impaired students. The study found at least four problems with this accommodation. First, readers varied widely in their accents, intonation, and fluidity. Second, readers occasionally mispronounced or misread words. Third, readers provided unintentional and intentional hints to the answer. Finally, participants were reluctant to ask for an item or part of an item to be re-read.[10] Although students were provided with a read aloud accommodation, it did not provide students with an adequate opportunity to show what they knew or could do because the accommodation was not delivered in a standardized or equitable manner. A third study found similar shortcomings with other test accommodations and concluded, "few tests are valid for use with students with sensory disabilities, and the adaptations made by uninformed professionals can result in both over- and under-estimates of an individual student's potential" (Bowen & Ferrell, 2003, p. 10).

Four factors make it difficult for traditional paper-based testing programs to provide adequate test accommodations. First, it is expensive to provide different versions—Braille, large print, one item per page—of paper-based test materials that meet the needs of individual students. Second, it is also expensive to provide individual test proctors who read or sign a test. Third, it is difficult for testing programs to standardize the delivery of accommodations provided by a test proctor. Finally, it is impossible to monitor the quality with which accommodations are provided in schools across the state. By combining computer-based technologies and the concept of universal design, however, each of these challenges can be addressed.

Spurred by the Americans with Disabilities Act, universal design is a direct response to design flaws in buildings—staircases, narrow entrances, escalators, high sinks, etc.—that made it difficult for people with physical disabilities to access buildings or use facilities within those buildings. Prior to the act, people with physical disabilities often required assistance from others to ascend staircases or maneuver through tight entryways. In other cases, they were required to use a separate entrance, such as loading docks or doors located on the side or back of a building. In the worst cases, a person was removed from a wheel chair and carried into a building. Universal design overcomes these obstacles by purposefully designing buildings so that they provide a choice of convenient and appropriate options when accessing a building, or using specific facilities.

Applying the principal of universal design to a high-stakes test assures that all students have access to the tools they need to demonstrate what they actually know and can do. Just as it is no longer acceptable to design and build a structure that requires a person with a physical disability to use a doorway located in the back of the building, a high-stakes test should not require students with disabilities and special needs to take a test that is separate and distinct from that which is used by all other students. Just as it is unreasonable to require people with a physical disability to bring their own ramp to ascend a staircase, a testing program should not require students or their school to purchase special software in order to take a test. Instead, a universally designed test should be usable by all students, regardless of their disability or special need.

Imagine for a moment four students. Beth reads at grade level and does not have any disabilities or learning challenges. She is representative of the 85% of students who perform most high-stakes tests without accommodations. Paul has dyslexia and an attention deficit disorder. He often needs assistance decoding text and finds it easier to concentrate while listening to background music or white noise. Sue has low vision and finds it easier to read text when it is presented in a larger font. Increasing contrast by using a yellow font on a black background also helps her see text more clearly. Finally, Sam is deaf and is reading below grade level. While he is able to read most text, it takes him a long time to do so. When taking mathematics, science, or social studies tests, he often finds it easier to focus on the problems if text is signed to him.

Today, these four students are taking a high-stakes mathematics test. When each student logs in, the computer-based testing system accesses his user profile to activate specific tools needed to enable him to demonstrate what he actually knows and can do. Beth does not need any accommodations. Her screen does not contain any additional tools or features, but simply presents each item and allows her to respond by clicking on what she believes is the correct answer (see Figure 9.1).

On Paul's screen, there are two tools (see Figure 9.2). The first tool reads aloud mathematics items so that Paul does not need to decode text. The second tool allows him to listen to white noise or pre-approved sound tracks while working on the items—a strategy that allows Paul to concentrate better.

Sue's screen displays each item in a magnified form (see Figure 9.3). As she works, she can adjust the magnification level depending on her need. When looking at graphs, she tends to increase magnification. When reading text, a lower level of magnification works best, for her. In addition, Sue's screen displays all text in yellow and has made the background black.

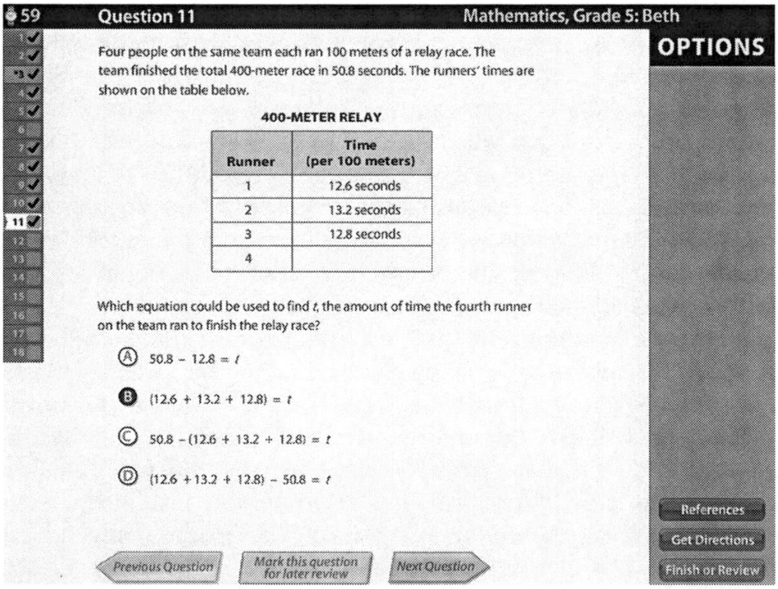

59 Question 11 Mathematics, Grade 5: Beth

OPTIONS

Four people on the same team each ran 100 meters of a relay race. The team finished the total 400-meter race in 50.8 seconds. The runners' times are shown on the table below.

400-METER RELAY

Runner	Time (per 100 meters)
1	12.6 seconds
2	13.2 seconds
3	12.8 seconds
4	

Which equation could be used to find *t*, the amount of time the fourth runner on the team ran to finish the relay race?

Ⓐ 50.8 − 12.8 = *t*

Ⓑ (12.6 + 13.2 + 12.8) = *t*

Ⓒ 50.8 − (12.6 + 13.2 + 12.8) = *t*

Ⓓ (12.6 + 13.2 + 12.8) − 50.8 = *t*

Previous Question | Mark this question for later review | Next Question

References | Get Directions | Finish or Review

Figure 9.1 Beth's screen with no accommodation tools activated. To view a color version of this figure, please visit www.infoagepub.com/madaus_paradoxes.

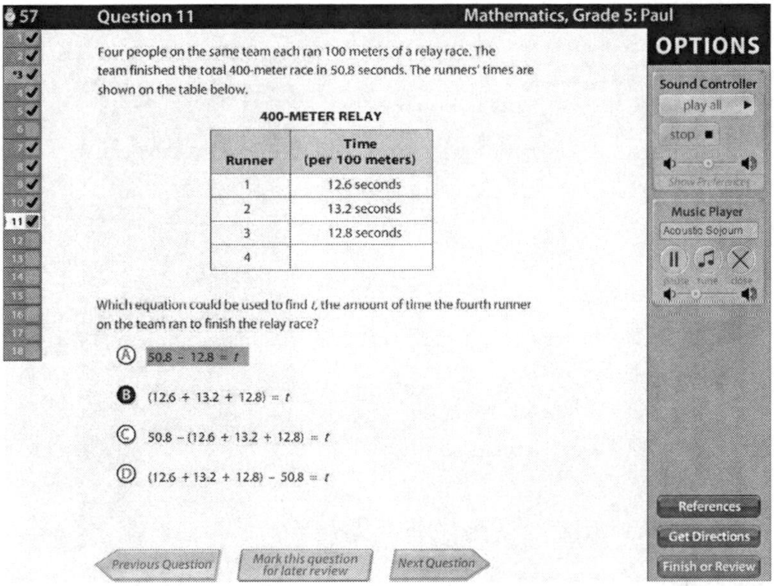

Figure 9.2 Paul's screen with the read aloud and auditory calming tools. To view a color version of this figure, please visit www.infoagepub.com/madaus_paradoxes.

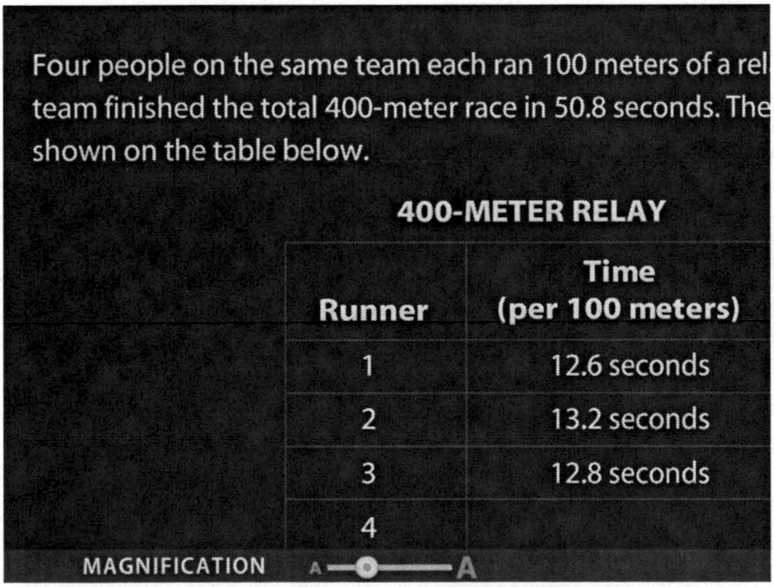

Figure 9.3 Sue's screen with magnification and yellow on black contrast. To view a color version of this figure, please visit www.infoagepub.com/madaus_paradoxes.

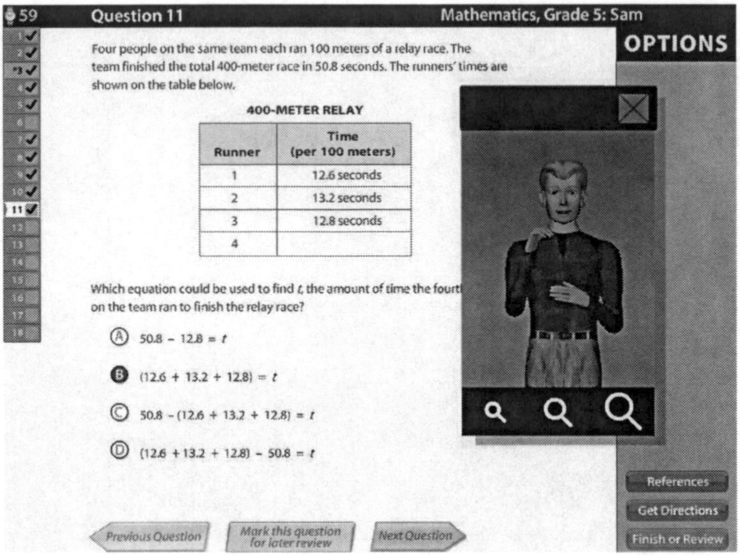

Figure 9.4 Sam's screen with signing. To view a color version of this figure, please visit www.infoagepub.com/madaus_paradoxes.

Finally, Sam's screen contains a window that displays a video of a person signing text (see Figure 9.4). As Sam begins an item, he can have the video display signing of the entire item. If he wants to re-read a portion of text, he highlights it and the video jumps to the corresponding section to display signing of that text.

Rather than creating and distributing separate versions of the test or requiring students to work in separate rooms with an individual test proctor, a universally designed computer-based system can deliver a test tailored to all students. Building in reading and signing assures that all students receive the same high quality presentation of text, with accurate pronunciation of all words, free from inadvertent (or intentional) clues. Students are then free to have text read or signed as many times as needed without feeling embarrassed or that they are overtaxing the test proctor. Clearly, combining principles of universal design with computer-based technologies holds tremendous potential to increase test validity for students with disabilities and special needs. Moreover, just as the option of displaying a television program with closed captioning has proven useful for many purposes beyond increasing access for the hearing impaired—watching television in a noisy bar or airport gate, or late at night while a spouse sleeps—it is likely that universally designed computer-based tests will come to benefit a wide spectrum of students in various unanticipated ways.

FREQUENT TESTS INTEGRATED WITH INSTRUCTION

For many students, teachers, and schools, a high-stakes test is like the Super Bowl. It is a culminating annual event, the outcome of which defines a student's attainment, a teacher's success, or a school's quality. When the goal of a program is to identify "winners" and "losers," an annual high-stakes test provides a definitive outcome. But, when the goal is to provide information that can improve performance, a one-time event has little utility. The Patriots might learn something from their Super Bowl loss, but those lessons cannot be applied until the next season, if at all. The same holds for a high-stakes test. There are three shortcomings of a once-a-year high-stakes test that limit its instructional value.

First, the long gap between when a student takes a test and when scores are reported renders most test scores ineffective for helping that student learn. A high-stakes test will indicate that some students are not performing as well as a teacher may have thought. But the teacher does not receive this information for several months. By then, the students have moved on to new topics, a new grade level, or a new school.

Second, many months pass between when a teacher helps a student learn a given skill or knowledge and when that skill or knowledge is measured by an annual high-stakes test. The gap between instruction and when a high-stakes test is administered precludes teachers from using the results to tailor instruction.

Third, using a single high-stakes test to sample an entire year's worth of content and skill means that the information available for any one content area or skill is extremely limited or non-existent. A teacher may spend several weeks teaching students about the water cycle, yet the test includes only one item on the concept.

To increase content coverage, some test items attempt to measure multiple skills. For example, a single item might require students to read a graph, create ratios, and then evaluate those ratios to solve a word problem. For a student who misses this single item, teachers cannot determine why. The student may have had difficulty reading the graph, creating ratios, evaluating the ratios, performing basic arithmetic, or some combination of these difficulties.

Reporting delays, timing delays, and limited content coverage combine to prevent current high-stakes tests from providing teachers with the specific information needed to help them improve student learning. Computer-based testing, however, holds potential to ameliorate these shortcomings.

Instead of administering a single test once a year, a testing program could provide a broader sample of the domain by creating a set of short computer-based tests. Each test might focus on a sub-set of skills or knowledge and take about 10 minutes to complete—similar to the short quizzes many readers experienced when they were students. As teachers help students master a given sub-set of skills or knowledge, they could access a menu of short computer-based tests and select the one best aligned with their current instruction. Unlike quizzes of old, teachers could immediately access the test results and decide whether individual students or the class as a whole have acquired sufficient understanding, or need additional instruction. When additional instruction is needed, teachers could then select a different version of the same test to help determine whether students' understanding improved.

For those who want empirical evidence that students are learning, a well-designed series of short tests also provides a database that documents the achievement of a student, classroom, school, district, or state. A set of short frequently administered computer-based tests would provide a larger body of evidence more representative of the domain of interest than does an annual high-stakes test.

Creating a series of tests that measure specific sub-areas of the curriculum is not a new idea. In the early 1960s, the concept of mastery learning was introduced. The underlying assumption of mastery learning was that all students could learn if properly taught. To inform instruction, mastery learning embraced the practice of frequently administering brief tests to determine whether a concept or skill had been mastered before advancing to new material.[11] Mastery learning, however, required teachers to develop their own tests rather than selecting from a set of tests developed by a testing program. In addition, mastery learning required teachers to administer paper-and-pencil tests and score them by hand.

Twenty years later, the Pittsburgh Public Schools modernized this concept by introducing data driven instruction. Each Friday, teachers administered short tests created by the district that measured what was supposed to be taught that week. Student answer sheets were sent to the central office and scored by machine. The results were then returned to teachers early the next week and teachers used those results to modify instruction while preparing students for the next test. Pittsburgh's approach was more efficient than prior attempts at mastery learning and was state-of-the-art at the time. Nonetheless, the testing program did not provide teachers with immediate access to results and required all teachers to administer the same test at the same time.[12]

In 2001, the Center for the Study of Testing, Evaluation, and Educational Policy proposed to take Pittsburgh's approach one step further by developing a testing program that allowed teachers to select from a menu of writing tests. The goal was to expand the sample of student writing by creating a series of test prompts, each linked to a different short story, novel, poem, or play included in the state standards. During the course of the year, teachers were to select and administer six of these writing prompts after covering the corresponding text. The idea gained support from a broad group including state educational leaders, state and federal legislators, teacher unions, school administrators, groups opposed to and favoring high-stakes testing. Ultimately, however, funding was not provided for the initiative—an opportunity cost that has slowed the integration of computer-based technologies and the technology of testing.

DIAGNOSTIC ASSESSMENT

For most teachers, the current approach to high-stakes testing is like the first few minutes of a visit to the doctor. Imagine that you are feeling ill and believe you have a fever. You go to the doctor, she takes your temperature, gets a reading of 102, and says that you do indeed have a fever. She then tells you to go home. Would you be satisfied? The thermometer confirmed what you already knew—you have a fever. But, you have not learned anything new. More importantly, you do not have a better understanding of what may be causing your fever or how to treat it.

Like a doctor telling a person with a fever that his temperature is 102, high-stakes tests provide information that confirms what most teachers already know. Several studies show that teachers can predict the test performance of their students with a high degree of accuracy.[13] Seeing that their students received a high or low score rarely tells them anything they did not already know. Unlike a doctor who performs follow up analyses to diagnose the cause of a fever, current high-stakes tests only provide information about a student's level of achievement. For students whose level of achievement is relatively low, these tests fail to provide diagnostic information about *why* they are struggling.

The lack of diagnostic information is a direct result of what current tests are designed to do. Just as a thermometer is designed to measure the relative warmth or coldness of an object by placing that measure on a scale calibrated in units called degrees, today's high-stakes tests are designed to measure the relative knowledge or ability of a student by placing that measure on a scale calibrated in levels of achievement. To measure knowledge or ability a set of items is presented to a student. For every item the student answers correctly, the test places the student higher on the achievement scale. Each test item is used to provide binary information—the student either answers the item correctly or incorrectly. Collecting and aggregating correct responses is an efficient method for placing a student on a scale that represents achievement. But, focusing solely on whether or not students respond correctly to each item does not provide insight into the cognitive processes the student used when answering each item.

In rare cases, an item asks students to describe their reasoning. Often, however, student descriptions are incomplete or inaccurate reflections of the thought process used when answering the item. As a result, these items provide indirect and crude insight into examinees' cognitive processes. Other items require students to show their work. The scoring criteria for these items, however, do not consider the strategies used to answer the item. Instead, the criteria focus on whether the procedures required to solve the problem were applied accurately.

Concern about the lack of diagnostic information provided by achievement tests, dates back several decades. For example, in the 1930s Ralph Tyler developed a test that provided four scores that provided teachers with information about the type of errors students made when answering items.[14] In the 1970s, researchers at MIT developed a computer-based tutoring system that presented students with mathematics items. The system, called BUGGY, then used a student's incorrect responses to identify procedural errors and offer additional instruction to help the student apply the correct procedure.[15]

More recently, the National Research Council resurrected calls to improve the diagnostic information provided by tests. Specifically, the Council recommended that student assessment should provide timely and informative feedback about the strategies children use when solving problems and that student thinking be made visible so that instructional strategies can be tailored to support learning.[16] Although these recommendations were made in 2001, seven years later they have not been embraced by any high-stakes testing program.

In 2004, however, the Technology and Assessment Study Collaborative launched the development of a diagnostic assessment system designed to increase the instructional value of testing. Known as the Diagnostic Algebra Assessment System, the initiative set out to develop a comprehensive computer-based assessment and instructional system that has three key features. First, the system provides teachers access to a series of on-line tests, each of which focuses on a specific algebraic concept. For each test, items are designed to measure students' understanding of the concept (e.g., equality). For a student who performs poorly, each test also provides information about whether a known misconception is interfering with the student's understanding.

Second, the system provides immediate feedback to teachers. An initial report sorts students into three categories. In the first category are students who performed well and appear to have a solid understanding of the tested concept. In the second category are students who did not perform well and who appear to hold a specific misconception. In the third category are students who also did not perform well, but do not appear to hold the misconception (e.g., they make a variety of errors unrelated to the measured misconception). These categories give teachers a better understanding of how well their students are performing and why some students are struggling with a given concept.

Third, the system links teachers to lessons and activities they can use to help students correct a given misconception. Students identified with a given misconception are also connected to learning activities that focus on that misconception. See http://www.bc.edu/research/intasc/researchprojects/DiagnosticAlgebra/daa.shtml for more information about the Diagnostic Algebra Assessment.

While the Diagnostic Algebra Assessment System is still in development, it is an example of how testing programs can capitalize on computer-based technology to provide teachers with diagnostic information they can use to tailor instruction for individual students.

COMPLEX INTERACTIVE TASKS

For decades, people have argued that multiple-choice items place too much emphasis on the recall of discrete facts rather than the application of skills and knowledge. As we saw in Chapter 7, these concerns led to the "beyond the bubble" movement in the 1990s that advocated the use of performance tests. Performance tests require students to apply diverse knowledge and multiple skills to solve a complex problem. Performance tests also often require students to use equipment and materials as they work on a problem. In science, a performance test might present students with unknown substances and ask them to apply a variety of techniques to determine which chemicals comprise each substance. A math task might present students with a lump of clay, a balance scale, a 10-gram weight, and a 25-gram weight. The student is asked to use these materials to produce a 15-gram ball of clay.

For a short period of time, some large-scale testing programs embraced performance tests. For example, New York adopted a performance test for science. The Standard Assessment Tasks used in primary schools throughout England employed performance tests in mathematics and science.[17] Two major international studies that compared achievement of students from many different countries also included several performance tasks.[18]

Enthusiasm for performance tests, however, was short-lived for three reasons. First, the equipment required for many performance tasks was expensive and difficult to distribute. Second, it was difficult to standardize the conditions under which students in different schools performed tasks. Third, scoring student responses was a challenging process. While the focus of many performance tasks—particularly in science and mathematics—was on the processes and procedures students applied to solve a complex problem, scoring often focused on written responses in which students described their solution. Rather than directly observing the processes and procedures employed by each student, asking students to write about them introduced noise into the testing process. Together, these challenges led to the abandonment of performance tests by testing programs in the United States. Nonetheless, computer-based testing holds tremendous potential to overcome these obstacles.

For several years now, computer-based performance tests have been used in many professions. Pilots use computer-based flight simulators to test their skills in dangerous situations. Army medics are tested on their ability to perform life-saving procedures on computer-based mannequins. The skills of anesthesiologist residents are also tested using computer-based mannequins that allow examiners to simulate life threatening conditions and observe how the resident reacts. Surgeons also test their laparoscopic skills using computer-based simulations of operations. In each case, computer-based technologies are used to present complex, and sometimes dangerous, situations that are impossible to replicate in a real-world environment, let alone on a paper-and-pencil test. In addition, these computer-based tests also capture every action and decision made while a person is working through a given scenario. This information is then used to analyze and provide immediate feedback about a person's performance.

For many subjects taught in elementary, middle, and high school, computer-based simulations hold tremendous potential to collect information about students decision-making and ability to successfully complete complex, multi-step tasks. Although computer-based tasks are more expensive to develop than a multiple-choice item, once created they can help assure that all students gain exposure to the same high-quality complex tasks, without requiring testing to distribute a variety of equipment.

Over the past ten years, there have been a handful of efforts to develop complex computer-based performance tasks that require students to conduct simulations. For example, researchers at the University of California, Los Angeles have developed a set of interactive multi-media exercises for mathematics, science, and social sciences. Each exercise simulates a real-world situation that requires students to apply their understanding of a specific concept or set of concepts to solve a complex problem. As just one example, a task simulates a situation in which an earthquake has caused chemicals to spill and students must perform tests to determine the composition of the spill. Based on the decisions and actions students make while solving a given problem, each simulation classifies the student's current level of understanding and their ability to apply their knowledge and skills in solving the problem.[19]

Initially, the interactive multi-media exercises were used to assess students' problem-solving skills within a given subject area in order to classify a student's current level of understanding. More recently, the exercises have been used to inform instruction and track student progress as they work on a series of problems related to a given subject area.[20]

Another example is found in a computer-based learning system called BioLogica that is designed to help students learn genetics. Funded by the National Science Foundation, the learning system comprises a series of modules, each of which focuses on a more complex genetic concept. As students explore a given concept, BioLogica asks students to demonstrate their understanding by conducting specific experiments that require them to apply their knowledge of that concept. As an example, in an early module, students are asked to breed dragons to create off-spring that have specific features, such as horns and forked tails. To do so, students must identify specific genetic codes within the dragons, determine which features are dominant and recessive, and then selectively breed the dragons to produce the desired features in the offspring.

Like UCLA's multi-media exercises, BioLogica collects information about each student's decisions as the task is performed. This information is used to classify the student's current level of understanding and their ability to apply their understanding to achieve a desired outcome. Depending on the classification, BioLogica presents opportunities for the student to refine his or her understanding of the concept or presents a more advanced concept.

The potential for computer-based simulations to provide deeper insight into student knowledge and skills has influenced the National Assessment of Educational Progress (NAEP), also known as the Nation's Report Card. In 2002, NAEP began exploring the use of interactive computer-based simulations when it launched the *Technology-Rich Environment* project. As part of this initiative, a computer-based performance task was developed and administered to a nationwide sample of students. This task assessed the application of specific scientific concepts to determine the relationship between the volume of gas in a balloon and the mass of the balloon's payload.

The computer-based simulation presented students with a balloon and different sized payloads. Students manipulated the volume of gas in the balloon, then attached a given sized payload, and observed how high the balloon ascended. Students plotted the values of each variable in a spreadsheet and generated a graph of the relationship between the variables. As students worked through the simulation, their actions and decisions were used to determine the extent to which they had developed each targeted skill.[21]

Although UCLA's interactive multimedia exercises, BioLogica, and the NAEP simulation have not yet been widely adopted, they provide a glimpse into the future of performance-based assessment. Like simulations used to assess pilots, medics, and doctors, these examples also foreshadow the complex tasks that will be used to assess students' knowledge, understanding, and skills across grade levels and subjects.

SUMMARY

In July of 2008, Austria's Heiligenkreuz Abbey monks' CD of Gregorian chants was released in the United States after topping the charts in Europe. The monk's music first surfaced when a young brother posted a video on YouTube. When asked during an interview what a monk was doing posting a video on YouTube, Father Karl Wallner responded: "Cistercian monks live with the rule of Saint Benedict, and it was written 1500 years ago, and even then Saint Benedict says that every monk has to have the instruments to write. And I say for nowadays this means that every monk has to have a computer and has to know how to deal with the new medias."[22]

Anyone who has watched children, sometimes as young as three, use a computer knows that today's kids intuitively know how to deal with the new media. All over the Internet, kids play games. Many of these games, like those found on pbskids.org, appear to be mere entertainment, but they are actually designed to teach at developmentally appropriate levels. One game, Clifford the Red Dog's *Measuring Up*, helps kids learn basic measurement concepts. Curious George's *Banana 411* helps toddlers learn how to use a phone. *History Scene Investigator* exposes older children to historical events as they solve mysteries. Other games, like *Ruinscape*, build in hints and clues that help kids navigate complex worlds as they perform various missions.

While these games are incredibly popular with today's kids, what often goes unnoticed is that their success depends, to a large extent, on the ongoing assessment of the child's acquisition of knowledge and skills that occurs as the game is played. Each game is really a series of mini-tests that require students to demonstrate their understanding, knowledge, and skills. Depending on how the student performs, the game advances, provides another opportunity, or reveals clues.

In hopes of capitalizing on the learning that can occur when students use computers, our schools have invested heavily in computer-based technologies. In the vast majority of schools, students now have easy access to computers and the Internet. As computers continue to become more affordable, and as companies develop computers specifically designed for education, student access to computers will only increase.[23]

To date, however, the testing industry has not fully capitalized on the power of computer-based technologies. True, many tests are being administered on computers. In Virginia, alone, more than 1.5 million tests were delivered on-line to students in 2007.[24] Yet, so far, the use of computers for testing has been limited to increasing the efficiency with which traditional tests are distributed, and answers are collected and scored. While increasing the efficiency of testing is a good place to begin, it barely scratches the surface of the benefits that can come by marrying the technology of testing with computer-based technologies.

Of course, the paradox of testing will apply to each of these advances—enhancements to the technology of testing will inevitably produce unintended positive and negative consequences. As we examine in the next chapter, no matter what technologies are employed, it is essential that independent monitoring of high-stakes testing programs is put into place in order to maximize the benefits and minimize the negative unintended consequences of testing.

NOTES

1. Buchanan, (1987).
2. See Cuban (1986), Oppenheimer (2003), and Stoll (1999).
3. Bausell (2008).
4. Stansbury (2008).
5. Bennett et al. (2008).
6. Although some observers believe that adaptive testing falsely punishes a student who mistakenly misses an item, the algorithms allow students to work up to items with an appropriate difficulty after presenting only a few additional items. As the technology of adaptive testing has matured, more complex algorithms have been developed to assure that the tests content adequately samples the domain of interest. By presenting students with different sets of items, adaptive testing also protects against cheating and breaches of security that have plagued some testing programs.
7. Borja (2003).
8. Dikli (2006).
9. *Chapman v. California Department of Education*, Case JCVCDOE224766 (2002).
10. Landau (2003).
11. See Bloom (1964), Bruner (1966), Carroll (1966), and Gagne (1965).
12. Wallace (1986).
13. See Cullen & Shaw (2000); Demaray & Elliott (1998); Hoge & Coladarci (1989); Mulholland & Berliner (1992).
14. Smith & Tyler (1942).
15. Krige (1998).
16. National Research Council (2001).
17. Madaus & Kellaghan, (1993).
18. Both the Third International Mathematics and Science Study (TIMSS) and the International Assessment of Educational Progress (IAEP) employed a set of performance tasks.
19. Vendlinski & Stevens (2002).

20. Russell (2006).
21. Bennett, Persky, Weiss, & Jenkins (2007).
22. All Things Considered (2008).
23. In the past two years, three major initiatives to develop low cost computers for schools have been launched. The most widely publicized is the One Laptop Per Child project (see www.laptop.org), which is an off-shoot of the MIT Media Lab. In addition, both Intel and Hewlett-Packard have developed "low" cost, scaled down laptops designed specifically for elementary, middle, and high school students.
24. Bennett et al. (2008).

CHAPTER 10

WHY AND HOW SHOULD HIGH-STAKES TESTING BE MONITORED?

The use of a multiple-choice test to sort and assign jobs to army recruits during World War I, kick-started the American test industry. Since the 1920s, the educational testing industry has evolved and expanded to provide schools with a variety of products and services that include pre-fabricated tests, customized products for high-stakes testing programs, computer-based test administration, scoring, and reporting. Educational testing is big business that generates more than a billion dollars in revenue each year.[1] On top of these expenditures, the indirect costs of high-stakes testing programs incurred by our teachers, school administrators, and students range from 4 to more than 50 times the direct costs.[2]

As we have seen throughout this book, high-stakes testing produces both benefits and harms for individuals and schools. Despite the harms, there is no independent organization to which policy makers, educators, parents, or students can turn to acquire assurances of the technical quality, valid use, or consequences of high-stakes tests.[3] Instead, those who have concerns about quality and consequences must rely on assurances by testing companies and state agencies in charge of high-stakes testing programs that tests are technically sound and produce no harm. What other entity in society

The Paradoxes of High Stakes Testing, pages 197–221

could subject 30 million children to a treatment without an independent mechanism to monitor the quality and effects of that treatment?

This chapter examines the need for a monitoring body for today's high-stakes testing programs. We begin by describing why a monitoring body is needed, and trace previous attempts to monitor the testing industry. Next, we discuss conditions that prompted the creation of regulatory and oversight bodies for other industries. We then examine several institutions that perform oversight functions for other industries and consider how those institutions can inform the design of a monitoring body for testing. Finally, we detail the challenges that must be addressed when establishing a test monitoring body.

Before exploring these issues, we want to emphasize that monitoring testing does not mean waiting for a "perfect test" before allowing a program to be launched. There is no such thing as a perfect test. Monitoring testing does not mean scrapping a program when the inevitable unanticipated negative consequences emerge or when misuses are detected. But, monitoring testing does mean that the tax payers who fund these programs, those who use test results, and the students, teachers, schools, and parents directly affected by such use will have assurances that the tests are technically sound, the benefits outweigh the harms, negative consequences are minimized, and errors and misuses are reduced.

THE NEED FOR AN INDEPENDENT MONITORING BODY

Testing is a useful but fallible technology. All technologies are subject to errors, misuse, and unintended consequences. This does not mean a useful technology should be abandoned. Instead its shortcomings should be identified and minimized. The technology of testing is no exception.

As we have seen in preceding chapters, the technology of testing relies on hidden algorithms, complex modeling, and computerized decision rules. These techniques are similar to those used for such things as credit checks, bank loans, and the triggering of an IRS audit. William Wallace, an expert on computer modeling, reminds us that hidden algorithms used for financial modeling affect the lives and opportunities of people. Wallace argues that checks are needed to prevent model builders or users from accidentally, deliberately, inaccurately, or irresponsibly misapplying these techniques.[4] Testing's arcane algorithms require the same checks.

Commenting on the ethics of hidden computer algorithms, John Staudenmaier, a scholar of technology, argues that refraining from bad behavior, taking care not to deliver poorly designed products, and exercising care in deciding which clients one will serve or refuse to serve are laudable. But these actions, alone, are not sufficient. Because of the complex nature of the technology and the economic and political pressures that influence its use, institutions must "face up to the responsibilities that come with sophisticated computer expertise."[5] Staudenmaier's advice is directly applicable to high-stakes testing. Institutionalized oversight is needed to monitor testing's arcane techniques.

When making the case for No Child Left Behind, George W. Bush argued that accountability is the cornerstone of educational reform. He also argued that testing is the key to holding teachers and schools accountable, demonstrating that students are learning, and ensuring taxpayers receive value for expenditures on education. If high-stakes testing is the key tool for educational accountability, then the tests themselves must be subject to independent, transparent accountability to ensure quality, validity, and proper use. Although there have been repeated calls for independent oversight of testing since the end of the 19th century, we do not have such assurances today.

A Little History

There is much to learn from previous attempts to monitor testing. History shows that establishing a monitoring body for testing is a daunting task that has eluded visionaries for more than a century.[6] In the sections that follow, we examine four distinct eras during which efforts were made to establish a test monitoring body. These eras include early efforts by individuals, institutional efforts, foundation supported efforts, and current calls for monitoring.

Early Individual Efforts

In 1925, Giles M. Ruch, the author of several standardized tests, argued "the test buyer is surely entitled to the same protection as the buyer of food products, namely, the true ingredients printed on the outside of each package."[7] By 1933, Ruch recognized the need for an external agency to monitor tests:

> There is urgent need for a fact-finding organization which will undertake impartial, experimental, and statistical evaluations of tests—validity, reliability, legitimate uses, accuracy of norms, and the like. This might lead to the listing of satisfactory tests in the various subject matter divisions in much the same way that Consumers' Research, Inc. is attempting to furnish reliable information to the average buyer.[8]

Despite his attempt to form such an organization, in the end Ruch was unsuccessful due to lack of funding and inability to generate sufficient interest among his contemporaries.

In 1938, however, Oscar K Buros, the editor and publisher of the renowned series, Mental Measurement Yearbooks (MMY), took up Ruch's call for a monitoring agency:[9]

> There is a real need for *the endowment* of a sort of 'Bureau of Standards' to assist test consumers in selecting the test, which will best meet their needs. This organization should not enter into the field of test construction but should devote all of its efforts to the critical appraisal of the construction, validation, and use of tests prepared by others.[10]

Buros' call for an endowment to support his proposed monitoring work was prophetic. As we shall see, a guaranteed revenue source to support the monitoring effort has been, and remains, a major obstacle in creating an independent monitoring organization.

Buros also argued that commercial test publishers, non-profit testing organizations, and sponsors of state testing programs *could not* effectively serve as unbiased critics of their own tests. Buros' insight about vested interests is still valid today.

Buros reported that he tried without success to start a test consumers organization. He noted, however, that despite interest in funding projects to develop new tests, "there seems to be little interest in an undertaking which would have as its main purpose the critical evaluation of tests."[11] Thirty years later, Buros offered this indictment of the testing industry:

> Test publishers continue to market tests, which do not begin to meet the standards of the rank and file of *MMY* and journal reviewers. At least half of the tests . . . should never have been published. Exaggerated, false, or unsubstantiated claims are the rule. . . . At present, no matter how poor a test may be, if it is nicely packaged and if it promises to do all sorts of things which no test can do, the test will find many gullible buyers.[12]

Institutional Efforts

In 1950, a committee of the American Psychological Association considered establishing a *Bureau of Test Standards* charged with applying and enforcing standards, and then granting a *Seal of Approval* to tests that met their standards.[13] The records of the American Psychological Association, however, note "the Council voted to take no action on these two recommendations, in view of the complicated problems they present."[14] Then, as now, it is difficult for a professional organization, with large numbers of members that rely on testing for part of their livelihood, to embrace monitoring or oversight of testing.

Twenty-five years later, the Department of Health Education and Welfare created the *Project on the Classification of Exceptional Children* to examine the classification and labeling of handicapped, disadvantaged, or delinquent children. In a description appropriate for today, the project proposed the creation of a federal test monitoring agency:

> Because psychological tests . . . saturate our society and because their use can result in the irreversible deprivation of opportunity to many children, especially those already burdened by poverty and prejudice, we recommend that there be established a *National Bureau of Standards for Psychological Tests and Testing.*[15]

The proposed Bureau would set standards for tests, test uses, and test users, act on complaints, operate a research program, and disseminate findings through a consumer reports section. The report acknowledged some reluctance to establish a new federal agency, but cited the failure of the states, professional organizations, and test publishers to control abuses. It also directly compared test regulation to food and drug regulation: "Poor tests or poor testing may be as injurious to opportunity as impure food or drugs are injurious to health."[16] Presumably the recommendation to form a federal test monitoring agency was considered at some level, but no action was taken.[17]

Not long after, however, the state of New York passed the *Standardized Testing Law of 1979.* The law was popularly called "truth in testing" and allowed examinees to see test items and the answer key to *admissions tests* after results were released.[18] The legislation was instrumental in uncovering incorrectly scored items on important tests like the SAT and Graduate Record Examinations. While "truth in testing" helped uncover errors, it does not permit challenges to the technical quality of a test, a test-based classification, a test's validity, the way in which a test is used, or unintended negative consequences.[19]

Foundation Supported Efforts

In 1990, a detailed study by the *National Commission on Testing and Public Policy,* sponsored by the Ford Foundation, concluded, "The enterprise of testing must be subjected to greater public accountability." The National Commission went on to recommend "the development of additional institutional means to examine the quality of tests and assessment instruments and to provide oversight of test use."[20]

In response to the National Commissions recommendation, a conference funded by the Carnegie and Ford Foundations solicited input from 20 experts on the feasibility of forming a test monitoring body. The experts' recommendations were incorporated in a report titled, *A Proposal For A Monitoring Body For Tests Used In Public Policy.*[21] The report led to the formation of the *National Board on Testing and Public Policy* (National Board) to monitor tests for technical adequacy and appropriate use. Housed at Boston College and with support from the Ford Foundation and the Atlantic Philanthropies, the National Board completed several studies on high-stakes testing and disseminated results broadly.[22] Nonetheless, the National Board's goal of monitoring tests for technical adequacy and appropriate use was unsuccessful for three reasons.

First, the National Board did not have a permanent source of funding such as an endowment or revenue stream. While generous, funding from foundations supported specific research projects related to testing, but was not sufficient to monitor testing more broadly. Of course, this was known to the National Board when it was launched. In fact, there is a saying that foundations can give birth to a baby, but cannot support it throughout its life. A lack of stable, long-term funding made it impossible for the National Board to maintain a permanent staff and infrastructure.

Second, the National Board could not adequately examine technical issues because it did not have access to data from testing companies or cooperation from State Departments of Education. As we shall see later in the chapter, lack of access and cooperation on the part of test developers and Departments of Education doom any effort at independent oversight.

Third, to avoid the impression that the National Board was anti-testing, a key goal was to form a Board of Directors comprised of visible, well known, and respected people from various walks of life. It was hoped that the Board of Directors would create national visibility and credibility, help disseminate research findings to a wider audience, and assist in raising money for an endowment to support operating expenses and a stable staff. While the National Board recruited some excellent members for the Board of Directors, it was unable to recruit the full combination of people that could provide adequate visibility, political clout, and fundraising capabilities.

An independent organization, *FairTest* has called attention to poor practices, mistakes, and unacceptable uses of testing for the past twenty years. *FairTest* has accomplished this through publications, web postings, lobbying, disseminating news stories about testing, and working to help the press understand problems with tests.[23] While these efforts have helped raise awareness of problems with tests, *FairTest* was not designed to systematically monitor tests for technical adequacy or oversee large-scale test use. Further, many in the testing community, the testing industry, and those running state testing programs consider *FairTest* to be anti-testing. To succeed, any attempt to monitor testing must address concerns raised by testing critics and those directly affected by testing without alienating groups with vested interests in a testing program—an exquisite balancing act.

In addition to their image problems within the testing community, *Fair Test* struggles financially. At the height of the 2006 SAT scoring error controversy, *The New Yorker* magazine and several newspapers called attention to *Fair Test's* work and pointed out that the small nonprofit organization was in danger of closing due to a lack of funding. *FairTest's* struggle to survive is another reminder of the necessity of a reliable and sufficient source of funding for any effort to oversee testing and test use.

CURRENT CALLS FOR TEST MONITORING

In the wake of the SAT 2006 scoring error, the chairman of the New York State Senate, Kenneth LaValle, called for the passage of a bill for stricter government oversight of the college admissions testing industry. In an interview with the New York Times, LaValle argued:

> The testing people are very cavalier about what this test is in the lives of the test takers. Test takers feel they have so much riding on this exam—acceptance into the college of their choice and whether they will get the careers they want. The testing companies just don't get how important it is.[24]

LaValle's bill strengthens the 1979 "truth in testing law" and would solve the problem of providing stable funding for test monitoring by levying a $1 tax on every college and graduate admission test given in the state. While the bill would make it easier to identify errors after the fact, it is narrowly tailored to college admissions tests and does not apply to the much larger testing programs mandated by states and NCLB.

Today, however, there are calls to oversee these larger high-stakes testing programs. In 2006, Thomas Toch published a comprehensive study titled, *Margins of Error: The Education Testing Industry in the No Child Left Behind Era.* In it, he highlighted the lack of "meaningful oversight of the sprawling NCLB testing enterprise."[25] Toch cited the call made sixteen years earlier by the *National Commission on Testing and Public Policy* to form a body to monitor the quality of tests and provide oversight of test use. Toch asked President Bush to create a bipartisan commission on standardized testing that would lead to the development of an independent oversight body for testing. Like Ruch and Burros before him, Toch envisioned a monitoring body functioning like other consumer protection agencies.

In 2006, *The Harvard Civil Rights Project* also noted Congress's failure to provide "serious oversight of the working of the law [NCLB]," and the Bush Administration's reluctance "to commission independent research on the implementation of the policy."[26] Unlike previous calls for an independent, non-governmental monitoring body, Toch and the Civil Rights Projects called on the federal government to perform this function. This is an important departure.

Previous proposals reasoned that government oversight of testing could not function independent of political pressure or lobbying from vested interests. It was also believed that governmental control was not acceptable to the professional communities involved with testing. State and national mandates for high-stakes testing have dramatically altered the landscape. We examine the pros and cons of governmental sponsorship of test monitoring later in this chapter.

WHAT CONDITIONS TRIGGER OVERSIGHT?

Regulation, monitoring, oversight, or auditing occur for an almost limitless range of products, practices, and actions. They occur across a vast array of consumer products such as automobiles, toys, and pet food, financial products and services, industrial practices, and commercial practices such as advertising and labeling. Professional behavior is subject to licensing by governmental authority, and to various codes of practice established by governmental and private entities. Certain types of personal behavior, such as wearing seat belts or smoking, are also subject to regulation. The overseers are many: federal, state, and local governments, professional organizations, private groups, and advocacy groups. Their actions are varied as well. They regulate behavior, evaluate products, set standards, enforce compliance, inspect, monitor, and investigate.[27]

Despite the impressive range of oversight and regulation that exists today, Americans historically have resisted intervention into private activities. This resistance is an inherent part of a social and political system based on personal freedoms, private property rights, belief in free market forces, and the importance of individualism in American life.[28]

The testing industry has opposed regulating or monitoring on the grounds that the government should not intervene into private proprietary business activities.[29] Yet, by its very nature, a mandated test is an intervention into the private life of individuals. Those who take a test must publicly reveal a part of themselves through their test performance, and then are objectified by the test score. Given this unavoidable intervention into their private life, shouldn't the interest of the individual test taker come before the interests of the testing industry? Absent monitoring, the test taker is not protected.

Why are so many things in our society monitored, yet testing is not? A helpful starting point in answering this question comes from the legal scholar Ernst Freund. In 1928 he pointed out that activities are likely to be regulated if they are hazardous to persons and their property, or if some persons are likely to abuse their positions of power at the expense of others. In 1989, Peter Sandman, an expert on risk analysis, added another ingredient necessary to trigger oversight—outrage.

Sandman proposed a simple 2 × 2 matrix that illustrates combinations of hazard and outrage.

TABLE 10.1 Sandman's Hazard/Outrage Matrix[30]

Cell 1 High Hazard—High Outrage **Intervention Likely**	*Cell 2* High Hazard—Low Outrage
Cell 3 Low Hazard—High Outrage	*Cell 4* Low Hazard—Low Outrage **Intervention Unlikely**

In Table 10.1 cells 1 and 4 are straightforward situations: with high hazard and high outrage, intervention occurs; with low hazard and low outrage, it does not.

To overcome American resistance to regulation, it takes high hazard and high outrage. The historian, John Burke, identifies the advent of steam power and a growing death toll from marine boiler explosions, as the key event that triggered American acceptance of government regulation.[31] Between 1816 and 1852 there were roughly 3,000 deaths due to marine boiler explosions. Four hundred and seven of these occurred in 1851 alone. In response to the growing carnage, Congress enacted a law regulating steam boilers, "an important step toward the inauguration of the regulatory and investigative agencies in the federal government."[32] Since then, many more industries have become regulated. Although the details of individual cases are debated, American people now accept government oversight and regulation as a matter of course.

While it makes sense that the combination of high outrage and high hazard triggers reaction, cases in which hazards are low but outrage is high are intriguing. Despite low hazards, such situations sometimes trigger regulation. As two examples, consider the development of the motion picture codes by the Motion Picture Association of America (MPAA) and, more recently, regulating what is broadcast by the cable television industry. More often, however, these cases do not lead to formal governmental regulation. Instead, industry self-regulates or private organizations engage in public awareness campaigns intended to pressure industries to adopt or reform their practices.[33] These efforts occur despite the fact that the hazard to people or property is low.

Hazards, Outrage, and High-Stakes Testing

High-stakes testing resides in cell 2, where the hazard is high but outrage is low. Yet, when the general public and policy makers think about testing, hazard rarely comes to mind.[34] As we have seen through this book, however, the hazards caused by high-stakes testing are high for many students, teachers, and schools. Students are retained in grade, placed in remedial programs, and denied diplomas. Teachers and principals are penalized for poor performance by their students, and in some cases fired. Schools alter their curriculum, decrease emphasis on non-tested subjects, are labeled as poor performing, and can be placed in receivership or closed entirely. In some cases, these high-stakes decisions and the resulting actions are justified. In other cases, the fallible nature of test scores produces faulty classifications and decisions. Despite the hazards caused by faulty decisions, generalized outrage is missing. There are at least four reasons why high-stakes testing does not generate generalized outrage.

First, testing is a common experience. While most readers may not have liked being tested, Americans generally regard taking tests as an ordinary part of going to school and growing up. Testing in school is rightly regarded as a necessary tool to assess learning. The very ordinariness and the public's tacit acceptance of testing convey an unwarranted transparency and acceptance of high-stakes tests by the public. Put simply, testing is viewed by many as a right of passage.

Second, many people realize that some students or groups of students do not do well on tests. Too often, though, poor performance is viewed as an accurate reflection of the student's achievement rather than the product of cultural, social, economic, and non-academic factors that influence the way a student interacts with a test and its individual items. Because poor performance is blindly attributed to poor achievement, there is little generalized outrage. And when poor test performance does provoke outrage, the response is for more testing, rather than questioning whether the test accurately reflects what students know and can do.

Third, when test errors become public, arguing that the effects are trivial minimizes them. For example, there was outrage when it was reported that 4,411 students received erroneously low scores and 613 received inflated scores on the 2006 SAT. Defenders of the SAT, however, were quick to point out that the error affected only eight tenths of one percent of the 495,000 students who took the test. While the SAT defenders acknowledged that the error was unacceptable and unfortunate, their argument implied that outrage was misplaced because it affected just a few examinees—collateral damage so to speak. Of course, for many of the *few* unfortunate students affected by the error, it had important personal consequences. In Chapter 4, we also saw the "its only a few" argument used in Bell Buckle, Tennessee. The Department of Education argued that the answer keyed as correct for a controversial multiple-choice item must be "correct" because only 1.4% of students did not select it.

Finally, testing differs in two important ways from many technologies used regularly by people. Unlike a car that pulls to the right or a computer that crashes, a test does not provide immediate, tangible feedback when something is amiss. In addition, unlike a car crash caused by failed breaks or loss of data caused by a faulty hard drive, the negative impact of high-stakes testing takes a long time to be revealed. Collectively, the lack of tangible feedback, delayed impact, and often-undocumented consequences of high-stakes testing prevent outrage.

Although these and other reasons explain why there is not general outrage about high-stakes testing, the hazards alone demand independent monitoring. But before any industry can be monitored, there must be clearly defined standards. For testing, these standards have been developed over many years and are already in place.

Standards and Guidelines for Testing

The *Standards for Educational and Psychological Testing (Standards)* and the *Code of Fair Testing Practices in Education (Code)* provide guidelines for test design, development, and use.[35] The *Standards* and *Code* comprise the principal criteria for evaluating work performed by the testing industry. In fact, many companies that develop tests claim their tests adhere to the *Standards* and the *Code*. The *Standards* are also used in court cases to both buttress and to counter claims about a particular test's technical adequacy.

The *Standards* and the *Code*, however, comprise very broadly stated standards open to interpretation. The *Standards* do not explain in simple terms the kinds of evidence needed for compliance. As a result, experts testifying in court have sharply disagreed over whether or not a particular test met a given standard. Compliance with the *Standards*, it seems, is in the eye of the beholder. More importantly, both the *Standards* and the *Code* lack any enforcement mechanism.[36] Nonetheless, the *Standards* and the *Code* provide a starting point for creating an independent test monitoring body.

WHAT CAN WE LEARN FROM OTHER EFFORTS TO MONITOR OR OVERSEE PRODUCTS OR PROGRAMS

A wide array of activities is subject to governmental, professional, and private oversight. The common focus across these oversight agencies is the quality of the object of oversight, such as food and drugs, products, manufacturing processes, the operations of securities markets, or the accreditation of professionals. In each case, oversight was put in place to protect the public from the actions of others, or themselves. Many of these interventions seek to educate and inform, to open up processes, and to foster decisions, by making available all relevant information free of misleading or deceptive spins.

To illuminate how a test monitoring body might function, we describe how oversight has worked in three areas; medical technology, injury prevention programs, and the introduction of new technology in industry. We then examine the important results from The Carnegie Corporation and the Ford Foundation's feasibility study of testing oversight. That study focused on 16 well-known agencies and examined their histories, operations, funding, strengths, weaknesses, costs, benefits, and economic and social impacts.[37]

Lessons From Regulation of Medical Technology

A lesson high-stakes testing can learn from medicine is it is never too late to monitor. The history of medicine is full of standard techniques, procedures, and innovations that later proved harmful or ineffective. One example is the use of DES (diethylstilbestrol) from 1938 to 1975 to reduce miscarriages and improve fetal growth. In the 1950s DES was shown to be ineffective. Nonetheless, its use continued until a 1970 study reported a rare cancer in young women whose mothers took DES during their pregnancy.[38]

Over time, the negative experiences of patients, and ensuing outrage convinces policy makers and the medical profession that medical technologies and drugs have to be proven beneficial before adoption, and then monitored after implementation.[39] The same holds for high-stakes educational testing.

As the LORAN Commission's report on the impact of medical technology states:

> Good decisions cannot be made without an adequate assessment of the relevant facts. First, there must be a diagnosis and prognosis. Then, a proposed treatment's possible outcomes must be evaluated. This evaluation should assess the likelihood of a favorable outcome and the benefits and burdens to the patient of all possible outcomes. Further, there should be candor not only about what is known, but also about what is unknown.[40]

Policy makers and the testing community take none of these actions before prescribing a high-stakes testing program. As is the practice in medicine, high-stakes testing treatments should be the subject of institutionalized, independent scrutiny before, during, and after implementation.

Lessons from Injury Prevention Programs

The increasingly sophisticated science of injury prevention tells us that injuries are not merely "accidents"—random uncontrolled acts of fate—but are events that are understandable, predictable, and preventable.[41] Similarly, test misuse, negative side effects, and errors are not unforeseen events; they are predictable and to some degree preventable.

The field of injury prevention relies on methods and tools similar to those used in the public health field. Like the outbreak of disease, injury is not the product of one cause, but of people's actions and interactions, as well as surrounding circumstances. Those working in the field of injury prevention study where, when, and how injuries occur, and to whom. They use this information to understand patterns of occurrence, to identify risk groups for specific injuries, and to design and implement preventive programs.[42]

Like injuries, the harms associated with testing do not have a single cause. They derive from the nature of the test itself, the characteristics of test takers, the uses to which test results are put, and the environment in which the test operates. Similar to injury prevention, a test monitoring body should mount field studies that monitor where, when, why, and how test misuse, negative side effects, and errors occur, and whom they affect. This knowledge would permit a test monitoring body to assist high-stakes testing programs to minimize the likelihood of such testing "accidents" and misadventures.

Lessons From The Introduction of New Technologies

Studies that examine the introduction of new technology in industry provide insight into the functions and approaches a test monitoring body might adopt. Studies of the introduction of new industrial technologies show that the introduction and utilization of advanced production technologies into the normal infrastructure of the plant often fail. W. Edwards Deming, a pioneer in quality control, describes this phenomenon:

> All these wonderful machines performed their intended functions, on test, but when they were put into operation in our plants, with our people, they were out of business so much of the time for this and that kind of failure that our overall costs, instead of going down, went up. No one had evaluated the overall probable failure rates and maintenance. As a result, we were continually caught with stoppages and with not enough spare parts, or with none at all; and no provision for alternate production lines.[43]

Making an innovation work in a plant is not simply a question of installing well-developed solutions. There is also a need to identify, diagnose, and address problems and opportunities that emerge only when the new technology is on line. Invariably existing systems and the new technology must be modified to define their roles, and exploit the technology's novel capabilities.[44]

A test monitoring body would benefit from the experience of industry in introducing a new technology, by helping ensure that carefully designed, small reversible steps are followed when introducing high-stakes testing in our schools. This approach would also provide continual monitoring of a testing program, evaluation of its consequences, and would help reduce, but not eliminate, human error.

WHAT WOULD A TEST MONITORING BODY LOOK LIKE?

There are a number of ways to configure a test monitoring body. To prime dialogue about what such a body might look like, we examine eight issues that must be considered when designing a test monitoring body:

The Goal
Fundamental Operating Principles
Sponsorship
Credibility
Staffing
Funding
Triggering Action
Access

For convenience we treat the eight issues separately, but they are closely interrelated. We recognize that the diverse values and vested interests of the many stakeholders involved in and affected by high-stakes testing assures competing views on each issue.

The Goal

The overarching goal of a test monitoring body should foster appropriate and responsible uses of high-stakes tests from preschool through secondary school.[45] To fulfill this goal, a test monitoring body should engage in three primary activities.

First, it should monitor testing programs to ensure that they are conceptually sound and satisfy all relevant technical and ethical standards. Second, it should document the benefits and harms associated with a high-stakes testing program. Finally, an effective test monitoring body should use non-adversarial, participatory procedures to forestall disputes and litigation concerning testing through early intervention.

The importance of forestalling disputes and litigation flows from the belief that conflict and disputes over testing programs create unnecessary hostility among parties who may share the same educational goals. Conflicts can impose unnecessary legal costs by advocacy groups, state departments of education, and aggrieved parents. Lawsuits soak up resources that could be more productively applied to other aspects of education.

To effectively forestall disputes and litigation, a test monitoring body must identify and involve affected stakeholders when negotiating differences regarding a testing program. The federal government and business communities employ well-established procedures to reach negotiated settlements that resolve conflicts and disagreements.[46] Similar procedures should be used by a test monitoring body.

Negotiation provides a forum for the parties concerned to share information, knowledge, expertise, and technical abilities. This approach contrasts with the more common adversarial method of bargaining where two camps are wary of divulging any more information than they feel absolutely necessary for fear of aiding their opponents' position. Reaching consensus on a negotiated decision also creates a sense of ownership by all participating parties. As a result, the final negotiated settlement is more likely to prove feasible, and will be easier to enforce.[47]

A test monitoring body's negotiations with stakeholder groups will inevitably focus on: a) technical aspects of test design, scoring, scaling, and equating, b) procedures for and evidence needed to validate inferences, descriptions, and decisions based on a test score, c) the technical and ethical standards that are applicable in a given situation, and d) the consequences associated with test use.

Without question, identifying stakeholder groups and then choosing candidates to represent them will not be easy. Nor will it be easy for stakeholders to reach consensus on the contentious issues that surround high-stakes testing. Nonetheless, a test monitoring body's overarching goal—fostering appropriate and responsible uses of high-stakes tests—cannot be reached without stakeholders first participating in the design of the body and then cooperating with the body as it performs its three primary activities.

Operating Principles

To meet its mission, a test monitoring body's work should be guided by five operating principles. The first principle is *beneficence*—all high-stakes tests should be useful, beneficial, and demonstrably more appropriate for their particular uses than are available alternatives. Given the many serious consequences associated with high-stakes tests that we explored throughout this book, assurances are needed that the tests are efficacious for their intended uses, and the benefits of use outweigh the harms.

The second principle is *evaluation in context.* No matter how sophisticated its design, or carefully it is developed, the value of a test or testing program is a function of how it is used. A high-stakes test must be evaluated in the particular context of its use. An evaluation must consider contextual factors such as the students tested, their communities, the resources and personnel available in their schools, and the high-stakes decisions made based on their test scores. As we have seen throughout this book, these and other factors affect how students interact with a test and how students, teachers, schools, and communities are affected by high-stakes decisions based on test results.

The third operating principle is *precedence of the interests of affected parties.* Individual rights and autonomy, and ethical issues such as informed consent and equity, are inherent in all high-stakes testing programs. Traditionally, these issues have been subordinated to the administrative convenience and efficiency for test developers and testing programs. Because of the potentially serious consequences of high-stakes tests, the rights of those affected should take precedence over the interests of developers and programs, and should be at the forefront of test monitoring activities.

The fourth operating principle is *open, critical inquiry.* The evaluation expert, Lee Cronbach, argued that, "The proper mission of evaluation is not to eliminate the fallibility of authority or to bolster its credibility. Rather, its mission is to facilitate a democratic, pluralistic process by enlightening all the participants."[48] Given that most work conducted by a test monitoring body is evaluative, all stakeholders benefit from open, participatory inquiry.

The final operating principle is *flexible application of recognized standards.* The *Standards* and the *Code* are the principle criteria for evaluating tests and test use. A test monitoring body, however, must apply the *Standards* in a consistent, yet flexible manner, taking into consideration the particular context of test use. A test monitoring body should also seek consensual agreement among disputing parties about the application of a standard in a given context.

Sponsorship

There are a variety of ways to sponsor a test monitoring body. Each comes with advantages and disadvantages.

One option is to have the National Academy of Education (NAE) and the National Academy of Sciences (NAS) jointly sponsor the test monitoring body. Both organizations are recognized for their independent and serious scrutiny of public policy matters. Sponsorship by either organization would lend immediate creditably to the body. This option, however, would require a Congressional mandate for funding and for guaranteed access to essential technical data from test developers and state testing programs.

A second option is a test monitoring board that is a federal agency. Federal sponsorship would ensure adequate and stable funding, as well as access to necessary data. In recent years, however, federal regulatory bodies like the Environmental Protection Agency, the Security and Exchange Commission, and the Federal Drug Administration, have succumbed to political pressure, partisan aims, and conflicts of interest.[49] For example, questions have arisen about the FDA not publishing studies with negative or questionable results, or publishing some of them in a way that conveyed positive results.[50] As an example, the Federal Fish and Wildlife Service office in Alaska directed their biologists not to discuss climate change, polar bears, or sea ice unless designated to do so.[51] Similarly, an apparent conflict of interest of a number of doctors who conducted clinical trails for the FDA of a technique to treat lower back pain has come of light.[52]

A third option is to establish a test monitoring body as a quasi-governmental organization. Existing examples include The Federal Reserve System, National Fire Protection Association, and Amtrak. Like a federal agency, a quasi-governmental organization would ensure stable funding and access to test data. In addition, it would be controlled by an independent board of prominent citizens and representatives of stakeholder groups. Of course, board members would need to be carefully selected so that partisan, political influence is minimized.

Credibility

To be effective over the long term, a test monitoring body must be a stable, enduring independent institution. Only then can it earn a reputation for credibility and fairness.[53] Any monitoring body will be ineffective if its results, advice, judgments, and evaluations are not credible to a wide audience. Credibility is a hard earned attribute and one easily lost. To protect its reputation for good judgment and integrity, a test monitoring body needs independence from political pressures, and a blend of technical expertise and leadership skills. If established as a quasi-governmental agency, a test monitoring body must have a self-perpetuating, non-political board of trustees representative of the various stakeholders.

Staffing

The design and development of high-stakes tests depend on arcane psychometric techniques. A test monitoring body must have staff with expertise in these techniques. Skilled psychometricians are in short supply. Few doctoral degrees in psychometrics are offered each year, yet the explosion in testing has created fierce competition for their services by companies with deep pockets. A test monitoring body must therefore offer competitive salaries.

A test monitoring body also needs staff with expertise in program evaluation, policy analysis, cost benefit analysis, mediation, computer-based technology, and human factor engineering. Of course, the body must have a highly qualified, nationally recognized director with political skills and the ability to assemble and direct a permanent staff. Secretarial and other support staff are also required.

Given the evolving nature of high-stakes testing, staffing patterns must be adaptable and able to react to emerging issues that inevitably will arise. In addition to the permanent staff, a test monitoring body needs the leadership, mechanisms, and funding to assemble ad hoc project teams and standing committees that have the necessary expertise to examine emerging issues. This expertise will likely draw from such disciplines as psychology, child development, sociology, political theory, economics, and computer science.

Funding

If a test monitoring body is to be viable and effective long term, it must have reliable funding sources. One source is the federal government that has mandated that states implement high-stakes testing programs. Another source of funding is state governments. Prior to federal mandates, several states independently implemented high-stakes testing programs. Today, it is these states who contract with test companies to develop their high-stakes tests. The federal government and state governments have an accountability obligation to taxpayers, students, teachers, and school systems to assure that their tests are technically sound and properly used. Monitoring and oversight of their testing programs provides this assurance. It is reasonable, therefore, to ask federal and state governments to help fund an independent test monitoring body.

Testing companies are another source of funding. These companies benefit enormously from the expansion of high-stakes testing. Because they have a vested interest in their product, companies cannot be expected to provide independent, credible monitoring of a high-stakes test. A small fee charged for each tested student would generate considerable funds for a test monitoring body.[54]

Regardless of the funding sources, reasonable estimates of startup and annual costs are needed prior to forming a monitoring body. These costs, we believe, represent a very small percent of the current money spent on high-stakes testing programs, and will be money well spent.

Triggering Action

Monitoring fifty different testing programs, affecting 30 million children, is a massive undertaking. Guidelines for conducting routine monitoring activities across the 50 states are essential. To periodically monitor the technical aspects of each state's testing program, the test monitoring body might examine the technical quality of 10 testing programs each year. When a state makes substantial changes in its tests, or technical questions arise, that state's program could be examined outside of the five year monitoring cycle.

When monitoring the consequences of test use, a test monitoring body could periodically examine the intended and unintended consequences of programs that attach similar stakes to test use. Within a set of programs that have similar stakes attached to test use, a sample of students, teachers, and schools could be examined to document how stakeholders are affected by test use.

A test monitoring body must be prepared to receive requests from stakeholders to examine a specific aspect of a testing program. Requests may come from state departments of education, advocacy groups, test developers or sponsors, or individual students, their parents, and teachers. Such requests could trigger immediate examination of a questionable high-stakes test or test use. For example, when a teacher or student disputes the correct answer for a test question, the test monitoring body could be asked to intervene. Anticipating that a test monitoring body will receive more requests than it could undertake, criteria and processes for deciding which projects to undertake will be essential. Two criteria for triggering a review might be the severity of the stakes and the number of students or schools affected.

Access

Access to data is essential for a monitoring body to examine the technical quality of high-stakes tests. Data that could be used to examine the psychometric characteristics of a test must come from each state or the company contracted to develop its tests. Currently, these data are not readily available.

How would a test monitoring body gain access to these data? If the body was a federal agency or a quasi-governmental organization, Congress could require states that take federal money for their testing program to provide test data to a test monitoring body, with appropriate privacy safeguards. If a test monitoring body is not a federal agency or quasi-governmental organization, high-stakes testing programs will need to agree to cooperate in sharing this data or Congress will need to require states who take federal money for testing to supply these data.

The eight issues presented above are certainly open to debate. When developing a test monitoring body, additional issues will surely emerge. To assure independence, fairness, viability, resources, and competence, these eight issues, and others that will emerge, must be confronted and addressed when crafting a test monitoring body.

THE TIME HAS COME

In the nineteen thirties Harvard University President James Conant envisioned a single organization devoted to testing and educational research that would enhance education in the United States. In 1947, part of his dream was realized when the American Council on Education, the Carnegie Foundation for the Advancement of Teaching, and the College Entrance Examination Board contributed a portion of their assets and key employees to form Educational Testing Service (ETS).[55] ETS became, and remains a premier psychometric organization—one that has greatly influenced American education. A test monitoring body would extend Conant's vision of assisting American education.

Monitoring high-stakes testing is long overdue. Since the end of the 19th century to the present, there have been repeated calls for such oversight. The benefits and risks to institutions and individuals linked to present high-stakes testing programs are real and serious. Today, however, students, educators, parents, and the public have only the assurances of those who build the test or control testing programs that the tests, procedures, uses, and consequences are fair and valid. Instead of leaps of faith about test quality, validity, use, and consequences we need assurances from an independent monitoring body.

State departments of education, and their contractors, may view independent test monitoring as threatening, opening doors best left closed, or, at the very least, inconvenient. Monitoring and oversight, however, should be viewed as an opportunity to improve testing, decrease testing error, and minimize the paradoxical harm caused by high-stakes testing. Test monitoring is an opportunity to ensure the quality and validity of tests used to hold students, teachers, and schools accountable. Independent oversight is owed to the millions of students, families, teachers, and schools affected by the paradoxical nature of high-stakes testing.

NOTES

1. A Government Accounting Office report estimated that the cost of testing over a 7-year period would range from $1.9 billion to $5.3 billion. The National Association of State Boards of Education (NASBE) estimated grades 3–8 assessment expenditures on NCLB mandated assessments range between $2.7–$7 billion between 2004 and 2008. In 2005, Eduventures, a company that provides information for the education market, reported assessment market revenues for 2003/04 and 2004/05 as of $1.192 billion and $1.347 billion respectively. Eduventures forecasts an annual growth in the assessment market of $1.468 billion in 2005/06 to $1.939 billion in 2008/09.
2. See Haney, Madaus, & Lyons (1993). While these estimates are from 1993 they probably underestimate indirect costs because of the increase in mandated testing under NCLB.
3. The independence of any oversight effort is of the utmost importance. For example, in 2007 the leaders of two major Olympic antidoping agencies criticized Major League Baseball for resisting George Michel's recommendation to have an independent organization do testing for HGH. See Wilson & Macur (2008).
4. Wallace (1994).
5. Staudenmaier (1989, p. 5, emphasis added).
6. In 1985 the American Psychological Association (APA) appointed a committee to investigate the feasibility of standardizing the collection of mental and physical measurements (Singleton, No date).
7. Ruch (1925), quoted in Buros (1938/1972, p. 2).
8. Quoted in Buros (1938/1972, p. 2).
9. The publications he initiated, the *Mental Measurements Yearbook* (MMY) and the *Tests in Print* (TIP) series became standard reference sources on tests. He began his work however, with the grander idea of more active monitoring of testing. For over forty years until his death in 1978, he directed the *Buros Institute of Mental Measurements,* and through it, a crusade to improve the quality of tests and their use. His wife Luella, who assisted him in the Institute, was instrumental in relocating the Institute to the University of Nebraska, where its work continues today.
10. Quoted in Buros (1938/1972, p. 3, emphasis added).
11. Buros (1938/1972, p. 4). The Buros Institute's work came to comprise the *MMY* and *TIP* series, and a series of monographs on tests in particular subject areas. The Institute maintains an on-line database with monthly updates of the publications. Their goal is to help test users by influencing test authors

and publishers to produce better tests and to provide more and better information about them.

12. Buros (1972, pp. xxvii–xxviii). In addition to what might better be called disappointments rather than failures—lack of interest in and funding for his idea—there are two major shortcomings in Buros' approach. First, critical reviews formed the core of his effort, and were undertaken by people who defined test quality very differently. Second, the focus of the Buros publications has been largely on the quality of tests produced and not on test use. But, it is clear that some of the most serious problems of testing have arisen not from shortcomings of the tests themselves, but rather from misuse of technically adequate products, or from the unintended paradoxical outcomes they trigger.
13. Adkins (1950).
14. Adkins (1950, p. 546, emphasis added).
15. The *Project's* report recognized that well-designed standardized tests could have value when used appropriately by persons skilled in their use, but concluded that tests were too often of poor quality and misused or abused, and that the "admirable efforts" of professional organizations and reputable test publishers were "insufficient to prevent widespread abuse" Ibid, p. 237.
16. Hobbs (1975, p. 238). It is interesting to note that in 2006 a report from the GAO found defects in the Food and Drug Administration's (FDA) procedures, "including bureaucratic infighting, disorganization and a lack of criteria for deciding what safety actions to take and when to take them" (New York Times, 2006). These charges need to be a red flag in developing a monitoring entity for tests and test use.
17. Edward Zigler, then Director of the *Office of Child Development*, who proposed the *Project*, recalls only, "the recommendation . . . was never followed up" (Zigler, 1991).
18. A similar law was passed in California.
19. Truth in Testing legislation generally worked well for large-volume aptitude tests like the SAT, where items of comparable quality can usually be written to replace released items. However, agencies and test developers maintain that full disclosure would be detrimental to many of their licensing and certification examinations. They argue that items measuring specific job-related knowledge are harder to write and expensive to replace. Thus, they claim disclosure could either decrease the validity of their tests, or make them prohibitively expensive, thereby thwarting the societal purpose they were intended to serve: protecting the public from candidates who lack the minimum skills and knowledge necessary for competent performance on the job.
20. National Commission on Testing and Public Policy (1990, p. 1–2).
21. The feedback from experts was solicited in a conference sponsored by Center for the Study of Testing, Evaluation and Educational Policy, and the RAND Institute on Education and Training. The participants included those from the foundations, state and public school test directors, testing companies, and the academic community of scholars from the fields of testing, evaluation and public policy. The authors of the final report were Madaus, Haney, Newton, & Kreitzer (1993). This chapter borrows heavily from this document and we

acknowledge the enormous contributions of Walt Haney, Kenneth Newton and Amelia Kreitzer in its development.

22. The studies *The Roles of Testing and Diversity in College Admissions; Testing and Diversity in Postsecondary Education: The Case of California, Perceived Effects of State-Mandated Testing Programs on Teaching and Learning: Findings from a National Survey of Teachers, Perceived Effects of State-Mandated Testing Programs on Teaching and Learning: Findings from Interviews with Educators in Low-, Medium-, and High-Stakes States, Errors in Standardized Tests: A Systemic Problem,* and *Testing in the News: A Frame Analysis of Educational Testing News* are posted on the NBETPP web site at www.bc.edu/research/nbetpp/.
23. *FairTest,* for example, was at the forefront of disclosure of the 2006 SAT scoring error calamity.
24. Arenson (2006, p. 2, emphasis added).
25. Toch (2006, p. 5).
26. Sunderman (2006, p. 6).
27. See Bellah, Madsen, Sullivan, Swidler, & Tipton (1991); Derthick & Quirk (1985); McCraw (1984); McGarity (1991); Spulber (1989); Wilson (1980) for more detailed treatments of the growth of regulatory bodies.
28. See Bellah et al. (1991).
29. For example, the industry mounted an extensive effort to defeat "Truth in Testing" legislation.
30. Formatting modified from Sandman (1989, p. 48).
31. Burke (1966).
32. Burke (1966, p. 23). For other examples of outrage leading to regulation see Quirk (1980) and Wilson (1980). Perhaps the most recent example of high hazard and high outrage occurred in 2007 with imports of toys from China tainted with lead paint.
33. Although the combination of hazard and outrage may be critical to governmental intervention, it is less so with private efforts. As suggested above, some private efforts result in part from government inaction because of insufficient outrage. One of the purposes of environmental advocacy groups, for example, is to mobilize public support by building outrage for problems that have not been adequately addressed. Al Gore's movie on global warming, *An Inconvenient Truth,* is an example. With other private efforts, consumer product evaluations, for example, the general level of hazard and outrage may simply not warrant governmental intervention, and the issue is simply better suited to voluntary private action.
34. An exception is "truth in testing" legislation.
35. These documents were jointly developed by the American Educational Research Association, (AERA), The American Psychological Association (APA), and the National Council on Measurement in Education (NCME). Most members of the testing community are members of one or more of the three organizations. Supplementing the *Standards* and the *Code,* scholars have produced works on testing and legal requirements for tests that should also guide test design and use. For, example Messick's (1988); Messick (1989) seminal work on validity and the Buckley amendment (20 U.S.C. § 1231(g)) addressed

issues of confidentiality of student records, including records of test performance.

36. As Arlene Kaplan Daniels has observed, professional "codes do not simply fulfill the function suggested by the professional ideology. Rather, they are part of the ideology, designed for public relations and justification for the status and prestige which professions assume vis-à-vis more lowly occupations" (Daniels, 1973, p. 49).
37. The sixteen were: Federal Deposit Insurance Corporation, Food And Drug Administration, Negotiated Rulemaking; Occupational Safety And Health Administration, American National Standards Institute; Consumer's Union, Good Housekeeping, Motion Picture Association Of America, National Collegiate Athletic Association, Standards And Poor's, Underwriter's Laboratory, American Bar Association, American Institute Of Certified Public Accountants, American Psychological Association, Consumer's Protection Division Attorney General's Office, Supreme Judicial Court–Bar Admissions & Lawyer Discipline.
38. See LORAN Commission (1988).
39. With the advent of biotechnology, assessing the possible social consequences of genetic engineering can have is an added criterion in evaluating many new drugs, see Roush (1991).
40. LORAN Commission (1988, p. 27).
41. National Committee for Injury Prevention and Control (1989).
42. For an example of a many faceted injury prevention program see the National Research Council News Report (1991).
43. Deming (1982, p. 13).
44. Tyre (1991).
45. While arguably high-stakes tests used by business for screening purposes, and tests used to certify candidates in medicine, law, accounting, and other high-stakes testing programs that employ psychological tests may be in need of oversight, this is too big a job, with different sets of political problems, for a test monitoring body to take on given the scope of test use in elementary and secondary education.
46. "Getting to Yes" is one process employed by the government. The process has been so successful and promising that Congress formalized it with the passage of the Negotiated Rulemaking Act of 1990 amended in 1996. See P.L. 104-320, (amending Pub. Law 101-648 and Pub. Law 102-354). Title 5, US Code. Subchapter III – Negotiated Rulemaking Act of 1996). Also see Fisher & Ury (1983); Singer (1990).
47. Breyer (1982).
48. Cronbach & Associates (1980, p. 1).
49. See Drew (2006).
50. See Turner, Matthews, Linardatos, Tell, & Rosenthal (2008).
51. See Revkin (2007).
52. See Abelson (2008).
53. The Consumers' Union and Underwriters Laboratories are noteworthy examples. In testing, the Buros Institute has a long and proud history of pro-

viding independent, credible, and useful information about educational and psychological tests free of the influence of the testing enterprise.

54. No doubt, a per tested student fee would be passed on to the tax payers by increasing the cost for developing and delivering a test.
55. From ETS web page at http://www.ets.org/portal/site/ets/menuitem.22f30af61d34e9c39a77b13bc3921509/?vgnextoid=a1e65784623f4010VgnVCM10000022f95190RCRD.

BIBLIOGRAPHY

Abelson, R. (2008, January 30). Financial ties are cited as issue in spine study. *New York Times.* Retrieved on October, 23 2008 at http://www.nytimes.com/2008/01/30/business/30spine.html?_r=1&oref=slogin.

Abrams, L. & Madaus, G. F. (2003). The lessons of high-stakes testing. *Educational Leadership, 61*(3), 31–35.

Abrams, L., Pedulla, J., & Madaus, G. F. (2003). Views from the classroom: Teachers' opinions of statewide testing programs. *Theory Into Practice, 42*(1), 18–29.

Acland, T. D. (1857). *Middle-Class Examination: Scheme of the West of England Examination and Prizes.* London: J. Ridgeway.

Adams, A. S. (1961). The pace of change. In Educational Testing Service. Paper presented at the Proceedings of the 1960 Invitational Conference on Testing Problems, Princeton, NJ.

Adkins, D. C. (1950). Proceedings of the fifty-eighth annual business meeting of the American Psychological Association, Inc., State College, Pennsylvania. 5, 544–575.

All Things Considered. (2008, July 6). YouTube Monks Storm European Pop Charts, retrieved on July 8, 2008 from http://www.npr.org/templates/story/story.php?storyId=92271550.

Allbeury, T. (1979). The Alpha List. New York: Methuen.

Alspach, K. (2005, October, 26). Board mulls raising MCAS standard. Sentinel & Enterprise. Retrieved on January, 15 2006 from http://www.sentinelandenterprise.com/local/ci_3153388.

American Educational Research Association, American Psychological Association, & National Council on Measurement in Education. (1999). Standards for Educational and Psychological Testing. Washington, DC: American Educational Research Association.

American Educational Research Association, American Psychological Association, & the National Council on Measurement in Education. (1985, revised 1999).

The Paradoxes of High Stakes Testing, pages 223–250

Standards for educational and psychological testing. Washington, DC: American Psychological Association.

Amerin, A. L. & Berliner, D. (2002). High-Stakes Testing, Uncertainty, and Student Learning. Education Policy Analysis Archives, 10(18), Retrieved on January 10, 2007 from http://epaa.asu.edu/epaa/v10n18/.

Anderman, E. M. & Maehr, M. L. (1994). Motivation and schooling in the middle grades. Review of Educational Research, 64, 287–309.

Angoff, W. H. & Dyer, H. S. (1971). The Admissions testing program. In W. H. Angoff (Ed.), The College Board Admissions Testing Program: A technical report on research and development activities relating to the Scholastic Aptitude and Achievement Tests (pp. 1–14). Princeton, NJ: Educational Testing Service.

Anrig, G. (1990). Letter to Lauro Cavazos, Secretary of Education.

Applebaum, H. (1992). The concept of work: Ancient, medieval, and modern. Albany: State University of New York Press.

Aratani, L. (2007, March 20). The Power of Peppermint Put to the Test Washington Post, p. B1.

Arenson, K. (2006, May 20). Senator Proposes Creating Board to Oversee College Admissions Tests. New York Times, Metropolitan p. 2.

Aries, P. (1962). Centuries of Childhood: A Social History of Family Life (R. Boldick, Trans.). New York: Vintage Books.

Arms, E. (2008). What Every Parent Should Know About Standardized Testing. Retrieved June 26, 2008, from http://family.go.com/parenting/pkg-learning/article-205674-what-every-parent-should-know-about-standardized-testing-t/

Arnold, M. (1867–1868). Annual Report of the Committee of Council on Education. London: Her Majesty's Stationary Office.

Asimov, N. (1994a, Feburary19). Alice Walker story pulled from state test. San Francisco Chronicle, p. A1 & A13.

Asimov, N. (1994c, February, 19). State rejects another story by Alice Walker. San Francisco Chronicle, p. A1 & A13.

Aspan, M. (2007, June 25). Prepare for the SAT Test, or Play With Your iPod Have it both Ways. New York Times, p. C7.

Ayres, L. (1918). Historical and present status of educational measurements. In G. Whipple, Montrose (Ed.), *The Seventeenth Yearbook of the National Society for the Study of Education; Part II The Measurement of Educational Products.* Bloomington, Illinois: Public School Publishing Company.

Baker, F. B. (1971). Automation of test scoring, reporting, and analysis. In R. L. Thorndike (Ed.), Educational measurement (pp. 202–234). Washington D. C.: American Council on Education.

Baker, R. (1984). Growing up. New York: Congdon & Weed Inc.

Ballou, F. (1916). Work of the Department of Educational Investigation and Measurements, Boston, Massachusetts. In G. M. Whipple (Ed.), The fifteenth yearbook of the National Society for the Study of Education Part I: Standards and Testing for the Measurement of the Efficiency of Schools and School Systems (pp. 61–68). Chicago: The University of Chicago Press.

Barker, L. (2006). Cosmo, The Fairly Accurate Knife Thrower, retrieved on September 10, 2006 from http://monologues.co.uk/Les_Barker/Cosmo_the_Knife.htm.

Barnard, H. C. (1961). A History of English Education from 1760. London: University of London Press.

Barton, P. E. & Coley, R. J. (2007). The Family: America's Smallest School. Princeton, NJ: Educational Testing Service.

Basalla, G. (1988). The Evolution of Technology. New York: Cambridge University Press.

Bausell, C. V. (2008). Tracking U.S. Trends: States vary in classroom access to computers and policies concerning school technology. Education Week, March 27.

Beaton, A., E. & Zwick, R. (1990). The effects of changes in the national assessment: Disentangling the NAEP 1985–86 reading anomaly. Princeton, N. J.: Educational Testing Service.

Beaton, A. E. (2000). Linking the VNT to NAEP: How much accuracy is necessary? Unpublished Paper.

Beckett, S. (1956). Malone Dies. New York: Grove Press.

Bell, R. & Grant, N. (1974). A Mythology of British Education. London: Panther.

Bellah, R., N., Madsen, R., Sullivan, W. M., Swidler, A., & Tipton, S. M. (1991). The good society. New York: Alfred A. Knopf.

Bennett, A. (2004). The History Boys. London: Gardner Books.

Bennett, R. E., Braswell, J., Oranje, A., Sandene, B., Kaplan, B., & Yan, F. (2008). Does it Matter if I Take My Mathematics Test on Computer? A Second Empirical Study of Mode Effects in NAEP. Journal of Technology, Learning, and Assessment, 6(9).

Bennett, R. E., Persky, H., Weiss, A. R., & Jenkins, F. (2007). Problem Solving in Technology-Rich Environments: A Report From the NAEP Technology-Based Assessment Project (NCES 2007–466). Washington DC: U.S. Department of Education, National Center for Education Statistics.

Bennett, W. J. (1994). The index of leading cultural indicators: Facts and figures on the state of American society. New York: Touchstone.

Benton, J. (2005, September 19). TAKS push not so equal. Dallas Morning News.

Berliner, D. C. (1993). Mythology and the American system of education. Phi Delta Kappan, 74(8), 632–640.

Berliner, D. C. & Biddle, B. J. (1995). The Manufactured crisis: Myths, fraud and the attack on America's public schools. Reading MA: Addison Wesley.

Bestor, A. (1958). What went wrong with U. S. schools. An interview with Prof. Arthur Bestor, University of Illinois. US News and World Report, January 24, 85–87.

Bick, J. (2006, May 28). SUNDAY MONEY: SPENDING; The Long (and Sometimes Expensive) Road to the SAT. New York Times. Retrieved on May 28, 2006 from http://select.nytimes.com/search/restricted/article?res=F70916FD70355A70910C70917B70918EDDAC70894DE404482.

Bijker, W., E. & Law, J. (1992). General introduction. In W. Bijker, E. & J. Law (Eds.), Shaping technology/Building society: Studies in sociotechnical change (pp. 1–14). Cambridge, MA: The MIT Press.

Blank, P. (2006). Shakespeare and the Mismeasure of Renaissance Man. Ithaca, NY: Cornell University Press.

Bloom, B. (1964). Stability and Change in Human Characteristics. New York: Wiley.

Bloomberg News. (2007, August 30). Comic books aim to prepare test-takers. The Boston Globe, p. C4.

Blumenthal, R. (2006, January 13). Houston Ties Teachers' Pay to Test Scores. New York Times. Retrieved on January 13, 2006 from www.nytimes.com/2006/2001/2013/national/2013houston.html.

Bojörklund, A., Clark, M. A., Edin, P.A., Fredriksson, P., & Krueger, A., B. (2005). The market comes to education in Sweden: An evaluation of Sweden's surprising school reforms. New York: Russell Sage Foundation.

Boles, J. K. (1982). Social movements as policy entrepreneurs: The family protection act and family impact analysis. Paper presented at the Paper delivered at the 1982 Annual Meeting of the American Political Science Association, Denver.

Booher-Jennings, J. (2005). Below the bubble: "Educational triage" and the Texas Accountability System. American Educational Research Journal, 42(2), 231–268.

Boorstin, D. (1961). The image: Pseudo-events in America. New York: Vintage.

Boorstin, D. (Ed.). (1989). Hidden history. New York: Vintage Books.

Boorstin, D. J. (1978). The Republic of technology. New York: Harper & Row, Publishers, Inc.

Boorstin, D. J. (1985). The discovers: A history of man's search to know his world and himself. New York: Vintage Books.

Borgmann, A. (1984). Technology and the character of contemporary life: A philosophical inquiry. Chicago: University of Chicago Press.

Borja, R. R. (2003). South Dakota Drops Online 'Adaptive' Testing. Education Week. 22(20), 16.

Boston Globe. (2008, May 25). B7.

Bowen, S. & Ferrell, K. (2003). Assessment in Low-Incidence Disabilities: The Day-to-Day Realities. Rural Special Education Quarterly, 22 (4), 10–19.

Bowler, R. F. (1983). Payment by Results: A study in Achievement Accountability. Unpublished doctoral dissertation, Boston College.

Boyd, R., Musick, M., & Glode, M. (1991). Letter to Stufflebeam et. al: NAGB, Washington, DC.

Bracey, G. W. (1992). The second Bracey report on the condition of public education. Phi Delta Kappan, 74(2), 104–117.

Bracey, G. W. (1993). The third Bracey report on the condition of public education. Phi Delta Kappan, 75(2), 104–117.

Bracey, G. W. (1997). The seventh Bracey report on the condition of public education. Phi Delta Kappan, 79(2), 120–137.

Bracey, G. W. (2004a). The fourteenth Bracey report on the condition of public education. Phi Delta Kappan, 86(2), 149.

Bracey, G. W. (2004b). Setting the record straight. Portsmouth, NH: Heinemann.

Bracey, G. W. (2005). Oh, Those NAEP Achievement Levels. Principal Leadership, 6(1), 76.

Bracey, G. W. (2006, May 21). Heard the One About the 600,000 Chinese Engineers? Washington Post. Retrieved online 11/19/2007 at http://www.washingtonpost.com/wp-dyn/content/article/2006/05/19/AR2006051901760.htm

Brancaccio, D. (2005). NOW Transcript. Retrieved January 15, 2008, from http://www.pbs.org/now/transcript/transcriptNOW135_full.html#esquith.

Brennan, R. L. (2004). Revolutions and Evolutions in Current Educational Testing: Center for Advanced Studies in Measurement and Education. Retrieved on January 30, 2008 from http://www.education.uiowa.edu/casma/wallace.casma.rpt.pdf.

Breyer, S. (1982). Regulation and Its Reform. Cambridge, MA: Harvard University Press.

Brigden, M. L. & Heathcote, J. C. (2000). What do unexpected results mean? Post Graduate Medicine On Line, 107(7).

Broadfoot, P. (Ed.). (1984). Selection, certification, and control: Social issues in educational assessment. New York: Falmer.

Brown, S. (1998). Professor of Medieval Philosophy, Boston College, translation.

Bruner, J. (1996). The culture of education. Cambridge, MA: Harvard University Press.

Bruner, J. S. (1966). Toward a theory of instruction. Cambridge, MA: Harvard University Press.

Buchanan, J. M. (1987). Opportunity Cost. The New Palgrave: A Dictionary of Economics, 3, 718–721.

Bull, R. & Stevens, J. (1979). The effects of attractiveness of writer and penmanship on essay grades. Journal of Occupational Psychology, 52, 53–59.

Burke, J. G. (1966). Bursting Boilers and the federal power. Technology and Culture, 7(1), 1–23.

Buros, O. K. (Ed.). (1938/1972). The nineteen thirty eight mental measurements yearbook. Highland Park, NJ: Gryphon (originally published in 1938 by the Rutgers University Press under the title The Nineteen Thirty Eight Mental Measurements Yearbook of the School of Education, Rutgers University; reissued by Gryphon with a 1972 imprint).

Buros, O. K. (Ed.). (1972). The seventh mental measurements yearbook. Highland Park, NJ: Gryphon.

Burton, E. (1979). Richard Lowell Edgeworth's Education Bill of 1979: A missing chapter in the history of Irish education. Irish Journal Of Education, 13(1), 24–33.

Bush, G. W. (2001). Remarks by President at Central Connecticut State University. Retrieved on April 20, 2001 from http://www.whitehouse.gov/news/releases/2001/04/20010418-3.html

Bush, G. W. (2005). No Unwinding No Child Left Behind: Excerpts from President George W. Bush's comments regarding No Child Left Behind at his April 29, 2005 press conference. Washington D.C.: U.S. Department of Education.

Callaghan, R. E. (1962). Education and the Cult of Efficiency. Chicago: University of Chicago Press.

Campbell, D. T. (1975). Assessing the impact of planned social change. In Social and Public Policies: The Dartmouth/OECD Conference. Hanover NH: Public Affairs Center, Dartmouth College.

Campbell, D. T. & Fiske, D., W. (1959). ''Convergent and Discriminant Validation by the Multitrait-Multimethod Matrix," Pychological Bulletin, 56, 81–105.

Cannell, J. J. (1987). Nationally Normed Elementary Achievement Testing in America's Public Schools: How all Fifty States are Above the National Average. Daniels, West Virginia: Friends for Education.

Cannell, J. J. (1989). The "Lake Wobegon" report: How public educators cheat on standardized achievement tests. Albuquerque, NM: Friends for Education.

Carroll, J. (1966). A model of school learning. Teachers College Record, 64, 723–733.

Carroll, L. (1982). Sylvie and Bruno. In The Penguin Complete Lewis Carroll. New York Penquin.

Carson, C. C., Huelskamp, R. M., & Woodall, T. D. (1992). Perspectives on education in America. Journal of Educational Research, 86(5), 259–309:entire issue.

Cellis, W. (1993, December 9). International report card shoes U.S. schools work. New York Times, pp. 1-A8.

Center on Educational Policy. (2006a). From the Capital to the Classroom: Year 4 of the No Child Left Behind Act: Summary and Recommendations. Washington DC: Center on Educational Policy.

Center on Educational Policy. (2006b). From the capital to the classroom: Year 4 of No Child Left Behind. Washington D.C.: Center on Educational Policy. Retrieved on March 30, 2006 from at www.cep-dc.org

Chapman v. California Department of Education, Case JCVCDOE224766 2002.

Chase, C. I. (1986). Essay test scoring: Interaction of relevant variables. Journal of Educational Measurement, 23(1), 33–41.

Chelimsky, E. (1992). U.S General accounting Office's interim report reviewing NAGB achievement levels and related matters. Washington, DC: Submitted to and at the request of the House of Representatives Committee on Education and Labor and the Subcommittee on Elementary, Secondary, and Vocational Education. GAO.

Christian, G. A. (1922). English Education From Within. London: Wallace Gandy.

Chrystal, K. A. & Mizen, P. (2001). Goodhart's Law: Its Origins, Meaning and Implications for Monetary Policy Prepared for the Festschrift in honour of Charles Goodhart. Retrieved on October 20, 2008 from http://www.cxoadvisory.com/blog/external/blog9-18-07/Goodharts_Law.pdf

Clarke, M. M., Haney, W., & Madaus, G. F. (2000). High Stakes Testing and High School Completion. Chestnut Hill, MA: National Board on Educational Testing and Public Policy, Boston College, Retrieved on December 20, 2001 from at http://www.bc.edu/research/nbetpp/.

Clarke, M. M., Shore, A., Rhoades, K., Abrams, L., Miao, J., & Li, J. (2003). Perceived effects of state-mandated testing programs on teaching and learning: Findings from interviews with educators in lo-,medium-,and high-stakes states. Chestnut Hill MA: National Board on Educational Testing and Public Policy, Boston College, at http://www.bc.edu/research/nbetpp/.

Clinton, B. (1987). Speaking of Leadership. Denver, CO: Education Commission of the States.

Coleman, J. S., Campbell, E. Q., Hobson, C. J., McPartland, J., Mood, A. M., Weinfeld, F. D., et al. (1966). Equality of Educational Opportunity. Washington, DC: Office of Education, U.S. Department of Health, Education and Welfare.

Colton, T. (1974). Statistics in medicine Boston: Little Brown.

Colvin, G. (2005, July 25). America Isn't Ready [Here's What To Do About It] In the relentless, global, tech-driven, cost-cutting struggle for business. FORTUNE Magazine, p. 70.

Commision on Behavioral and Social Sciences and education (CBASSE). (1999). Grading the Nation's Report Card: Evaluating NAEP and Transforming the Assessment of Educational Progress (Vol. http://books.nap.edu/books/0309062853/html/7.html). Washington D.C.: The National Academies Press.

Connolly, W. E. (1991). Identity/difference: Democratic negotiations of political paradox. Ithaca NY: Cornell University Press.

Coolahan, J. M. (1975). The Origins of the Payment by Results Policy in Education and the Experience of it in the National and Intermediate Schools of Ireland. Unpublished Master's thesis, Trinity College, Dublin.

Corbett, H. & Wilson, B. (1999). Testing, reform, and rebellion. Norwood, NJ: Ablex.

Crialese, E. (2007) THE GOLDEN DOOR Miramax Films A MARTIN SCORESE FILM.

Cronbach, L. J. & Associates. (1980). Toward reform of program evaluation. San Francisco: Jossey-Bass.

Crosby, A. W. (1997). The measure of reality: Quantification and western society 1250–1600. New York: Cambridge University Press.

Cuban, L. (1986). Oversold & Underused: Computers in the Classroom. Cambridge, MA: Harvard University Press.

Cullen, J. & Shaw, S. (2000). The Accuracy of Teacher Predictions of Student Test Performance for Students Referred to Special Education: Connecticut: Department of Education and Educational Psychology, Western Connecticut State University.

Cunningham, A. (1989). Enney, Meeny, Minie, Moe: Testing Policy and Practice in Early Childhood, Paper commissioned by The National Commission on Testing and Public Policy. Chestnut Hill MA: Boston College.

Daniels, A. K. (1973). How free should professionals be? In E. Freidson (Ed.), The professions and their prospects (pp. 39–57). Beverly Hills, CA: Sage.

Darling-Hammond, L. & Falk, B. (1997). Using standards and assessment to support student learning. Phi Delta Kappan, 79(3), 1990–1999.

Datta, L. (1982). Employment-related basic skills. In The 81st Yearbook of the National Society for the Study of Education Part 2 (pp. 140–221). Chicago: University of Chicago Press.

Dearing, R. (1993). The national curriculum and its assessment: An interim report. London: School Examinations and Assessment Council, Newcombe House, 45 Notting Hill Gate, London W11 3JB.

Demaray, M. K. & Elliott, S. N. (1998). Teachers judgments of students' academic functioning: A comparison of actual and predicted performance. School Psychology Quarterly, 13(1), 8–24.

DeMarco, P. (2005, August 7). Tufts dean offers new view on smarts: Psychologist argues tests not ideal measure. Boston Globe, p. B8.

Deming, W. E. (1982). Out of the crisis. Cambridge, MA: The MIT Center for Advanced Engineering Study.

Derthick, M. & Quirk, P. J. (1985). The politics of deregulation. Washington, D.C.: The Brookings Institution.

Deyhle, D. (1986). Success and failure: A micro-ethnographic comparison of Navajo and Anglo students' perceptions of testing. Curriculum Inquiry, 16(4).

Dikli, S. (2006). An Overview of Automated Scoring of Essays. Journal of Technology, Learning, and Assessment, 5(1).

Dillon, J. (2005b, November 26). Students Ace State Tests but Earn D's From U.S. New York Times, p. A1.

Dillon, J. & Hershbell, J. (1991). Iamblichus On the Pythagorean way of Life: Text, Translation, and Notes. Atlanta, GA: Scholars Press.

Dillon, S. (2005a, August 22). Connecticut takes U.S. to court over Bush education initiative. New York Times. Retrieved on August 30, 2005 from http://www.nytimes.com/2005/08/22/nyregion/22cnd-child.html?ex=1282

Dillon, S. (2006, March 26). Schools Cut Back Subjects to Push Reading and Math. New York Times, p. 1.

Dionne, E. J. J. (1992). Why Americans hate politics. New York: Touchstone.

Diuguid, L. (2005, December 28). ADDRESSING CLASSISM WILL IMPROVE SCHOOL PERFORMANCE. Kansas City Star, Retrieved on December 30, 2005 from http://www.kansascity.com/mld/kansascity/news/columnists/lewis_w_diuguid/13495997.htm.

Dossey, J. A., Mullis, I. V., S., Lindquist, M. M., & Chambers, D. L. (1988). The mathematics report card: Are we measuring up. Princeton, NJ: Educational Testing Service.

Downey, M. T. (1965). Ben Wood: Educational reformer. Princeton, NJ: Educational Testing Service.

Doyle, D. P. (1991, September). Empowering Teachers. The Atlantic Monthly, 15.

Drew, E. (2006, June 22). Power Grab. The New York Review of Books, 53, Retrieved on June 30, 2006 from http://www.nybooks.com/contents/20060622.

Duffy, M. (1962). That's how it was. New York: Doubleday.

Economic Focus. (1993, December 25). The richer, the slower. The Economist, 329, 92.

Edes, G. (2008, January 18th). Lowell living large: Series star enjoys his new celebrity. Boston Globe.

Educational Testing Service. (1954). Proceedings of the 1953 Invitational Conference on Testing Problems. Princeton, NJ: Author.

Eduventures. (2006). K–12 Solutions Learning Markets & Opportunities 2005. Boston: Eduventures.

Ellul, J. (1964). The Technological Society (J. Wilkinson, Trans.). New York: Vintage Books.

Ellul, J. (1990). The technological bluff. Grand Rapids, MI: Williams B. Eerdmans Company.

Elton, G. R. (1991). Return to essentials: Reflections on the present state of historical studies. Cambridge, UK: Cambridge University Press.

Eulau, H. (1977). Technology and civility: The skill revolution in politics. Stanford CA: Hoover Institution Press.

Fassold, M. A. (1996). Adverse Racial Impact of the Texas Assessment of Academic Skills. San Antonio TX: Mexican American Legal Defense and Education Fund.

Feldt, L. S. & Brennan, R. L. (1989). Reliability. In R. Linn (Ed.), Educational measurement. New York: Macmillan, pp. 105–146.

Fielder, J. (1992). Autonomous technology, democracy, and the nimbys. In L. Winner (Ed.), Democracy in a technological society (Official publication of the Society for Philosophy and Technology, 9 ed., pp. 105–121). Boston: Kluwer Academic Publishers.

Fisher, L. M. (1992, June 23). Sears's auto centers to halt commissions. New York Times: Business Day, p. D1 & D5.

Fisher, R., & Ury, W. (1983). Getting to Yes: Negotiating agreements without giving in Harmondsworth, Middlesex England: Penguin Books.

Fitch, J. (1864–65). *Annual Report of the Committee of Council on Education.* London: Her Majesty's Stationary Office.

Fitzmyer, J. A. (1992). Response to 101 Questions on the Dead Sea Scrolls. Boston: Paulist Press.

Flannery, T. (2006, February, 23). The Ominous New Pact. The New York Review of Books, LIII, 24.

Foden, F. (1989). The examiner. James Booth and the origins of common examinations. Leeds: School of Continuing Education, University of Leeds.

Foucault, M. (1979). Discipline and punish: The birth of the prison. Harmondsworth, England: Penguin.

Franke, W. (1963). The reform and abolition of the traditional Chinese examination system. Boston: East Asian Research Center, Harvard University.

Fuller, B., Gesicki, K., Kang, E., & Wright, J. (2006). Is the No Child Left Behind Act Working The Reliability of How States Track Achievement Working Paper 06-1. Oakland: Policy Analysis for California Education University of California, Berkeley.

Gagne, R. M. (1965). Conditions of Learning. New York, NY: Holt, Rineheart, and Winston.

Galbraith, J. K. (1992). The culture of contentment. Boston: Houghton Mifflin Company.

Gao, X., Shavelson, R. J., & Baxter, G., P. (1994). Generalizability of large-scale performance assessments in science: Promises and problems. Applied Measurement in Education, 7(4), 323–342.

Gardner, H. (1991). The unschooled mind. New York Basic Books.

Gardner, H. (1997). Frames of Mind. Basic Books: New York.

Gilbert, F. (2008, February 9). Our confederacy of dunces. The Tablet (http://www.thetablet.co.uk), pp. 58–59.

Ginsburg, A. L., Noell, J., & Plisko, V. W. (1988). Lesson from the wall chart. Educational Evaluation and Policy Analysis, 10(1), 1–12.

Gipps, C., McCallum, B., McAllister, S., & Brown, M. (1991). National assessment at seven: some emerging themes: University of London, Institute of Education and Centre for Educational Studies King's College, Unpublished draft paper presented at BERA conference 1991.

Gladwell, M. (2005, October 10). A Critic at Large. Getting in: The Social Logic of Ivy League Admissions. The New Yorker, 80–86.

Gleick, J. (1987). Chaos: Making a new science. New York: Viking Penguin Inc.

Gonzalez, J. (2008, May 21). Bronx 8th-graders boycott practice exam but teacher may get ax. New York Daily News. Retrieved October 22, 2008 from http://www.commondreams.org/archive/2008/05/22/9123.

Goodkin, S. & Gold, D. G. (2007, August 27). The Gifted Child Left Behind. Washington Post, p. A 13.

Gordon, P. & Lawton, D. (1978). Curriculum change in the 19th and 20th centuries. New York: Holmes and Meier.

Gordon, S. C. (1968). Reports and Repercussions in West Indian Education, 1835–1933. London: Ginn.

Gould, S., Jay. (1981). The Mismeasure of man. New York: W. W. Norton & Company.

Grabmann, (1927) Baeumker, Clemens und Grabmann, Martin, Studien und Charakteristiken zur Geschichte der Philosophie insbesondere des Mittelalters (Beitraege zur Geschichte der Philosophie des Mittelalters, Text und Untersuchungen, Bd. 25, Hft. 1/2). Muenster in Westf.: Aschendorff.

Graham, D. & Tyler, D. (1993). A lesson for us all: The making of a national curriculum. London: Routledge.

Graves, F. P. (1920). A History of Education during the Middle Ages (2nd ed.). Westport, CT: Greenwood Press Publishers.

Green, R. (2006, August 8). If Kids Can't Read, What Can They Do Later? Hartford Courant. Retrieved on September 1, 2006 from: http://pqasb.pqarchiver.com/courant/access/1096964101.html?dids=1096964101:1096964101&FMT=ABS&FMTS=ABS:FT&type=current&date=Aug+1096964118%1096964102C+1096962006&author=RICK+GREEN&pub=Hartford+Courant&edition=&startpage=B.1096964101&desc=IF+KIDS+CAN%1096964127T+READ%1096964102C+WHAT+CAN+THEY+DO+LATER%1096964103F.

Griffin, B. & Heidorn, M. (1996). An examination of the relationship between MCT performance and dropping out of high school. Educational Evaluation and Policy Analysis, 18(243–251).

Groopman, J. (2000). Second Opinions. New York: Viking.

Gusfield, J., R. (1981). The culture of public problems: Drinking-driving and the symbolic order. Chicago: The University of Chicago Press.

Haertel, E. (1989). Student achievement tests as tools of educational policy: Practices and consequences. In B. Gifford (Ed.), Test Policy and Test Performance: Education, Language and Culture (pp. 25–50). Boston: Kluwer Academic Publishers.

Hall, E. T. (1977). Beyond culture. New York: Anchor Books.

Hallahan, D. P. & Kaufmann, J. M. (2006). Exceptional learners: an introduction to special education (10th ed.). Boston: Allyn Bacon.

Hamilton, W. (1853). Discussions in Philosophy and Literature, Education and University Reform (2nd ed.). London: Longman.

Haney, W. (2001a). The myth of the Texas miracle in education. Education Policy Analysis Archives, 8(41).

Haney, W. (2001b, January 13). Revisiting the Myth of the Texas Miracle in Education: Lessons about Dropout Research and Dropout Prevention. Paper prepared for the "Dropout Research: Accurate Counts and Positive Interventions" Conference. Paper presented at the Dropout Research: Accurate Counts and Positive Interventions" Conference, Cambridge, MA.

Haney, W. (2005, December 13). Overcoming Obstacles to Progress. The Washington Post, p. A12.

Haney, W., Madaus, G. F., Abrams, L., Wheelock, A., Miao, J., & Gruia, I., M. (2004). The Education Pipeline in the United States, 1970–2000. Chestnut Hill, MA: Education Pipeline Project, National Board on Educational Testing and Public Policy Center for the Study of Testing, Evaluation, and Educational Policy Lynch School of Education Boston College at http://www.bc.edu/research/nbetpp/statements/nbr3.pdf.

Haney, W., Madaus, G. F., & Lyons, R. (1993). The Fractured Market Place for Standardized Testing. Boston: Kluwer Academic Publishers.

Haney, W. & Scott, L. (1987). Talking with children about tests: An exploratory study of test item ambiguity. In R. Freedle & R. Duran (Eds.), Cognitive and linguistic analyses of test performance: Vol 22 of Advances in Discourse Processes. Stamford CT: Ablex Publishing Corporation, pp. 69–87.

Hansard's Parliamentary Debates a. Third Series, cols. 198–199. London: T. C. Hansard.

Hanson, F. A. (1993). Testing testing: Social consequences of the examined life. Berkeley, CA: University of California Press.

Harasta, C. (2000, September 21). Cathy Harasta's Olympic sports column: Equipment error doesn't measure up to standards. The Dallas Morning News. Retrieved July 2, 2001, from: http://www.dallasnews.com.

Hartog, P. & Rhodes, E. C. (1935). An Examination of Examinations. London: Macmillan.

Hauser, R. M. (2000). Should we end social promotion? Truth and consequences. Paper presented at the Paper Presented at the Conference of the Harvard Civil Rights Project on Civil Rights and High Stakes Testing December 1998, Retrieved 11/18/2002 from http://www.edrs.com (ED445015), New York, NY.

Hays, C. L. (2004, December 20). For Some Parents Its Never to Early for S.A.T. Prep. New York Times. Retrieved January 25, 2004 from http://www.nytimes.com/2004/12/20/technology/20toy.html

Hearn, W. E. (1872). Payment by the Results in Primary Education. Melbourne: Stellwell and Knight.

Helderman, R. (2002, November 7). Passing rate increases on Va. exams. The Washington Post. Retrieved on November 8, 2002 from http:www.washingtonpost.com.

Henry, J. (1963). Culture against man. New York: Vintage Books.

Herbert, A. (Ed.). (1889). The Sacrifice of Education to examinations: Letters from "all sorts and conditions of men". London: Williams and Norgate.

Hickok, E. (2006, October 11). No Undergrad Left Behind. New York Times. Retrieved on November 15, 2006 from http://select.nytimes.com/search/restricted/article?res=F00F12FE03B540C728DDDA90994DE404482.

Hill, C. & Larsen, E. (2000). Children and reading tests (Vol. 65). Stamford CT: Ablex Publishing Corporation.

Hobbs, N. (1975). The futures of children. San Francisco: Jossey-Bass.

Hoge, R. D., & Coladarci, T. (1989). Teacher-based judgments of academic achievement: A review of the literature. Review of Educational Research, 59, 297–313.

Holmes, E. G. A. (1911). What is and what might be: A study of education in general and elementary in particular. London: Constable.

Holt, P. (Ed.). (1996). Alice Walker Banned. San Francisco: Aunt Lute Books.

Hopkins, J. S. (2004, September 22). Tutoring Spin Off of Sylvan Expects IPO of 15 Million Shared This Week: Educate Inc. Would Trade On NSDAQ Stock Market. Baltimore Sun, Retrieved on October 10, 2004 from http://www.baltimoresun.com/business/investing/bal-bz.sylvan22sep22,21,3610596.story?coll=bal-investing-headlines

Horkay, N., Bennett, R. E., Allen, N., Kaplan, B., & Yan, F. (2006). Does it Matter if I Take My Writing Test on Computer? An Empirical Study of Mode Effects in NAEP. Journal of Technology, Learning, and Assessment, 5(2).

Horn, C., Ramos, M., Blumer, I., & Madaus, G. F. (2000). Cut scores: Results may vary. NBETPP Monographs, 1(1), 1–31.

Hoskins, K. (1968). The examination, disciplinary power and rational schooling. History of Education, 8, 135–146.

Howell, A. (1991). The fine art of motivation. Bobbin, 33(2), 20, 22, 24–26.

Hubbard, J. (2006, September 19). Bibb Students Face 70 Days of Testing. The Macon Telegraph, p. 1 & 4.

Huelskamp, R. A. (1993). Perspectives on education in America. Phi Delta Kappan, 74(9), 718–721.

Hughes, R. N. (1979, March 15). Education could pay. New York Times.

Hughes, T. P. (1989). American genesis: A century of invention and technological enthusiasm. New York: Penguin Books.

Huxley, T. H. (1870). The School Boards: What They Can Do, and What They May Do. Contemporary Review, 16(December, 1870), 1–15.

Jacob, B. (2002). Accountability, Incentives and Behavior: The Impact of High-Stakes Testing in the Chicago Public Schools. Cambridge MA: Social Science Research Network. Retrieved on December 30, 2002 from http://ssrn.com/abstract=314639.

Jimerson, S. R., Anderson, G. E., & Whipple, A. D. (2002). Winning the battle and losing The war: Examining the relation between grade retention and dropping out of high school. Psychology in the Schools, 39(4), 441–457.

Jones, M., Jones, B., Hardin, B., Chapman, L., & Yarbough, T. (1999). The impact of high-stakes testing on teachers and students in North Carolina. Phi Delta Kappan, 81(3), 199–203.

Jones, T. (2005). Formulaic thrills: A review of the Oxford Murders by Guillermo Martinez, Translated by Sonia Soto. The London Review of Books, 27(2).

Judd, C. H. (1918). A look forward. In G. M. Whipple (Ed.), The Measurement of Educational Products. Bloomington, Ill: Public School Publishing Co.

Kamii, C. (1990). Achievement testing in early childhood education: The games grown-ups play. Washington, DC: National Association for the Education of Young Children.

Keenan, J. F. (1993). What's your worst moral argument? America, 169(42), 17–18, 28–30.

Keillor, G. (1985). Lake Wobegon Days. New York: Viking.

Kellaghan, T. (1996). IEA studies and educational policy. Assessment in Education, 3, 143–160.

Kellaghan, T. (2000). Educational equity and inclusion. Paper presented at the Paper presented at the Mexico-Irish Conference, Ministry of Education, Mexico City, October 5–6 2000.

Kellaghan, T. & Greaney, V. (1992). Using examinations to improve education. A study in fourteen African countries. Washington D.C.: World Bank.

Kellaghan, T. & Madaus, G. F. (1993). Using public examinations to improve student motivation. Paper presented at the annual meeting of the American Educational Research Association, 1993, Atlanta GA.

Kellaghan, T., Madaus, G. F., & Raczek, A. (1996). The use of external examinations to improve student motivation. Washington, D.C.: American Educational Research Association.

Kelley, D. E. (2006). Helping Hands: 17 January (Season 2 Episode 12), ABC.

Kelly, A. V. (1989). The Curriculum. Theory and Practice (3rd ed.). London: Chapman.

Kermode, F. (1988). I am only equivocally Harol Brodkey: Excerpted from Stories in an almost classical mode. New York Times Book Review, September 18, p.3.

Koretz, D. (1988). Arriving in Lake Wobegon. Are standardized tests exaggerating achievement and distorting instruction? American Educator, 12(2), 8–15, 46–52.

Koretz, D. (1995). Sometimes a cigar is only a cigar, and often a test is only a test. In D. Ravitch (Ed.), Debating the future of American education. Do we need national standards and assessments? Washington, D.C.: Brookings Institute, pp. 154–166

Koretz, D., Barron, S., Mitchell, K., & Keith, S. (1996). Perceived effects of the Maryland school performance assessment program (Technical Report 409): CRESST/RAND Institute on Education and Training.

Koretz, D. & Deibert, E. (1994). Interpretations of National Assessment of Educational Progress (NAEP) anchor points and achievement levels by the print media in 1991. Washington DC: Institute on Education and Training RAND.

Kotkin, J. & Kishimoto, Y. (1988, January 17). Let's quit whining and get to work! Forget those gloom-mongering prophecies–America's economy is the envy of the world. Washington Post, p. C1&2.

Kracke, E. A. (1953). Civil Service in Early Sung China- 960–1067. Cambrige MA: Harvard University Press.

Kreitzer, A. E., Haney, W., & Madaus, G. F. (1989). Competency testing and dropouts. In E. F. Lois Weis, and Hugh G. Petrie (Ed.), In Dropouts from school: Issues, dilemmas, and solutions, Part II (pp. 129–152). New York: State University of New York.

Krige, A. (1998). Intelligent tutoring systems: BUGGY. Retrieved July 17, 2008 from http://tecfa.unige.ch/staf/staf-d/krige/staf11/buggy.html.

Kritzman, L. D. (Ed.). (1990). Michel Foucault: Politics, philosophy, culture: Interviews and other writings 1977–1984. New York: Routledge.

Kroft, S. (Writer) (2007). Unlikely Terrorists on No Fly List, 60 Minutes: CBS News.

Kula, W. (1986). Measures and men (R. Szreter, Trans.). Princeton, NJ: Princeton University Press.

Laffer, A. B. (1982). For better schools, pay achievers. *Education Week.* Retrieved on January 10, 2005 from www.edweek.org/ew/articles/1982/05/19/02290002.h01.html

Landau, S., Russell, M., Gourgey, K., Erin, J., & Cowan, J. (2003). Use of the Talking Tactile Tablet in mathematics testing. Journal of Visual Impairment and Blindness, 97(2), 85–96.

Lang, S. (2006). Press Release: New Bedford Mayor Scott W. Lang's Statement. Retrieved on 10/30/07 at http://susanohanian.org/atrocity_fetch.php?id=6182.

Larkin, P. (1947). Jill. London: Fortune Press.

Lens, W. (1994). Motivation and learning. In T. Husén & T. N. Postlethwaite (Eds.), The international encyclopedia of education (2nd ed.) (pp. 3936–3942). Oxford: Pergamon.

Levine, D. M. (Ed.). (1971). Performance Contracting in Education. An Appraisal: Toward a Balanced Perspective. Englewood Cliffs, NJ: Educational Technology Publications.

Lewy, A. (1996). Postmodernism in the field of achievement testing. Studies in Educational Evaluation, 22(3), 223–244.

Lichtblau, E. (2005, September 2). FBI Abandons disputed test for bullets from crime scenes. New York Times. Retrieved on October 22, 2008 from http://www.nytimes.com/2005/09/02/politics/02bullets.html

Lindsay, J. (2001, May 23). Students find mistake in math portion of MCAS test. Retrieved from the Associated Press May 23, 2001, http://www.masslive.com.

Linn, R., Graue, E. M., & Sanders, N. M. (1990). Comparing state and district test results to national norms: Interpretations of scoring 'above the national average'. (CSE Technical Report 308). Los Angeles: University of California at Los Angeles, Center for Research on Evaluation, Standards and Student Testing.

Little, A. (1982). The role of examinations in the promotion of the 'Paper Qualification Syndrome'. In International Labour Organization (Ed.), Paper Qualifications Syndrome (POS) and Unemployment of School Leavers. A Comparative Sub-Regional Study. Addis Ababa: International Labour Office.

Little, A. (1993). Toward an international framework of understanding assessment. Paper presented at the Conference on Learning, Selection and Monitoring: Resolving the Roles of Assessment, International Centre for Research on Assessment, Institute of education, University of London.

Locust, C. (1988). Wounding the spirit: discrimination and traditional American Indian belief systems. Harvard Educational Review, 58(3), 315–330.

Loewe, M. (1986). The former Han dynasty. In D. Twitchett & M. Loewe (Eds.), The Cambridge history of China (Vol. 1, pp. 103–198). Cambridge: Cambridge University Press.

Lomax, R., G, West, M., Maxwell, Harmon, M., E, Viator, K., A, & Madaus, G., F. (1996). The impact of mandated standardized testing on minority students. Journal of Negro Education, 64(2), 171–185.

LORAN Commission. (1988). Report of the LORAN Commission to the Harvard Community Health Plan: Harvard Community Health Plan, Boston MA.

Lowrance, W. W. (1986). Modern science and human values. New York: Oxford University Press.

Lyman, R. (1989). Give 'em the razor, sell 'em the blades. Graphic Arts Monthly, January, 74–76.

Maclaverty, B. (1979). The miraculous candidate. Belfast: Blackstaff.

MacPherson, K. (2004, July 12). School Leaving arts behind many feel. Pittsburgh Post-Gazette, pp. A-1.

Mad Hot Ballroom (2005). Directed by Marilyn Agrelo. With Heather Berman, Emma Therese Biegacki, Paul Daggett purchased by Paramount Classics and Nickelodeon.

Madaus, G. (Ed.). (1983). The courts, validity and minimum competency testing. Boston: Kluwer-Nijhoff Publishing.

Madaus, G., F, Haney, W., Newton, K., B, & Kreitzer, A. (1993). A proposal for a monitoring body for tests used in public policy. Paper presented at the Conference on The Evaluation of Test-based Educational Reforms, Executive Education, Babson College Wellesley, MA.

Madaus, G., F. & Kellaghan, T. (1993). The British experience with 'authentic' testing. Phi Delta Kappan, 74(6), 458–469.

Madaus, G. F. (1979). Testing and funding: Measurement and policy issues, 1, 53–62.

Madaus, G. F. (1988). The influence of testing on the curriculum. In L. Tanner (Ed.), Critical Issues in Curriculum (Vol. 87th Yearbook of the National Society for the Study of Education, Part 1, pp. 83–121). Chicago: University of Chicago Press.

Madaus, G. F. (1993). A national testing system: Manna from above: An historical/technological perspective. Educational Assessment, 1(1), 9–26.

Madaus, G. F. (1994). A technological and historical consideration of equity issues associated with proposals to change the nation's testing policy. Harvard Educational Review, 64(1), 76–95.

Madaus, G. F. (2004). Ralph W. Tyler's contribution to program evaluation. In M. C. Alkin (Ed.), Evaluation Roots: Tracing Theorists' Views and Influences (pp. 69–79). Thousand Oaks, CA: Sage Publications.

Madaus, G. F., Airasian, P. W., & Kellaghan, T. (1980). School Effectiveness: A Reassessment of the Evidence. New York: McGraw Hill.

Madaus, G. F., Clarke, M., & O'Leary, M. (2003). A century of standardized mathematics testing. In G. M. Stanic & J. Kilpatrick (Eds.), In A Recent History of

Mathematics Education in the United States and Canada. Reston, VA: National Council of Teachers of Mathematics.

Madaus, G. F. & Kellaghan, T. (1992). Curriculum evaluation and assessment. In P. W. Jackson (Ed.), Handbook of research on curriculum (pp. 119–154). New York: Macmillian.

Madaus, G. F. & Macnamara, J. (1970). Public examinations: A study of the Irish leaving certificate. Dublin: Educational Research Centre, St. Patrick's College.

Madaus, G. F. & O'Dwyer, L. (1999). A short history of performance assessment: Lessons learned. Phi Delta Kappan, 80(9), 688–695.

Madaus, G. F., Ryan, J., Kellaghan, T., & Airasian, P. W. (1987). Payment by results: an Analysis of a Nineteenth Century Performance Contracting Program. Irish Journal of Education, 21, 80–91.

Madaus, G. F. & Stufflebeam, D. (1989). Educational Evaluation: The Classic Works of Ralph W. Tyler. Boston: Kluwer-Nijhoff.

Madaus, G. F., West, M. M., Harmon, M. C., Lomax, R. G., & Viator, K. (1992). The influence of testing on teaching math and science in grades 4–12: Report of a study funded by the National Science Foundation (SPA8954759). The Center for the Study of Testing, Evaluation and Educational Policy, Boston College, Chestnut Hill, MA.

Mann, H. (1845). The Common School Journal, 7(19), Reprinted in Caldwell and Courtis, 1924 p. 1238.

Margulies, J. (Artist). Cartoon. (2007). The Record (Hackensack, NJ), Reprinted in the New York Times, September 9, 2007, p 14.

Markham, L. R. (1976). Influences of handwriting quality on teacher evaluation of written work. American Educational Research Journal, 13(4), 277–283.

Marshall, J. C. & Powers, J. C. (1969). Writing neatness, composition errors, and essay grades. Journal of Educational Measurement, 6, 97–101.

Mathews, J. (2000). *Testing the market, The Washington Post.* Retrieved June, 2 2000, from: http://www.washingtonpost.com

McCarthy, C. (2006, March 18). Teach to the Test'? What Test? Washington Post, p. A21.

McCormick, R. A. (1993). Value variables in the health-care reform debate. America, 168(19), 7–13.

McCraw, T. K. (1984). Prophets of regulation: Charles Francis Adams, Louis D. Brandeis, James M. Landis, Alfred E. Kahn. Cambridge, MA: Belknap Press of Harvard University Press.

McGahern, J. (1977). The Dark. New York: Quartet.

McGarity, T. O. (1991). Reinventing rationality: The role of regulatory analysis in the federal bureaucracy. New York: Cambridge University Press.

McMillan, J., Myran, S., & Workman, D. (1999, April 19–23). The impact of mandated statewide testing on teachers' classroom assessment and instructional practices. Paper presented at the Paper presented at the annual meeting of the American Educational Research Association, , Montreal, Quebec, Canada.

McNeil, L. M., Coppola, E., Radigan, J., & Heilig, J. V. (2008). Avoidable losses: high-stakes accountability and the dropout crisis. Education Policy Analysis

Archives, 16(3). Retrieved on October 20, 2008 from http://epaa.asu.edu/epaa/v16n3/

McShane, D. (1989). Testimony. Paper presented at the effects of testing on American Indians, Albuquerque, NM.

Medina, J. (2007, June 9). Schools plan to pay cash for marks. New York Times, p. B 1.

Medina, J. (2008, January 21). New York measuring teachers by test scores. New York Times. Retrieved on March 20, 2008 from http://www.nytimes.com/2008/01/21/nyregion/21teachers.html?_r=1&oref=slogin&ref=education&pagewanted=all

Medwar, P. (1982). Pluto's Republic. Oxford: Oxford University Press.

Meisels, S. J. (1989). High-stakes testing in kindergarten. Educational Leadership, 46(7), 16–22.

Meng, H. W. (1993). The role of assessment in China: A shift in direction from selection to monitoring. Paper presented at the Conference on Learning, Selection and Monitoring: Resolving the Roles of Assessment, International Centre for Research on Assessment, Institute of education, University of London.

Merton, R. K. (1936). The unintended consequences of purposive social action. American Sociological Review, 1(6), 894–904.

Merton, R. K. (1964). Foreword. In E. Jacques (Ed.), The technological society (pp. v-viii). New York: Vintage Books.

Meskill, J. (1963). The Chinese Civil Service: Career open to talent. Boston: Heath.

Messick, S. (1988). The once and future issues of validity. Assessing the meaning and consequences of measurement. In H. Wainer & H. Braun (Eds.), Test validity (pp. 33–45). Hillside, NJ: Lawrence Erlbaum.

Messick, S. (1989). Validity. In R. L. Linn (Ed.), Educational Measurement 3rd ed. (pp. 13–103). New York: Macmillan.

Milne, A. (1930). Autobiography. New York: Dutton.

Milton, V. J. (2008, March 15, 2008). Today's Lesson: Courage, Brocton fourth-graders learn about sacrifice as their teacher leaves the classroom to begin his tour of duty in Iraq. Boston Globe. Retrieved on May 8, 2008 from http://www.boston.com/news/local/articles/2008/03/15/todays_lesson_courage/

Miyazaki, I. (1976). China's Examination Hell. New York: Weatherhill.

Montgomery, R. J. (1967). Examinations: An account of Their Evolution as Administrative Devices in England. Pittsburgh: University of Pittsburgh Press.

Moore, T. (1989, September). The Cholesterol Myth. The Atlantic Monthly, 264 (3), p. 37.

Morgenson, G. (2002, July 14). MARKET WATCH; An Idea Gone Haywire: Linking Executive Pay to Sales. New York Times. Retrieved on July 28, 2002 from http://select.nytimes.com/search/restricted/article res=FB0613F0683A0540C0778DDDAE0894DA404482.

Morris, G. C. (1969). Educational objectives of higher secondary school science. Unpublished Unpublished doctoral dissertation, University of Sydney, Australia.

Morris, N. (1961). An historian's view of examinations. In S. Wiseman (Ed.), Examination and English Education (pp. 1–43). Manchester: Manchester University Press.

Mulholland, L. A. & Berliner, D. C. (1992). Teacher experience and estimation of student achievement, Annual Meeting of the American Educational Research Association. San Francisco, CA.

Murphy, R. (1975). The Reading Lesson. In D. Marcus (Ed.), Irish Poets (pp. 43). London: Pan.

Myers, K. C. (2001). *State use of MCAS exams 'wrong': The head of company running the tests said he does not think tests should be used s a requirement for high school lgraduation. The Cape Cod Times.* Retrieved May 22, 2001, from htpp//www.capecodtimes.com

Myers, K. C. (2003, July 16). A dream denied: Aspiring chef rethinks her future a Falmouth school board bows to state pressure on MCAS. *Cape Cod Times,* Retrieved July 16, 2003 from http://www.capecodonline.com/cctimes/adream2016.htm.

Naipaul, S. (1984, September 17). A Trinidad childhood. The New Yorker, 57–78.

Nasar, S. (1993, October 22). More signs of a productive U.S. New York Times, p. D1&6.

National Center on the Educational Quality of the Workforce & Bureau of the Census. (1995). The EQW national employer survey. Washington, D.C.: Office of Educational Research and Improvement, U.S. Department of Education.

National Commission on Excellence in Education. (1983a). *A Nation at Risk.* Washington D.C.: U.S. Government Printing Office.

National Commission on Excellence in Education. (1983b). *Meeting the Challenge: Recent efforts to improve education across the nation.* Washington D.C.: U.S. Government Printing Office.

National Commission on Testing and Public Policy. (1990). From gatekeeper to gateway: transforming testing in America. Chestnut Hill, MA: National Commission on Testing and Public Policy, Boston College.

National Committee for Injury Prevention and Control. (1989). Injury prevention: Meeting the challenge. New York: Oxford University Press.

National Defense Education Act of 1958. U.S. Code Sept 2 1958, P.L. 85–64. 72 Stat. 1580, Section 101.

National Indian Education Association. (2005). Preliminary Report on No Child Left Behind (NCLB). Washington, D.C.

National Institute of Education. (1981, July 8, 9, 10). Transcript of the Minimum Competency Testing clarification Hearings prepared by Alderson Reporting Co, Washington D.C.

National PTA. (2006). Recess Is At Risk, New Campaign Comes To The Rescue. Retrieved April 4, 2006, from http://www.pta.org/ne_press_release_detail_1142028998890.html

National Research Council. (2001). *Understanding Dropouts: Statistics, Strategies, and High- Stakes.* Washington DC: Committee on Educational Excellence and Testing Equity, National Research Council.

National Research Council. (2007). Lessons Learned About Testing: Ten Years of Work at the National Research Council. Position DC: National Research Council.

National Research Council News Report. (1991). (Vol XLI, No 6). Broad measures proposed to save fishermen's lives: A national program to increase vessel safety.

Needham MA, P. S. (2006). Stingfest. Needham Public Schools, Needham, MA.

Neill, M. (2005). Response to Public Education Network (PEN) Report *Open to the Public: Speaking Out on "No Child Left Behind"*, Retrieved on Januay 2, 2006 from http://www.fairtest.org/joint%20statement%20civil%20rights%20grps%2010-21-04.html

Neufeld, S. (2007, January 23). Schools to offer pay for scores: city incentives up to $110 per student for graduation tests. Baltimore Sun. Retrieved on October 22, 2008 from www.baltimoresun.com/news/local/baltimore_city/bal-te.ci.schools23jan23033219,0,4929013.story

New York Times. (2006, April 25). EDITORIAL: Drug Safety After the Fact. New York Times, p. A 26.

New York Times Editorial. (2007, September 7). Really Leaving No Child Behind. New York Times, p. A28.

New York Times Editorial. (2008, June 19). Testing and learning. Retrieved June 26, 2008, from http://www.nytimes.com/2008/06/19/opinion/19thu2.html?ref=opinion

Nichols, S. L. & Berliner, D. C. (2005). The inevitable corruption of indicators and educators through high stakes testing: Education Policy Studies Laboratory. Education Policy Research Unit, Arizona State University.

Nichols, S. L., Glass, G., & Berliner, D. (2005). High-Stakes Testing and Student Achievement: Problems for the No Child Left Behind Act. Tempe AZ: Education Policy Research Unit (EPRU) Education Policy Studies Laboratory, College of Education. Division of Educational Leadership and Policy Studies, Arizona State University. Retrieved on December 15, 2005 from http://www.asu.edu/educ/epsl/EPRU/documents/EPSL-0509-105-EPRU.pdf.

Nivison, D. S. (1963). The critera of excellence. In J. M. Menzel (Ed.), The Chinese civil service: Career open to talent (pp. 92–106). Boston: D. C. Heath.

NOW with David Brancaccio. (2005, September 2). *Interview with Rafe Esquith.* Retrieved September 5, 2005, from http://www.pbs.org/now/archive_transcripts.html

Now with David Brancaccio (Writer) (2005). Are you getting the truth from the media in America? Media reformer Robert McChesney [Television], http://www.pbs.org/now/archive_transcripts.html.

O'Connor, S. D. & Romer, R. (2006, March 25). Not By Math Alone. Washington Post, p. A19.

Oakes, J. (1991). The many-sided dilemmas of testing. In Voices from the field: 30 expert opinions on America 2000, the Bush administration strategy to "reinvent" America's schools: William T. Grant Foundation Commission on Work, Family and Citizenship Institute for Educational Leadership.

Olson, L. (2005). State Test Programs Mushroom as NCLB Mandate Kicks In: Nearly half of states are expanding tests into more grades in 2005-06 school year.

Education Week, p. http://www.edweek.org/ew/articles/2005/2011/2030/2013assesstest.h2025.html?querystring=entirely%2020multiple%2020choice.

Ong, W. (1977). Interfaces of the Word: Studies in the evolution of consciousness and culture. Ithaca NY: Cornell University Press.

Ong, W. (1971). Rhetoric, romance, and technology. Ithaca, NY: Cornell University Press.

Oppenheimer, T. (2003). The flickering mind: The false promise of technology in the classroom and how learning can be saved. New York: Random House.

Orwell, G. (1968). New Words. In I. Angus & S. Orwell (Eds.), The collected essays, journalism, and letters of George Orwell. My country right or left, 1949–1943. New York: Harcourt, Brace, & Jovanovich.

Parenti, M. (1978). Power and the powerless. New York: St. Martin's Press.

Paul, A. M. (2004). The Cult of Personality Testing: How personality test are leading us to miseducate our children, mismange our companies, and misunderstand ourselves. New York: Free Press.

Pear, R. (2005, September 30). Audit assails the White House for public relations spending. New York Times. Retrieved on November 10, 2005 from http://www.nytimes.com/2005/09/30/politics/30cnd-educ.html?hp

Pedulla, J., Abrams, L., Madaus, G. F., Russell, M., Ramos, M., & Miao, J. (2003). Perceived effects of state-mandated testing programs on teaching and learning: Findings from a national survey of teachers. Chestnut Hill MA: National Board on Educational Testing and Public Policy, Boston College. Retrieved on December 15, 2003 from http://www.bc.edu/research/nbetpp/.

Peristein, L. (2004, May, 31). School Pushes Reading, Writing, Reform; Sciences Shelved in Effort to Boost Students to 'No Child' Standards. Washington Post, p. A01.

Peterson, P. E. (1983). Background paper commissioned by Pauly. In Making the Grade. New York: The Twentieth Century Fund.

Popham, WJ (1983) Measurement as an instructional catalyst, in Ekstrom, RB (Ed. Measurement, Technology and Individuality in Education: Proceedings of the 1982 ETS Invitational Conference. New Directions for Testing and Measurement, 17, San Francisco: Jossey-Bass, 19–30.

Popham, W. J. (1987). The merits of measurement-driven instruction. Phi Delta Kappan, 68(9), 679–682.

Popham, W. J., Cruse, K. L., Rankin, S. C., Sandifer, P. D., & Williams, P. L. (1985). Measurement-driven instruction: It's on the road. Phi Delta Kappan, 66(9), 628–635.

Porter, T. M. (1995). Trust in numbers: the pursuit of objectivity in science and public life. Princeton, NJ: Princeton University Press.

Postman, N. (1992). Technolopoly: the surrender of culture to technology. New York: Alfred A. Knopf.

Powers, D., Fowles, M., Farnum, M., & Ramsey, P. (1994). Will they think less of my handwritten essay if others word process theirs? Effects on essay scores of intermingling handwritten and word-processed essays. Journal of Educational Measurement, 31(3), 220–233.

Prescico, J. J. (1990). Employment motivation: Beliefs vs. reality. Quality, 29(3), 51–53.

Quirk, P., J. (1980). Food and drug administration. In J. Q. Wilson (Ed.), The politics of regulation (pp. 191–235). New York: Basic Books.

Rafferty, M. (1985). Examinations in literature: Perceptions from non technical writers of England and Ireland from 1850 to 1984. Unpublished Doctoral Dissertation, Boston College, Chestnut Hill, MA.

Rapp, D. (2006). NCLB Outrages. Montpelier, VT: Vermont Society for the Study of Education.

Rapple, B. (1994). Payment by Results: An Example of Assessment in Elementary Education from Nineteenth Century Britain. Education Policy Analysis Archives, 2(1), http://epaa.asu.edu/epaa/v2n1.htm.

Rapple, B. (2004). Standardized testing in America's schools: Lessons from Matthew Arnold's Britain. Contemporary Review, 285(1665), 193–198.

Reardon, S. F. (1996, April). Eighth Grade Minimum Competency Testing and Early High School Dropout Patterns. Paper presented at the Annual Meeting of the American Educational Research Association, New York.

Reed, J. (1987). Robert M. Yerkes and the Mental Testing Movement. In M. M. Sokal (Ed.), Psychological Testing and American Society: 1890–1930 (pp. 75–94). New Brunswick NJ: Rutgers University Press.

Reid, T. R. (1992, January 8). Tokyo: U.S. workers outproduce Japanese. Washington Post, p. C1 & 6.

Reutter, H. (2006, Aug 3). Education official says Nebraska's Assessments Work. The Grand Island Independent.

Revkin, A. (2007, March 8). Memos Tell Officials How to Discuss Climate. New York Times. Retrieved on April 2, 2008 from http://www.nytimes.com/2007/03/08/washington/08polar.html

Rhoades, K. & Madaus, G. F. (2003). Errors in standardized tests: A systemic problem. Chestnut Hill, MA: National Board on Educational Testing and Public Policy, Boston College.

Romano, L. (2005, October 19). Students Show Few Gains Since 'No Child' Math Up Slightly, Reading No Improvement. Washington Post. Retrieved on October, 20, 2005 from http://www.washingtonpost.com/wp-dyn/content/ article/2005/10/19/AR2005101900708_pf.htm

Romberg, T., Zarinia, E., & Willams, S. (1989). The influence of mandated testing on mathematics instruction: Grade 8 teachers' perceptions. Madison, WI: National Center for Research in Mathematical Science Education, University of Wisconsin-Madison.

Rose, L. C. & Gallup, A. M. (2007). The 39th Annual Phi Delta Kappa/Gallup Poll Of the Public's Attitudes Toward The Public Schools. Phi Delta Kappan, *89*(1), 33–48

Rotberg, I. (1990). I never promised you first place. *Phi Delta Kappan, 72*(4), 296–303.

Rothstein, R. (2004). Class and Schools: Using Social, Economic, and Educational Reform to Close the Black-White Achievement Gap New York: Teachers College Press.

Roush, W. (1991). Who decides about biotech? The clash over bovine growth hormone. Technology Review, 94(5), 66–68.

Royal Commission on Education (Great Britain). (1886). Minutes of Evidence. London.

Rubin, J. (2004, November 28). Are Schools Cheating Poor Learners? Officials say federal rules compel them to focus on pupils more likely to raise test scores. Los Angeles Times, pp. http://www.history.ucsb.edu/projects/ge/iv/news/LAT04v-28AreSchoolsCheating.htm.

Ruch, G. M. (1925). Minimum essentials in reporting data on standard tests. Journal of Educational Research, 12, 349–358.

Russell, M. (1999). Testing writing on computers: A follow-up study comparing performance on computer and on paper. Educational Policy Analysis Archives, 7(20).

Russell, M. (2006). Technology and assessment: The tale of two interpretations. Greenwich, CT: Information Age Publishing.

Russell, M. & Abrams, L. (2004). Instructional uses of computers for writing: How some teachers alter instructional practices in response to state testing. Teachers College Record, 106(6), 1332–1357.

Russell, M. & Haney, W. (1997). Testing writing on computers: An experiment comparing student performance on tests conducted via computer and via paper-and-pencil. Educational Policy Analysis Archives, 5(3).

Russell, M., Higgins, J., & Hoffmann, T. (2004). Examining the effect of text editor and robust word processor use on student writing test performance. Chestnut Hill: MA: Technology and Assessment Study Collaborative, Boston College.

Russell, M., O'Dwyer, L., Bebell, D., & Miranda, H. (2004). Technical report for the USEIT study. Boston, MA: Boston College: Technology and Assessment Study Collaborative.

Russell, M. & Plati, T. (2001). Effects of computer versus paper administration of a state-mandated writing assessment. Teachers College Record. Retrieved on July 23, 2007 from http://www.tcrecord.org/PrintContent.asp?ContentID=10709

Russell, M. & Tao, W. (2004a). The influence of computer-print on rater scores. Practical Assessment, Research, and Evaluation, 9(10). Retrieved on July 2, 2007 from http://pareonline.net/getvn.asp?v=9&n=10

Russell, M. & Tao, W. (2004b). Effects of handwriting and computer-print on composition scores: A follow-up to Powers et al. Practical Assessment, Research, and Evaluation, 9(1). Retrieved on July 2, 2007 from http://pareonline.net/getvn.asp?v=9&n=1

Sable, J. & Garofano, A. (2007). Public Elementary and Secondary School Student Enrollment, High School Completions, and Staff From the Common Core of Data: School Year 2005-06 (NCES 2007-352). Washington, D.C.: U.S. Department of Education, National Center for Education Statistics.

Sacchetti, M. (2006, October 19). More districts aim for the top on MCAS In shift, proficient isn't good enough. Boston Globe, p. at: http://www.boston.com/news/local/massachusetts/articles/2006/2010/2019/more_districts_aim_for_the_top_o.

Saltman, K. J. (2005). The Edison Schools: Corporate schooling and the assault on public eduction. New York: Routledge.

Samelson, F. (1987). Was early mental testing: (a) racist inspired, (b) objective science (c) a technology for democracy, (d) the origin of multiple-choice exams, (e) none of the above? In M. M. Sokal (Ed.), Psychological testing and American society, 1890–1930. (pp. 113–127). New Brunswick, NJ: Rutgers University Press.

Samuelson, R., J. (2004, June 2). Seduced by reform. Washington Post, p. A25.

Sanchez, C. (2006). Students Sue over Incorrect SAT Scores, All Things Considered (http://www.npr.org/templates/story/story.php?storyId=5362382 ed.). USA: National Public Radio.

Sandman, P. M. (1989). Hazard versus outrage in the public perception. In V. Covello, T., D. McCallum, D. & M. Pavola, T., (Eds.), Effective risk communication (pp. 45–49). New York: Plenum.

Sandoval, G. (2005, June 3). Laptops now more popular than desktops. San Francisco, Associated Press.

Sarason, S., B. (1993). Letters to a serious education president. Newbury Park, CA: Corwin Press.

Saulny, S. (2005, January 19). Meaning of proficient varies across the country. New York Times, p. Section B 8.

Saulny, S. (2006, February 12). TUTOR PROGRAM OFFERED BY LAW IS GOING UNUSED. New York Times. Retrieved on February 20, 2006 from http://select.nytimes.com/search/restricted/article?res=F70613FE70395A70610C70718DDDAB70894DE404482.

Saunders, D. (1995, February 1). There is no one answer. San Francisco Chronicle, p. A.21.

Schiesel, S. (2008, June 9). Former justice promotes web-based civics lessons. New York Times, p. B7.

Schnurman, M. (2005, August 10). Business lessons apply to school ratings Fort Worth Star-Telegram. Retrieved on August 30, 2005 from http://www.dfw.com/mld/dfw/news/12347592.htm.

Shanker, A. (1986, October 26). Power v. Knowledge in St. Louis: Professional under fire. New York Times.

Shavelson, R. J., Baxter, G., P., & Pine, J. (1992). Performance assessments: Political Rhetoric and measurement reality. Educational Researcher, 21(4), 22–27.

Shavelson, R. J., Gao, X., & Baxter, G., P. (1993). Sampling variability of performance assessments (CSE Tech Report, No, 361). Santa Barbara, CA: National Center for Research in Evaluation, Standards and Student Testing.

Sheed, W. (1982). Transatlantic blues. New York: E. P. Dutton.

Shepard, L. A. (1990). Inflated Test Score Gains: Is the Problem Old Norms or Teaching. Educational Measurement: Issues and Practices, 9(3), 15–22.

Shepard, L. A. & Smith, M. L. (1986). Synthesis of research on school readiness and kindergarten retention. Educational Leadership, 44(3), 78–86.

Shepard, L. A. & Smith, M. L. (1988a). Escalating academic demand in kindergarten: Counterproductive policies. Elementary School Journal, 89(2), 135–145.

Shepard, L. A. & Smith, M. L. (1988b). Flunking Kindergarten: Escalating curriculum leaves many behind. American Educator, 12(2), 34–39.

Shepard, L. A. & Smith, M. L. (1989). Escalating academic demand in kindergarten: Counterproductive policies. Elementary School Journal, 89(2), 135–146.

Shepard, L. A. & Smith, M. L. (1990). Synthesis of research on grade retention. Educational Leadership, 48(8), 84–88.

Shepard, L. A. & Smith, M. L. (Eds.). (1989a). Flunking Grades: Research and Policies on Retention. London: Falmer Press.

Sheridan, J. D. (1949). Midsummer Madness: In Half in Earnest. Dublin: Talbot.

Shorrocks, D., Daniels, S., Stainton, R., & Ring, K. (1993). Testing and assessing 6 and 7 year olds: The evaluation of the 1992 Key Stage 1 National Curriculum Assessment. Final Report of National Union of Teachers and School of Education, University of Leeds. London: The College Hill Press LTD.

Singer, L. R. (1990). Setting disputes: Conflict resolution in business, families and the legal system. Boulder, CO: Westview Press.

Singleton, M. C. (No date). Historical survey of issues considered by the committee on psychological test and assessment: 1895–1976: American Psychological Association, Washington D.C, Unpublished paper.

Skinner, B. F. (1953). Science and human behavior. New York: Macmillan.

Smith, F. (1931). English Elementary education. London: University of London Press.

Smith, M. (1991). Put to the test: The effects of external testing on teachers. Educational Researcher, 20(5), 8–11.

Smith, M. L. & Shepard, L. A. (1988). Kindergarten readiness and retention: A qualitative study of teachers' beliefs and practices. American Educational Research Journal, 25(3), 307–333.

Smith, E., & Tyler, R. (1942). *Appraising and recording student progress.* New York: Harper & Row.

Smith, M. R. (1987). Army ordnance and the 'American System' of manufacturing: 1815–1861. In M. R. Smith (Ed.), Military enterprise and technological change (pp. 39–87). Cambridge, MA: MIT Press.

Snow, R. (1982). Education and intelligence. Cambridge: Cambridge University Press.

Sokal, M. M. (Ed.). (1987). Psychological testing and American society: 1890–1930. New Brunswick, CT: Rutgers University Press.

Soukup, P. (1993). Communication and the media. In T. Sanks, Howland & J. Coleman, A (Eds.), Reading the signs of the times: Resources for social and cultural analysis. Mahwah, NJ: Paulist Press.

Spaulding, F. T. (1938). High school and life: The Regent's inquiry into the character and cost of public education. New York: McGraw Hill.

Spector, M. (2002, May 27). Do finger prints lie? The gold standard of forensic evidence is now being challenged. The New Yorker, 96–105.

Spulber, D. F. (1989). Regulation and markets. Cambridge, MA: The MIT Press.

Stansbury, M. (2008). Researchers identify key ed-tech trends. eSchool News, May 15. Retrieved May 20, 2008 from http://www.eschoolnews.com/news/top-news/index.cfm?i=53795&page=1

Staples, B. (2005, November 21). Why the United States Should Look to Japan for Better Schools. New York Times, p. Section A P 22.

Starch, D. & Elliot, E. C. (1912). Reliability of grading high school work in English. School Review, 21, 442–457.

Starch, D. & Elliot, E. C. (1913). Reliability of grading work in mathematics. School Review, 21, 254–259.

Staudenmaier, J. (1988). Technology and faith [audio cassette]. Kansas City: Credence Cassettes.

Staudenmaier, J. M. (1985). Technology's storytellers: Reweaving the human fabric. Cambridge MA: MIT Press.

Staudenmaier, J. M. (1989). U.S. technological style and the atrophe of civic commitment. In D. L. Gilpi (Ed.), Beyond individualism toward a retrieval of moral discourse in America (pp. 120–152). South Bend: Notre Dame Press.

Staw, B. M. (1976). Intrinsic and extrinsic motivation, pp. 1–23. Morristown, NJ: General Learning Press.

Stecher, B., Barron, S., Chun, T., & Ross, K. (2000). Reforming schools by reforming assessment: Consequences of the Arizona student assessment program (ASAP): Equity and teacher capacity building (CSE Technical Report 525). Los Angeles: National Center for Research on Evaluation, Standards, and Student Testing.

Stecher, B., Barron, S., Kaganoff, T., & Goodwin, J. (1998). The effect of standards-based assessment on classroom practices: Results of the 1996–97 RAND survey of Kentucky teachers of mathematics and writing: National Center for Research on Evaluation, Standards and Student Testing (CRESST)/RAND Education, Technical Report 482.

Stedman, L. C. & Kaestle, C. F. (1987 Winter). Literacy and reading performance in the United States from 1880 to present. Research Reading Quarterly, 22(1), 8–46.

Sternberg, R. J. (2006, February, 22). Creativity Is a Habit. Education Week, pp. 47, 64.

Sticht, T. (1988). Military testing and public policy: The enlisted corps. Alexandria, Virginia: Applied Behavioral and Cognitive Sciences, Inc.

Stigler, S. M. (1986). The history of statistics. Cambridge, MA: Harvard University Press.

Stoll, C. (1999). High-tech heretic. New York: Random House.

Stufflebeam, D. L., Jaeger, R. M., & Scriven, M. (1991). Summative evaluation of the National Assessment Governing Board's inaugural 1990–91 effort to set achievement levels on the National Assessment of Educational Progress: The Evaluation Center Western Michigan University.

Stufflebeam, D. L., Jaeger, R. M., & Scriven, M. (1992). A retrospective analysis of summative evaluation of NAGB's pilot project to set achievement levels on the National Assessment of Educational Progress. Paper presented at the Annual Meeting of the American Educational Research Association, San Francisco, CA.

Suen, H. K. & Yu, L. (2006). Chronic consequences of high-stakes testing? Lessons from the Chinese civil service exam. Comparative Education Review, 50(1), 46–63.

Sunderman, G. (2006). The Unraveling of No Child Left Behind: How Negotiated Changes Transform the Law. Cambridge, MA: The Civil Rights Project, Harvard. Retrieved on December 28, 2006 from http://www.civilrightsproject.harvard.edu/research/esea/NCLB_Unravel.pdf.

Sutherland, G. (1973). Elementary Education in the Nineteenth Century. London: London Historical Association.

Tanner, D. (1993). A nation 'truly' at risk. Phi Delta Kappan, 75(4), 288–297.

Taylor, F. W. (1911). The principles of scientific management. New York: Harper.

Taylor, G., Shepard, L. A., Kinner, F., & Rosenthal, J. (2003). A survey of teachers' perspectives on high-stakes testing in Colorado: What gets taught, what gets lost. Los Angeles: University of California, Center for Research on Evaluation, Standards, and Student Testing (CSE Technical Report 588).

The Economist. (1994b, January 15). Ready to take on the world. The Economist, 330, 65–66.

The Epoch Times. (2006, February 22). Miniature Qing Dynasty Cheating Books Revealed in China. The Epoch Times International. Retrieved on March 10, 2006 from http://www.theepochtimes.com/tools/printer.asp?id=38541.

The Michigan Diabetes Research and Training Center. MDRTC Lipid Measurement Fact Sheet, Retrieved on August 15, 2007 from http://www.med.umich.edu/MDRTC/cores/ChemCore/lipids.htm

Thomas, L. (1980). the medusa and the snail: More notes of a biology watcher. New York: Bantam Books.

Thorndike, E. L. (1918). The nature, purposes and general methods of measurements of educational products. In The Measurement of Educational Products (pp. 16–24). Bloomington, Ill: Public School Publishing Company.

Thorndike, R. & Lohman, D. (1990). A century of ability testing. Chicago: Riverside Publishing Company.

Toch, T. (2006). Margins of Error: The Education Testing Industry in the No Child Left Behind Era. Washington. DC: Education Sector.

Travers, R. M. W. (1983). How Research Has Changed American Schools: A History from 1840 to the Present. Kalamazoo, MI: Mythos Press.

Traxler, A. E. (1954). The IBM Test Scoring Machine: An evaluation. In Educational Testing Service (Ed.), Proceedings of the 1953 Invitational Conference on Testing Problems (pp. 139–146). Princeton, NJ: Educational Testing Service.

Turbayne, C. (1962). The myth of the metaphor. New Haven CT: Yale University Press.

Turner, E., Matthews, A., Linardatos, E., Tell, R., & Rosenthal, R. (2008). Selective publication of antidepressant trails and its influence on apparent efficacy. New England Journal of Medicine, 358:252–260.

Twentieth Century Fund Task Force on Federal Elementary and Secondary Education Policy. (1983). Making the Grade. New York: Twentieth Century Fund.

Tyack, D. & Hansot, E. (1982). Managers of Virtue: Public School Leadership in America. New York: Basic Books.

Tyack, D. B. (1974). The one best system: A history of American urban education. Cambridge MA: Harvard University Press.

Tyler, R. W. (1979). Educational Objectives and educational testing: Problems now faced. In Testing, teaching and learning. Report of a conference on research on testing. Washington, D.C.

Tynan, M. (1985). Catholic Instruction in Ireland 1720–1950. Dublin: Four Courts Press.

Tyre, M. J. (1991). Managing innovation on the factory floor. Technology Review, 94(7), 58–65.

U.S. Congress Office of Technology Assessment. (1992). Testing in American schools: Asking the right questions (Publication No. OTA-SET-519), . Washington, DC: U.S. Government Printing Office. (NTIS No. PB92-170091).

Vandenberg, D. (1983). Human rights in education. New York: Philosophical Library.

Vendlinski, T. & Stevens, R. (2002). Assessing student problem-solving skills with complex computer-based tasks. Journal of Technology, Learning, and Assessment, 1(3). Retrieved on August 18, 2002 from http://escholarship.bc.edu/cgi/viewcontent.cgi?article=1010&context=jtla

Vermes, G. (2004). The Complete Dead Sea Scrolls in English. London: Penguin Books.

Volti, R. (1992). Society and technological change (Second ed.). New York: St. Martin's Press.

Waite, M. (2004, May 28th). Group blasts school rating measures Florida's accountability system and No Child Left Behind give conflicting assessment. St Petersburg Times. Retrieved on May 29, 2008 from http://www.sptimes.com/2004/05/28/State/Group_blasts_school_r.shtml

Wallace, R. C. (1986). Reports on topic areas data-driven educational leadership. American Journal of Evaluation, 7(3), 5–15.

Wallace, W. A. (1994). Introduction. In W. A. Wallace (Ed.), Ethics in modeling. London: Pergamon Press.

Wallace, W. A. (Ed.). (1994b). *Ethics in modelling*. London: Pergamon Press.

Webber, C. (1989). The mandarin mentality: Civil service and university admissions testing in Europe and Asia. In B. R. Gifford (Ed.), Testing policy and the politics of opportunity allocation (pp. 33–60). Boston: Kluwer Academic Publishers.

Wells, H. G. (1892). On the true level of education. Educational Review, 4, 380–385.

Wells, H. G. (1934). An experiment in biography. New York: Macmillian.

West, M. M. & Viator, K. (1992). Teachers' and administrators' views of mandated testng programs. In G. F. Madaus, M. M. West, M. Harmon, E, R. G. Lomax & K. Viator (Eds.), The influence of testing on teaching math and science in grades 4–12. Chestnut Hill, MA: Report of a study funded by the National Science Foundation (SPA8954759). The Center for the Study of Testing, Evaluation and Educational Policy, Boston College.

Westbury, I. (1992). Comparing American and Japanese achievement: Is the United States really a low achiever? *Educational Researcher, 21*(5), 18–24.

Westbury, I. (1993). American and Japanese achievement... again. *Educational Researcher, 22*(3), 21–25.

White, E. E. (1888). Examinations and promotions. Education, 8, 519–522.

Whole Child Education Reform. (date unknown). Dangerous Folk, Educational Songs of Resistance, Retrieved on January 10, 2007 from http://www.wholechildreform.com/home.html

Will, G. (2003, March 2). Shame: School Reform's Weak Weapon. Washington Post, A27.

Wills, G. (2000). *Papal sin: Structures of deceit.* New York: Doubleday.

Wilson, A. (2005). Radio Golf. In American Theatre (Vol. 22, pp. 87–108).

Wilson, D. & Macur, J. (2008, January 17). Antidoping officials give baseball leaders failing grade. New York Times. Retrieved on January 20, 2008 from http://www.nytimes.com/2008/01/17/sports/baseball/17baseball.html?fta=y

Wilson, J. Q. (Ed.). (1980). The politics of regulation. New York: Basic Books, Inc.

Winerip, M. (2005, July, 13). Study Great Idea, but Teach to the Test. *New York Times.*

Winerip, M. (2006, March, 22). Standardized Tests Face a Crisis Over Standards. New York Time, p. A21.

Winner, L. (1977). Autonomous technology: Technic-out-of-control as a theme in political thought. Cambridge MA: MIT Press.

Winner, L. (1986). The Whale and the reactor: A search for limits in an age of high technology. Chicago: The University of Chicago Press.

Wolfe, T. (1987). The bonfire of the vanities. New York: Bantam Books.

Woolcok, N. (2008, July 15). School test fiasco may result in Educational Testing Service being sacked. The Times of London. Retrieved on July 20, 2008 from http://www.timesonline.co.uk/tol/life_and_style/education/article4333852.ece

Zenderland, L. (1998). Measuring Minds: Henry Herbet Goddard and the Origins of American Intelligence Testing. New York: Cambridge University Press.

Zigler, E. (1991). Letter to Kenneth B. Newton.

Zimmerman, N. (1990). Motivation or Manipulation. Incentive(June), 82–85.

INDEX

A

B

C

The Paradoxes of High Stakes Testing, pages 251–254

D

E

F

G

H

I

J

K

L

S

T

U

V

W

Y

Z

Printed in the United States
137687LV00003B/17/P

9 781607 520276